# Dickens: The Dreamer's Stance

# DICKENS:

## *The Dreamer's Stance*

### *By* TAYLOR STOEHR

Cornell University Press
*Ithaca, New York*

CORNELL UNIVERSITY PRESS

*First published 1965*

Library of Congress Catalog Card Number: 65-18567

PRINTED IN THE UNITED STATES OF AMERICA

BY W. F. HUMPHREY PRESS

*For Rosie*

# Preface

THE main purpose of this book is to describe Dickens' literary manner—what I call in the text "the Dickensian manner," or "the dream manner," or "super-naturalism."

The first three chapters are primarily theoretical in approach, and prepare the way for a long chapter of practical analysis, in which Dickens' last six, "dark" novels, from *Bleak House* to *Our Mutual Friend,* are approached from this new theoretical perspective. A fifth chapter considers the results of this reading of the novels, and explores its implications for our understanding of the grounds of Dickens' achievement. A final chapter treats some aspects of Victorian art and society which correspond to elements in the Dickensian dream manner, with a view to suggesting the place of his work in literary and cultural history.

The first section concentrates on those devices of language and rhetoric that produce the characteristic ring of Dickens' style. The features described there are also associated with some interesting qualities of Dickens' peculiar kind of mimesis, and these are dealt with in Chapter 2. What emerges from the two chapters is the nucleus for a theory of Dickens' literary manner—the interrelations between his style and his stance, at once a world-view and a methodology of the imagination. Dickens is neither realist nor fantast, but something in between. I try to clarify this by means of an analogy proposed in Chapter 3, where I compare Dickens' literary manner to Freud's notion of dreamwork. The theoretical considerations of the preceding two chapters are thus codified in terms of a familiar, systematic view of certain kinds of imaginative experience.

With this analogy, the initial theoretical statement of the book is complete. The first three chapters bear on one another in two ways: first, the ideas and terminology developed in one section are intended to open paths to further questions and to a new approach in the section that follows; second, all three chapters deal with the same set of interrelated elements, studied in their different aspects—as a group of stylistic traits, as a fictive view of reality, and as a literary manner with dreamlike characteristics.

With this rationale for regarding the novels as like dreams, I move on to practical criticism in Chapter 4, where six novels are interpreted as if they actually were dreams. The theoretical apparatus of the first three chapters is not so much *used* as it is *tested* in these analyses: that is, although the dream analogy provides the perspective, the method of analysis is rather like ordinary formal criticism, except that psychological interpretation of the structural elements assumes more than the usual importance. And so in my fifth chapter, where the results of such analysis are assessed, my aim is not only to show how the formal/psychological characteristics of the novels add up to a single meaning ("The Meaning of the Dream"), but also to show—what is implicit in the perspective of Chapter 4—that this meaning is largely determined and conveyed by the literary dream manner. With this section, the main line of argument and proof in my book is concluded.

The account of Dickens' dream manner seems to me to integrate a number of well-known, important, and characteristic traits of his work in a way that is more comprehensive and illuminating than anything the ordinary approaches of literary criticism have been able to manage. Furthermore, it seems to suggest a new orientation toward Dickens' place in literary history, for to understand his literary manner as a kind in itself (with other exemplars, in his time and ours), rather than merely as an amalgam of realism, naturalism, symbolism—the traditional categories of manner—is to see Dickens in a new context and to give him new stature, much as Defoe has his reputation partly by virtue of his standing at the headwaters of realism. My final chapter explores some of the possibilities of such an orientation, by mentioning a number of literary and cultural phenomena which seem to have in common the dreamlike characteristics found in Dickens. In this section I have not attempted anything like the full-scale study that would be necessary to settle super-naturalism, or the dream manner, into a comfortable place alongside realism or naturalism. Many books will have to be written before that is possible. Nor have I tried to show Dickens as an originator or an influence on other writers, although much might be done along those lines. My purpose is to show that Dickens' literary manner, like others better known, grew up out of cultural needs and pressures, and is reflected in the artistic and social scene of the century, especially in England. It would be somewhat misleading to speak of Dickens as the originator of super-naturalism, just as it would be to take Defoe as literally the inventor of realism. But that Dickens was the greatest artist working this vein in Victorian England seems clear enough, and this is the reason for making him a touchstone in assessing the sources and quality of supernaturalism in the age.

# ACKNOWLEDGMENTS

I have acknowledged my specific indebtedness to a number of scholars in the footnotes, but students of Dickens will recognize that many others have affected my thinking although they go unmentioned.

I should like to express my special gratitude to Mr. Henry Charles Dickens for permission to quote from the manuscript of Dickens' "Memoranda" book (1855–1870).

I am grateful also to the Oxford University Press for permission to quote from the *New Oxford Illustrated Dickens;* to the New York Public Library for permission to examine and quote from the "Memoranda" book, which is in its Henry W. and Albert A. Berg Collection, and to the Curator of the Berg Collection, Mr. John D. Gordan, for his kind assistance; to Mr. J. Hillis Miller for permission to quote from his Harvard dissertation, "Dickens' Symbolic Imagery."

Parts of my book, in its earliest stages, were written while I held a Kofoid Fellowship in English at the University of California at Berkeley. For this and other assistance I wish to thank the Committee on Graduate Scholarships, the Committee on Research, and the Department of English at Berkeley. The Grant-in-Aid Fund of the Cornell English Department has liberally supported my research and paid for the preparation of the manuscript. The Cornell University

Press and its staff have been extremely helpful and patient; in particular, the Press editors have been as shrewd and painstaking as one could hope for.

The following friends, colleagues, and teachers have read portions of the manuscript in its various stages and offered suggestions for improvements beyond my power to discover for myself. I thank them now: Jonathan and Alison Bishop, Anthony Caputi, John Dings, Angus Fletcher, Paul Goodman, Neil Hertz, David Sachs, Mark Schorer, and Walter Slatoff. In recording these debts, I must omit others, some equally great, which were incurred less conspicuously in the years during which the book was growing. I hope those of my readers who see their influence in the following pages will understand my silent gratitude.

TAYLOR STOEHR

*Ithaca, New York*
*December 1964*

# Contents

CONTENTS

Dickens: The Dreamer's Stance

# 1

# The Style

DICKENS' style has a characteristic flavor. It is, as specialists sometimes say, Dickensian. The following analysis is not intended as a comprehensive study of his style, but is rather an attempt to isolate some outstanding features of it which seem to me to produce its characteristic flavor, especially (1) Dickens' use of detail as an active ingredient in setting and plot, (2) his use of rhetorical devices such as anaphora and metonymy to order and connect these details, and (3) the effect of such usages on Dickensian characterization and plotting. As the reader will see, particularly in the treatment of Dickens' principle of ordering, I am not so much concerned with any single instance of his use of detail or rhetoric as I am with the general nature of these elements; consequently, terms like "anaphora" and "metonymy" should be interpreted very broadly in this context, as designating tendencies of method in Dickens' work rather than specific tricks in his bag of artistic expedients.

Because I want to ground my study in close analysis of stylistic features and their inner consistency and integrity,

I concentrate here on a single novel. In later chapters, as the argument progresses, there will be more and more reference to other novels, but in the beginning *A Tale of Two Cities* must serve as a representative text. The *Tale* will be familiar to almost any reader I can expect to reach, including those who are not specialists in the field; yet it is a novel which, unlike most of the major works in the Dickens canon, has not received the critical attention it deserves from our generation. The *Tale* provides familiar material about which readers are likely to have fewer critical preconceptions than they have about other Dickens novels—an obvious advantage in presenting a new reading of an old master.

*A Tale of Two Cities* has sometimes been thought atypical of Dickens; if this were true, of course, it would not be suitable for the kind of representative analysis offered here. In some ways the *Tale* is special and unusual, but its peculiarities do not prejudice the case any more than the specialness of *Bleak House* or *Great Expectations* would. Each of Dickens' novels differs from its predecessors and sequels, because Dickens was a serious artist, who learned something from each book he wrote. Yet always much persisted of his style and manner, and it is what persists that we think of as Dickensian, the essence of his art. *Pickwick, Oliver Twist, Martin Chuzzlewit, David Copperfield, Hard Times, Little Dorrit*—it is hard to name a novel that does not seem unrepresentative of the canon in one respect or another, and yet they are all quite Dickensian too. In *A Tale of Two Cities* Dickens is perhaps at his most rhetorical; but he is always a highly rhetorical writer, and the heightening that may be seen in the *Tale* is not un-Dickensian so much as it is ultra-Dickensian. For stylistic analysis, this has not seemed to me a drawback but rather an advantage.

## Unnecessary Detail

Like other novelists, Dickens has his stylistic ups and downs, his moments of brilliance and his lapses into self-parody. In his best writing and in his worst, the habits that constitute his style persist, and here as in the work of other great stylists these habits call attention to themselves, regardless of the success or failure of particular passages. Nevertheless, the passages of greatest excellence—what in poetry used to be called the "beauties"—deserve our closest attention, for we are interested in Dickens' style, after all, only because it is so often brilliant.

Dickens lovers and scholars have always been disposed to praise those parts of *A Tale of Two Cities* in which the revolutionary scene predominates—the Wine-Shop chapter, the murder of the Marquis, the storming of the Bastille—so it seems natural to begin with these. Nothing is more typical than the way the Wine-Shop chapter opens:

A large cask of wine had been dropped and broken, in the street. The accident had happened in getting it out of a cart; the cask had tumbled out with a run, the hoops had burst, and it lay on the stones just outside the door of the wine-shop, shattered like a walnut-shell.*

The beginning of interest lies in the concrete object, the thing; Dickens sets the scene, almost cinematically, by focusing on such particulars. Here the effect is that of a high-angle view, centered on the splintered cask, slowly moving down on the square. As we are brought closer, description slides into narration, still determined by the objects in the setting:

*All quotations from Dickens' novels follow the *New Oxford Illustrated Dickens* (21 vols.; London, 1947–1958), ultimately based on the Charles Dickens edition, the last "authorized" edition to pass through his hands.

All the people within reach had suspended their business, or their idleness, to run to the spot and drink the wine. The rough, irregular stones of the street, pointing every way, and designed, one might have thought, expressly to lame all living creatures that approached them, had dammed it into little pools; these were surrounded, each by its own jostling group or crowd, according to its size.

Everything "run[s] to the spot"; people are mere adjuncts of the stones and wine. It is the scene that sticks in the memory. Places, buildings, all kinds of physical objects take up most of the available space in the Dickensian world. Later, when the revolutionary characters are introduced and made to come alive in their dazzling way, we discover that even in the delineation of character Dickens depends on the physical setting, the *mise-en-scène,* the concrete object, for his favorite effects. In the passage quoted it is the objects that have character, that exist "expressly to lame all living creatures that approached them"; in other passages the people derive much of their special kind of life from the things which invariably accompany them: Madame Defarge and her knitting, Doctor Manette and his cobbler's bench, Jerry Cruncher and his spiky hair, Gaspard and his nightcap are typical examples. This insistence on the bits and pieces of physical reality has attracted the attention of most of Dickens' readers in one way or another. George Orwell, perhaps the most interesting of the critics who discuss the problem, has even suggested that the abundance of "unnecessary detail" is "the outstanding, unmistakable mark of Dickens's writing." Orwell likens such details to "florid little squiggle[s] on the edge of the paper"—and he includes among them not merely physical objects given in the setting, but also bits of narrative, scraps of dialogue, all the trivia of plot and character. "Everything is piled up and up, detail on detail, embroidery on

4

embroidery," and the result, concludes Orwell, is like a wedding cake, as much beyond criticism as the rococo— "either you like it or you do not like it."[1]

The notion that the details in Dickens are "unnecessary" is not as simple as it sounds, for Orwell does not mean that the "little squiggles" do not function in the work; otherwise he would not have said that "it is by just these details that the special Dickens atmosphere is created." But exactly how do the details operate in the total impression? In what way are they both necessary and unnecessary?

There is a sense in which the details may be regarded as unnecessary by reason of their sheer abundance. And in an age that invented photography and built the Crystal Palace, that filled its parlors with papier-mâché gimcrackery and its galleries with the *tableaux vivants* of Maclise, Hunt, and Frith, and that quibbled over the species of Tennyson's "sea-blue bird of March," we are not surprised to find the novel—especially the popular novel—laden with true-to-life bric-a-brac. Something of the collector's mania is at work in Dickens' style, and not even Defoe (the all-time English champion in reporting the trivial) lavishes fonder attention on movables and properties. Dickens' novels are rightly termed "crowded," not only because of the large cast of characters he always used, but also because of the super-abundance of "things" in his imaginative world, a super-abundance that goes much further than the demands of verisimilitude, cluttered as his real world was.

But all this is merely to say that other novelists might not find it convenient to fill their novels so full as Dickens fills his—that, to return to Orwell's neat analogy, there is a difference between wedding cakes and cakes of other kinds. We have to do with different intentions and perhaps even different perceptions. That the details in Dickens are unnecessary from a certain point of view does not mean that they fail to contribute to the total effect. Indeed, from another point of view they *are* the effect. (Similarly, Victorian society might be usefully contemplated as merely the embodiment of that taste for objects and things which, as we say, characterized it.) Thus is the apparently superfluous detail indispensable simply by virtue of being a prominent part of the whole.

One can go further than this, however, in specifying the function of detail in Dickens' novels. He himself gives something of his views on the use of setting and props in a letter of advice written to a would-be contributor to his magazine:

Suppose yourself telling that affecting incident in a letter to a friend. Wouldn't you describe how you went through the life and stir of the streets and roads to the sick-room? Wouldn't you say what kind of a room it was, what time of day it was, whether it was sunlight, starlight, or moonlight? Wouldn't you have a strong impression on your mind of how you were received, when you first met the look of the dying man, what strange contrasts were about you and struck you? I don't want you, in a novel, to present *yourself* to tell such things, but I want the things to be there.[2]

Such injunctions might come from any writer of fiction, but Dickens' suggestions are particularly interesting because they so very exactly describe his narrative method in the Wine-Shop passages. He begins with the larger situation, given in concrete detail yet suggesting the whole framing context. He moves next to some unit already mentioned in the description of the larger context (the sickroom, the sharp stones). Finally characters are introduced, in some close relation to the objects. The emphasis throughout is on things, not so much things that happen, that can be recounted (though they are important too, obviously enough), as things that are *there*,

in the novel and in the novel's world. Once the scene has
become a human one, the narrative continues to be organized
around the bits and pieces of the physical context:

Some men kneeled down, made scoops of their two hands joined,
and sipped, or tried to help women, who bent over their shoulders,
to sip, before the wine had all run out between their fingers.
Others, men and women, dipped in the puddles with little mugs
of mutilated earthenware, or even with handkerchiefs from
women's heads, which were squeezed dry into infants' mouths;
others made small mud embankments, to stem the wine as it ran;
others, directed by lookers-on up at high windows, darted here
and there, to cut off little streams of wine that started away in
new directions; others devoted themselves to the sodden and lee-
dyed pieces of the cask, licking, and even champing the moister
wine-rotted fragments with eager relish.

Here, as in the passages already quoted, the details of the
setting seem to determine the movement of the narrator's
eye: the wine is sipped and dipped, squeezed out and dammed
up and cut off; mugs and handkerchiefs, mud and fragments
of wood, figure more prominently than the people handling
them. Even the dramatic feeling—the passion and despair of
the characters, the meanness of their daily lives—is given
through these vulgar objects and their uses.

It is worth pressing this point, for by just such means do we
feel the pressure of atmosphere which is so powerful in
Dickens, the impression that the world is thick with moods
and presences, that will affect the course of events and drive
the characters to their fate. The "unnecessary details" and
"needless ramifications" fill up this world, and whether
needless or not they constrain and determine action as the
pebbles of a gravelly soil at once guide and hinder the
searching roots.

Furthermore, Dickens only seems to pack his world full to bursting with the merely incidental and fortuitous; more often than not the apparently needless and accidental details form part of a meticulous weaving which, as the novel progresses, leaves less and less to chance. Consider the following passage, which occurs after all the wine has disappeared from the street:

The man who had left his saw sticking in the firewood he was cutting, set it in motion again; the woman who had left on a door-step the little pot of hot ashes, at which she had been trying to soften the pain in her own starved fingers and toes, or in those of her child, returned to it; men with bare arms, matted locks, and cadaverous faces, who had emerged into the winter light from cellars, moved away, to descend again; and a gloom gathered on the scene that appeared more natural to it than sunshine.

The wine was red wine, and had stained the ground of the narrow street in the suburb of Saint Antoine, in Paris, where it was spilled. It had stained many hands, too, and many faces, and many naked feet, and many wooden shoes. The hands of the man who sawed the wood, left red marks on the billets; and the forehead of the woman who nursed her baby, was stained with the stain of the old rag she wound about her head again. Those who had been greedy with the staves of the cask, had acquired a tigerish smear about the mouth; and one tall joker so besmirched, his head more out of a long squalid bag of a night-cap than in it, scrawled upon a wall with his finger dipped in muddy wine-lees—BLOOD.

The time was to come, when that wine too would be spilled on the street-stones, and when the stain of it would be red upon many there.

When one first comes upon it in the novel, this passage foreshadows little more than the explicit prophecy of the last sentence, but as we read further we find that the little details thrown out so lavishly, and as it were so casually, have their echoes throughout the story. We meet the same woodsawyer again, and we begin to connect him with the "Woodman Fate" of the opening chapter. We see and hear the stained feet again—the echoing footsteps in Lucie's life, the dancing feet of the Carmagnole, the cruel foot of Madame Defarge as she steadies the governor's head for her knife. The "tigerish smear about the mouth" is our first introduction to the "life-thirsting, cannibal-looking, bloody-minded juryman, the Jacques Three of St. Antoine." The tall citizen in the night-cap is Gaspard, who has in him still another note, also to be "scrawled," after the murder of the Marquis: *Drive him fast to his tomb. This, from* JACQUES."

The whole narrative is webbed with such interconnections, based always on the foreshadowing or echoing detail. Such repetitions have the obvious function of promoting the unity and probability of the novels, but an even more important result is the creation of a density of atmosphere beyond the power of mere verisimilitude or circumstantiality to achieve: we are presented with a cosmos everywhere interdependent, so that even objects in the landscape contribute to the sense of an interlocking system. With their multiple linkages, the "unnecessary detail" and "needless ramifications" of Dickens' style and plot provide the very fiber and fabric of his tightly knit world. The notorious coincidences of his novels are not the weak expedients of melodrama, but have behind them this same cosmic rationale. Thus Dickens' friend and biographer John Forster reports:

On the coincidences, resemblances, and surprises of life, Dickens liked especially to dwell, and few things moved his fancy so pleasantly. The world, he would say, was so much smaller than we thought it; we were all so connected by fate without knowing it; people supposed to be far apart were so constantly elbowing each other; and to-morrow bore so close a resemblance to nothing half so much as to yesterday.[3]

Again and again, Dickens' stories depend on the "unnecessary," coincidentally related details of this small world. *Little Dorrit* begins with a "chance" grouping of characters in Marseilles, and Dickens' notes for the first number show him imagining their coincidental relationships from the very beginning: "People to meet and part as travellers do, and the future connections between them in the story not to be now shown to the reader but to be worked out as in life."[4] Similarly, in the early pages of the *Tale* Lucie and her father are casually brought into contact with the Defarges, then with Darnay—all of whom, it turns out, are intimately connected with Doctor Manette's secret story. As one critic has said, "whoever has read one Dickens novel takes up a second with the happy confidence that the persons he meets there, however remote from each other they may at first appear, will all interlock in a tightening pattern and each make his influence felt by the others, as in a folk tale the ragged old woman casually befriended by the third son is sure to reappear in his hour of need."[5] In the typical Dickens novel, then, the concrete detail not only gives a framework for the movement of the narrative (as in the Wine-Shop passages) and a medium for the establishment of unity and coherence in the total action of the plot (by means of foreshadowing and other devices based on repetition), but also creates, in its very abundance and multiplication, the characteristic Dickensian atmosphere, a world in which all seemingly trivial, unrelated objects, people, and events finally mesh in an intricate and self-contained pattern.

## *The Principle of Ordering*

Dickens' extravagant fondness for enumerating the flotsam and jetsam of life (one way of viewing the needlessness of the detail) is combined with a similarly extravagant passion for order (so that the details must be made necessary). Every new impulse to expand and amplify is accompanied by a corresponding desire to curb and control. Thus generalized, of course, the paradox is recognized as a central fact of all art, and we must look further in order to discover anything of special relevance to our understanding of Dickens. We must consider the particular character of Dickens' materials, how he chooses them, orders them, and so forth; and this in turn will lead us into questions about Dickens' vision of the world and the choices it offers to any man.

Let us approach the problem in terms of *A Tale of Two Cities* itself. As is his usual practice, Dickens begins by mystifying us. We are rushing along the Dover Road, in the dead of night, to what distant event we know not. Later we discover the purpose of that journey, but for each solution to a mystery some new and even more tangled puzzle is introduced. Why was Doctor Manette imprisoned? Who is Charles Darnay? Why is Doctor Manette so disturbed by him? Whose are the footsteps that echo in Lucie's chamber? What did Defarge find in his search of 105 North Tower? By the end of the novel every question has been answered, but meanwhile the world presented to us is a rather strange one. It is not so much mysterious, even, as it is peculiarly discontinuous. We are offered, to be sure, a sequence of events: one thing leads to another, time passes, the ground goes by under foot. But there seems to lurk behind the façade of normal occurrences some secret meaning, every now and then intruding itself as though in warning of imminent catastrophe.

These intrusions are woven into the pattern of ongoing events in such a way that the train is never broken, but they strike us differently, as isolated bits of another story somehow underlying the one that takes up the actual time and space of the narrative. The denouement consists of the discovery that these apparently disconnected elements are in fact related, and even form a logical sequence—the true action of the story that we have been reading.

Such is the scheme of all Dickens' later novels. Two aspects of this method should be of particular interest to us: (1) the author's habit of seeing experience as full of isolated signs and hints beyond our immediate comprehension and therefore in a sense "extra," "superfluous," or "unnecessary"; and (2) the equally insistent view of these mysterious events as all part of an intricately ordered and self-contained whole, so that everything is relevant, even necessary, to the total design. Much as this looks like a paradigm for the detective novel, there is a crucial difference, for the clues in Dickens do not belong to the plot in the way those of the usual mystery story do, but are rather like Orwell's "squiggles," puzzling incidentals that seem mere flourishes until their pattern begins to emerge. There is nothing here like the knife with bloody fingerprints or the door locked from the inside.

One guesses that Dickens did not plan out his network of coincidences and connections in any very systematic way, but preferred to let his imagination run free, inventing wildly, and then securing the significance of each detail by repetition in new contexts, gradually allowing the hidden (at first, perhaps, even unknown) implications to unfold. From the negative evidence of his memoranda and notes for the novels, we must assume that Dickens kept these intricate patterns and networks in his head. Even the conjecture that there might have been some master plans, now lost, cannot explain the incredible control which he exercises over the details of foreshadowing and echo. It is much easier to believe that his mind was of that special sort (called sometimes "compulsive," though perhaps misleadingly so) which organizes experience, including its own inventions and musings, according to such powerfully overriding principles that every item of conscious life has its place in the scheme and is related by rule and code to every other item, as in a gigantic filing system. It should be emphasized that such a system need not be in any sense organic, that is, directed toward some end or furthering some pressure of meaning; on the contrary, the principle is much more likely to be without any direction at all, a kind of tidying-up without plan. But purposeful or not, Dickens' passion for order is itself a rewarding subject for investigation; in fact, I hope to show that the order is more important than the things ordered or than the ostensive goals of arrangement. Dickens' principle of ordering, once understood, will help us see why his details seem both necessary and unnecessary, and why the abundance of realistic detail does not add up to a realistic novel.

We have already seen, both in his advice to an aspiring lady novelist and in his own practice, how Dickens often uses details of setting as a framing device for narrative structure, landscape and props determining action rather than the other way round. This predominance of setting over plot may occur in varying degrees, of course, and different kinds of relations are also possible between the scenes of a novel and the actions played out in them (as for example the difference between the haphazard parceling out of plot in Defoe's goods-ridden world of tradesmen, and the shaping influence of Hardy's Wessex, where the maleficent landscape works like fate itself, inexorably drawing the characters to their ends).

In Dickens, both the insistent circumstantiality and the larger, subtler pressure of fate may be discerned, but neither is a mark of his style. The essence of his style is not found in the kinds of details, or the general direction in which they seem to lead, but in the principle that governs their disposition in particular sentences and paragraphs. To see what this principle is and how it works, let us return to the Wine-Shop chapter; Dickens is describing Saint Antoine and its citizens, who have now lapped up all they can of the spilled wine:

The children had ancient faces and grave voices; and upon them, and upon the grown faces, and ploughed into every furrow of age and coming up afresh, was the sign, *Hunger*. It was prevalent everywhere. *Hunger* was pushed out of the tall houses, in the wretched clothing that hung upon poles and lines; *Hunger* was patched into them with straw and rag and wood and paper; *Hunger* was repeated in every fragment of the small modicum of firewood that the man sawed off; *Hunger* stared down from the smokeless chimneys, and started up from the filthy street that had no offal, among its refuse, of anything to eat. *Hunger* was the inscription on the baker's shelves, written in every small loaf of his scanty stock of bad bread; at the sausage-shop, in every dead-dog preparation that was offered for sale. *Hunger* rattled its dry bones among the roasting chestnuts in the turned cylinder; *Hunger* was shred into atomies in every farthing porringer of husky chips of potato, fried with some reluctant drops of oil. [my italics]

There is much that will bear analysis in this passage, but for our present purposes what is interesting is the articulation of the narrative and descriptive materials by the use of the rhetorical device of *anaphora*, the repetition of the key word "Hunger" to introduce and mark off the successive items of the presented scene. This device, which may be seen at work very frequently in Dickens—for instance, in the Wine-Shop passages already quoted—epitomizes Dickens' method of ordering his imagined world. The details of the scene are not merely piled up, one upon another; rather, there is a kind of logic in their arrangement. Everything here is mentioned because it is a concomitant of hunger, because it is a familiar result or cause or symptom or contingency of that condition. Observation and report are controlled, selection is determined, by the key word. One cannot, however, argue the converse, that what is given in the scene necessitates the choice of the word "Hunger," for it is the word which tells the reader what to notice, how to take the descriptive elements. Substitution of another word—say, "Poverty" or "Misery"—would result in a different set of meanings for the same reported observations. Thus the principle of *relevance* in the passage seems to be determined by the choice of the anaphoric expression. But the principle of *order* in the passage seems to be differently derived. The reader is presented with a cinematic rendering of continuous space in continuous time, the narrator functioning as a camera-eye; details make their appearance according to their position in the imagined scene, one thing next to another, and still another next to that. We are invited to attend to the houses, to the clotheslines stretched from their windows, to the man sawing firewood in front of the houses, to the chimneys which show no sign of wood being burned inside, and back again to the street and its shops and shop signs, its chestnut stand, costermongers and their wares. Although the selection of details is determined by the anaphora, the ordering seems to be given by the scene itself, by the mere contiguity of things. Of course, one can discover other principles of order here—for instance, the gradual movement of the attention toward what little food there is—but the

description is handled in such a way that these other principles of arrangement seem to be mere corollaries of the
physical arrangement of the actual scene, as if one could
not avoid seeing things in this order. Indeed, the camera-eye
effect, the rendering of continuous space in continuous time,
seems to imply a strict necessity to report everything just
as it is; and if Dickens actually had been under such a
necessity, there could be no order at all except the "natural"
order of the observed scene. Such is, in fact, the impression
one often gets in reading his descriptions. He manages this
effect, without seeming to wander aimlessly and endlessly
over the scene, by means of the same rhetorical device that
allows him to exercise selectivity. The obligation to record
everything is avoided by the use of anaphora, which acts as
a delimiting device, a kind of lens and shutter marking off
selected bits of the scene, moving the reader's attention from
representative sample to representative sample, and thus
building an impression of the whole from the enumerated
parts. The rhetoric controls the time and space of perception
and report by opening (and, at each new opening, also thereby closing) the windows of the linguistic medium, our
access to the author's world.

Anaphora, then, seems to give Dickens his means both of
exercising selectivity and of presenting a scene as if he were
exercising no selectivity at all, as if he were merely reporting what is there to be seen, without any authorial influence
or distortion. Clearly enough, this is not a use of rhetoric
merely for its own sake. The flavor of the passage is not
rhetorical at all; what one notices is the vehemence of gaze
which so impressed Taine:

The imagination of Dickens is like that of monomaniacs. To
plunge oneself into an idea, to be absorbed by it, to see nothing
else, to repeat it under a hundred forms, to enlarge it, to carry

it, thus enlarged, to the eye of the spectator, to dazzle and over-whelm him with it, to stamp it upon him so firmly and deeply that he can never again tear it from his memory,—these are the great features of this imagination and style.[6]

The cumulative process by which the word-idea *Hunger* becomes a distinctive figure against the background of the street scene, a whole to which all the parts contribute and cling, is analogous to the mechanism of visual perception: a series of ocular fixations (with corresponding eye-movements) is essential to the perception of even the simplest figure, and, within limits, the vividness of the image depends on the number as well as the "intensity" of fixations and move-ments.[7] In the passage from the Wine-Shop chapter the vividness of the description may be partially accounted for by the anaphoric construction, each repetition of the word "Hunger" acting as a signal for "fixation" on that part of the whole which follows it.

While the anaphora is exercising its shuttering effect, superimposing a single-minded orderliness on the scene, the details thus framed exhibit their own internal logic, though it could hardly be called a planned progression. The principle of movement from detail to detail is the principle of con-tiguity, of juxtaposition and next-to-ness. The anaphora articulates and enumerates the parts, but without progress; whatever direction there is arises from the nature of the details themselves, in their physical associations with each other. Nor is this principle of movement by contiguity merely a function of Dickens' delight in objects, in the physical manifestations of reality, though the world of space, of visible, measurable dimensions, probably lends itself to such an organization more readily than any other. But beyond that, there is a *literalness* of vision in Dickens which condi-tions his apprehension of all phenomena, even in the realm of feeling or of ideas. He takes the world at surface value: his vision is not naive, but he takes experience as a child might, in concrete terms. In the Hunger passage, for example, we are given something like an ostensive definition of hunger, not by the citing of examples or equivalents, but by the presentation of concomitants of hunger, the things that go with it, that are part and parcel of it. Strictly speaking, one might not want to call the language of the passage metonymical, since none of the images here has the neatness of the usual textbook illustrations of metonymy; but in broader terms, Dickens' whole procedure may be described as metonymical, insofar as it depends on the principle of association by contiguity. As the linguist Roman Jakobson has theorized,

The development of a discourse may take place along two different semantic lines: one topic may lead to another either through their similarity or through their contiguity. The *metaphorical way* would be the most appropriate term for the first case and the *metonymical way* for the second, since they find their most condensed expression in metaphor and metonymy respectively.[8]

Let us return to the Wine-Shop passage: two kinds of order may be seen at work there—the order by juxtaposition given in the details themselves, and the directionless order superimposed by the anaphora. Contiguity determines both arrangements: on the one hand, the movement from detail to detail; on the other, the schematizing repetition and emphasis of the rhetorical frame. The details attract the eye and provide the continuity of a contiguous world. The anaphora marks off these details, or groups of them, one by one, drawing attention to the juxtaposition; but here the effect is not so much an emphasis on continuity as it is the opposite, a sort of discontinuity—a rhetorical net in which the details are caught in motion, like the arrested activity of a snapshot. Because the anaphora is neutral, in that it suggests no *particular* progression in the elements it frames, and yet at the same time does very strictly impose *some* order, the whole scene is thrown into a kind of relief. To borrow another cinematic concept, the effect is like that of a montage-cluster, a series of detail shots juxtaposed in time, as for example in the Odessa Steps sequence in *Potemkin*—or, perhaps even closer to Dickens' montage, the collocation of stills-in-sequence which Barnaby Conrad edited for his remarkable "movie," *The Death of Manolete* (others have borrowed the technique, as viewers of American television commercials can testify). In such models, it almost seems as if one thing does not lead to another; everything exists at once, juxtaposed, superimposed, articulated in the consciousness by the anaphoric pattern. The details are both isolated from and joined to each other by the rhetorical boundaries. The isolation in time and space—the caught moment—exactly identifies the photographic realism that is characteristic of Dickens' treatment of detail. Similarly, it is the articulation, the juxtaposition, the superimposition of such details that gives, by its combination of order and disjunction, the strangely unreal effect which we also associate with Dickens, the sense of a world all in pieces, where every fragment is nonetheless intimately and mysteriously involved with every other fragment.

## Metonymies of Character and Plot

Sometimes the "montage-clusters" of details which Dickens invents seem to take particularly strong hold on his mind, and he repeats them, or parts of them, in other contexts. Anaphora and other schematizing devices can have the effect of freezing the separate units together in the memory as an associational whole, and thus provide the basis for still another metonymic principle of connection between the larger parts of a novel. For example, Kenneth Burke has explained how any part of such an "associational cluster" may do synecdochic duty for the whole:

And as regards our speculations upon the nature of "clusters" or "equations," would it not follow that if there are, let us say, seven ingredients composing a cluster, any one of them could be treated as "representing" the rest? In this way such an image as a "house" in a poem can become a "house plus," serving as proxy for the other ingredients that cluster about it (e.g., for the beloved that lives in the house, and is thus "identified" with it). Usually, several of these other ingredients will appear surrounding the one temporarily featured.[9]

The cluster of details that forms the basis of a structural synecdoche like this may derive its original cohesiveness in several ways. Positional contiguity—the fact that the elements first occur in close proximity to each other, often strongly marked by anaphoric devices—may determine the connection. Then again, the pattern need not be set up in a single paragraph or even a single chapter. Take the example of the Stone Face cluster in *A Tale of Two Cities*: throughout several chapters of Book 2 various ingredients are associated through their connection (again, by contiguity) with the Marquis St. Evrémonde's face. The Marquis is introduced in Chapter VII of the second book:

He was a man of about sixty, handsomely dressed, haughty in manner, and with a face like a fine mask. A face of a transparent paleness; every feature in it clearly defined; one set expression on it. The nose, beautifully formed otherwise, was very slightly pinched at the top of each nostril. In these two compressions, or dints, the only little change that the face ever showed, resided. They persisted in changing colour sometimes, and they would be occasionally dilated and contracted by something like a faint pulsation; then, they gave a look of treachery, and cruelty, to the whole countenance.

In the same chapter, after running down a child with his coach, the Marquis betrays his anger through this physiognomical peculiarity:

"You dogs!" said the Marquis, but smoothly, and with an unchanged front, except as to the spots on his nose: "I would ride over any of you very willingly, and exterminate you from the earth."

Chapter ix begins with a description of the Marquis' château, and introduces the image of the stone face:

It was a heavy mass of building, that château of Monsieur the Marquis, with a large stone court-yard before it, and two stone sweeps of staircase meeting in a stone terrace before the principal door. A stony business altogether, with heavy stone balustrades, and stone urns, and stone flowers, and stone faces of men, and stone heads of lions, in all directions. As if the Gorgon's head had surveyed it, when it was finished, two centuries ago.

. . . . .

The great door clanged behind him, and Monsieur the Marquis crossed a hall grim with certain old boar-spears, swords, and knives of the chase; grimmer with certain heavy riding-rods and riding-whips, of which many a peasant, gone to his benefactor Death, had felt the weight when his lord was angry.

Later in the chapter, the Marquis' face begins its transformation to stone:

Every fine straight line in the clear whiteness of his face, was cruelly, craftily, and closely compressed, while he stood looking quietly at his nephew, with his snuff-box in his hand.

In the Marquis we have a perfect model, almost a prototype, for the well-known Dickens caricature, complete with social mask, hidden motives, and an exaggerated oddity—the nose—

which provides the necessary key to the connection between the apparent and the real character. The cluster of information about the Marquis—his cold indifference (to the child's death), his heritage of cruelty (the riding-whips), his crafty hatred (of Darnay, his nephew)—circles persistently about the central image of his masklike face with its pinched and dinted nose. Everything comes back to that mask, that nose, and those dints, which finally take on more life than the Marquis himself.

Similar cases in others of Dickens' novels immediately suggest themselves: Merdle in *Little Dorrit,* whose hands are always taking each other into custody; or Rigaud-Blandois, also in *Little Dorrit,* whose character is summed up in his disgusting smile; or Bucket in *Bleak House,* whose function in the story may be reduced to his accusing finger. In each of these caricatures the major image is accompanied by a cluster of associated images, as a sun by its planets, and the attention is largely limited to the repeated orbitings within this system, a single image dominating the whole in intensity and centrality.

As Burke points out, there is a special advantage to these circling yet fixed patterns of association, in that a single part of any cluster may be used synecdochically to suggest the whole. Typically in Dickens there is some pivotal detail that serves in this way; the image of the stone mask with its pinched nose sets off the train of associations. Thus at the end of Chapter IX, where Dickens sums up all the Marquis' sins and their punishment, he returns to this dominant image:

The Gorgon had surveyed the building again in the night, and had added the one stone face wanting; the stone face for which it had waited through about two hundred years.

It lay back on the pillow of Monsieur the Marquis. It was like a fine mask, suddenly startled, made angry, and petrified.

The mask has usurped the field; nothing else of the cluster remains. The Marquis has been totally dehumanized, and exists only as a stone face. Taine has pointed out this dehumanizing effect of Dickens' caricature:

The tenacity of your imagination, the vehemence and fixity with which you [that is, Dickens] impress your thought into the detail you wish to grasp, limit your knowledge, arrest you in a single feature, prevent you from reaching all the parts of a soul, and from sounding its depths.[10]

But Taine short-changes Dickens' genius. This static, almost staring effect in the characterization of the Marquis, the fascination with his nose, accounts for the vividness of the characterization, just as the repetitive, "fixing" devices such as anaphora account for the vividness of the scenes. Actually Taine's complaint has to do with the lack of conventional realism in Dickens—we do not see "all the parts of a soul," the contradictory motives, the paradoxes of behavior that give an illusion of depth. But Dickens' verisimilitude is of another sort: the static quality is necessary to the photographic precision and clarity, while the third dimension—apparent depth—is given in the *meaning* of the character, by the use of associational clusters circling round a central image.

Dickens' iconography is in no sense unsophisticated or unpsychological. In the example of the Marquis' nose, the Marquis' defining quality is not ordinary anger but rage, habitually suppressed and therefore white-hot. In the stone mask with the pinched, pulsating dints in the nose, Dickens manages to express both the fury and its suppression. Moreover, while the Marquis' nose gives us the key to his character, other elements in the scene itself are used to elaborate this indirect presentation. When the Marquis leaves the town house of Monseigneur, furious because he is out of favor, the anger is allowed to show only in his pulsating nose.

But for once the image is not adequate to the power of the feeling, which is actually expressed in the scene that follows, when the Marquis' *coach* runs down a helpless child—thus conveying, by a perfectly appropriate metonymy, the murderous rage that possesses him. In general, the Marquis cannot be allowed to have any direct contact with the fulfillment of his fiery desires, since it is his character to suppress his feelings. His ancestors wielded the riding whips, his coach acts out his fury, his nose betrays his hidden passion.

The extreme of his detachment is given in the vengeance he takes for his own murder, for now he exists *only* as a stone mask with a dinted nose:

A rumour just lived in the village—had a faint and bare existence there, as its people had—that when the knife struck home, the faces changed, from faces of pride to faces of anger and pain; also, that when that dangling figure [of Gaspard] was hauled up forty feet above the fountain, they changed again, and bore a cruel look of being avenged, which they would henceforth bear for ever. In the stone face over the great window of the bedchamber where the murder was done, two fine dints were pointed out in the sculptured nose, which everybody recognised, and which nobody had seen of old. [2, XVI]

In Chapter XXIII of the second book, the Marquis' anger reaches its climax when the revolutionaries have seized power and are destroying his château. Appropriately enough, the Marquis is himself consumed in his own rage, symbolized in the scene by the holocaust:

The château was left to itself to flame and burn. In the roaring and raging of the conflagration, a red-hot wind, driving straight from the infernal regions, seemed to be blowing the edifice away. With the rising and falling of the blaze, the stone faces showed as if they were in torment. When great masses of stone and timber fell, the face with the two dints in the nose became obscured:

anon struggled out of the smoke again, as if it were the face of the cruel Marquis, burning at the stake and contending with the fire.

Dickens says "as if it were the face of the cruel Marquis," but indeed the Marquis' face has become stone, and we finally see him in his true aspect, concealed so long behind the mask: "burning at the stake and contending with the fire."

The same synecdochic use of an image to express character or even theme occurs again and again in the *Tale* and in Dickens' other novels. In any one novel, several clusters will combine to spread their network of relationship throughout the entire narrative. These connections are based on a closed system of metonymies and synecdoches, one cluster being related to another by means of some common part which can represent either whole. Dickens' use of such patterns as a plotting device has been noticed by J. Hillis Miller:

Images in a novel get their significance not simply in their immediate relation to the narrative line, but in relation to all the images in their contexts before and after. In Dickens this spatial quality results in part from the intricate plots in which everything that happens and all the characters turn out in the end to be somehow related. The revelations at the end cause the whole pattern of the novel to fall into place almost with an audible click.[11]

Although I would not agree that the unraveling of relationships is always withheld until the end, Miller is certainly right about this "spatial quality." A Dickens novel is like a crossword puzzle, worked out temporally, one item at a time, but existing finally in space, all at once, in a network of interconnections. Joseph Frank has pointed out similar systems in other writers, where "relationships are juxtaposed independently of narrative progress; the full significance of the scene [in Dickens' case, one could say of the whole novel] is given only by the reflexive relations among the units of meaning."[12] In such a novel, foreshadowing is only one part of the reflexive structure. Elements refer both forward and backward, and clusters of associations not only provide a context for new materials, but are themselves influenced by their repetition in varying circumstances, so that foreshadowing is modified in the memory by what it foreshadows. Consider, for example, the gradual accumulation of meaning in the successive reappearances of the Wine-and-Scarecrow motif introduced in the Wine-Shop chapter:

Those who had been greedy with the staves of the cask, had acquired a tigerish smear about the mouth; and one tall joker so besmirched, his head more out of a long squalid bag of a night-cap than in it, scrawled upon a wall with his finger dipped in muddy wine-lees—BLOOD.

. . . . .

A narrow winding street, full of offence and stench, with other narrow winding streets diverging, all peopled by rags and night-caps, and all smelling of rags and nightcaps, and all visible things with a brooding look upon them that looked ill. . . . every wind that blew over France shook the rags of the scarecrows in vain, for the birds, fine of song and feather, took no warning. [1, v]

The rooms [of Monseigneur], though a beautiful scene to look at, and adorned with every device of decoration that the taste and skill of the time could achieve, were, in truth, not a sound business; considered with any reference to the scarecrows in the rags and nightcaps elsewhere (and not so far off, either, but that the watching towers of Notre Dame, almost equidistant from the two extremes, could see them both), they would have been an exceedingly uncomfortable business. . . . [2, VII]

Saint Antoine had been, that morning, a vast dusky mass of scarecrows heaving to and fro, with frequent gleams of light above the billowy heads, where steel blades and bayonets shone in the sun. [2, XXI]

Lovely girls; bright women, brown-haired, black-haired, and grey; youths; stalwart men and old; gentle born and peasant born; all red wine for La Guillotine, all daily brought into light from the dark cellars of loathsome prisons, and carried to her through the street to slake her devouring thirst. [3, V]

Rags, nightcaps, patched scarecrows, greedy drinkers of wine—all change, from signs of poverty, to causes of revolution, to effects of revolution. In this change a kind of temporal succession is implied; however, the meaning of these relations among the images finally exists not in a sequence but rather all at once, "spatially" configured as Miller and Frank suggest. As in dreams, the logical connections of the surface narrative carry less of the meaning than does the logic hidden in the combination of images: the hungry scarecrows will drink the blood of the lords and ladies in all their finery; the aristocracy is the natural prey of the proletariat.

This atemporal reflexive technique is most easily observed in the special case where a cluster is arranged in point-by-point correspondence with the whole novel, making an all-inclusive narrative metonymy. Again Miller has described the device:

In a sense the opening chapters of a novel should imply the entire novel by giving us a situation in which a certain action is potentially inevitable. The various arrows of expectancy I have analyzed in the first two chapters of *Little Dorrit* serve such a synecdochic purpose. They contain yet do not reveal all that will come after, as an embryo hides and yet implies all its future development.[13]

One can distinguish three different methods of foreshadowing that may be involved. First, there is the kind present to some extent in all novels, which is scarcely foreshadowing at all, but merely a limitation of the possibilities of action, as circumscribed by conditions given in the beginning. Second, there is normal foreshadowing, the introduction of "arrows of expectancy," in Dickens often accompanied by some such verbal signal as "The time was yet to come when. . . ." Finally, there is the "embryonic" foreshadowing, in which the whole pattern of events is prefigured in considerable detail. This last device seems to be more than mere foreshadowing. Of the three methods it alone is truly synecdochic, a part of the novel representing the whole.

Although it does so in *Little Dorrit,* the embryonic episode need not occur at the beginning or in any other special place; in *A Tale of Two Cities,* Chapter vi of the second book contains such a synecdochic foreshadowing, from which the lines of correspondence stretch out both forward and backward to encompass the whole novel. The passage, long as it is, must be quoted nearly in full to preserve its peculiar effect:

The night was so very sultry, that although they sat with doors and windows open, they were overpowered by heat. When the tea-table was done with, they all moved to one of the windows, and looked out into the heavy twilight. Lucie sat by her father; Darnay sat beside her; Carton leaned against a window. The curtains were long and white, and some of the thunder-gusts that whirled into the corner, caught them up to the ceiling, and waved them like spectral wings.

"The rain-drops are still falling, large, heavy, and few," said Doctor Manette. "It comes slowly."

"It comes surely," said Carton.

They spoke low, as people watching and waiting mostly do; as people in a dark room, watching and waiting for Lightning, always do.

There was a great hurry in the streets, of people speeding away to get to shelter before the storm broke; the wonderful corner for echoes resounded with the echoes of footsteps coming and going, yet not a footstep was there.

"A multitude of people, and yet a solitude!" said Darnay, when they had listened for a while.

"Is it not impressive, Mr. Darnay?" asked Lucie. "Sometimes, I have sat here of an evening, until I have fancied—but even the shade of a foolish fancy makes me shudder tonight, when all is so black and solemn—"

"Let us shudder too. We may know what it is."

"It will seem nothing to you. Such whims are only impressive as we originate them, I think; they are not to be communicated. I have sometimes sat alone here of an evening, listening, until I have made the echoes out to be the echoes of all the footsteps that are coming by-and-by into our lives."

"There is a great crowd coming one day into our lives, if that be so," Sydney Carton struck in, in his moody way.

The footsteps were incessant, and the hurry of them became more and more rapid. The corner echoed and re-echoed with the tread of feet; some, as it seemed, under the windows; some, as it seemed, in the room; some coming, some going, some breaking off, some stopping altogether; all in the distant streets, and not one within sight.

"Are all these footsteps destined to come to all of us, Miss Manette, or are we to divide them among us?"

"I don't know, Mr. Darnay; I told you it was a foolish fancy, but you asked for it. When I have yielded myself to it, I have been alone, and then I have imagined them the footsteps of the people who are to come into my life, and my father's."

"I take them into mine!" said Carton. "*I* ask no questions and make no stipulations. There is a great crowd bearing down upon us, Miss Manette, and I see them—by the Lightning." He added the last words, after there had been a vivid flash which had shown him lounging in the window.

"And I hear them!" he added again, after a peal of thunder. "Here they come, fast, fierce, and furious!"

It was the rush and roar of rain that he typified, and it stopped him, for no voice could be heard in it. A memorable storm of thunder and lightning broke with that sweep of water, and there was not a moment's interval in crash, and fire, and rain, until after the moon rose at midnight.

In the first paragraph the still developing relations among the characters are sketched: Doctor Manette, his loyal daughter, her future husband, and, removed from them all, Carton, in a characteristic posture. The mention of "spectral wings" suggests that what follows may not be merely what it seems. And indeed almost every detail—even bits of the syntax— reaches outside the scene. The triad "large, heavy, and few," which Doctor Manette uses to describe the rain, gives place by the end of the scene to "fast, fierce, and furious," and this in turn looks forward to the phrase "headlong, mad, and dangerous," which later in the novel will be used to describe the outbreak of the revolutionary storm. In accord with the quickening tempo implied in this sequence, the tempest begins slowly, if surely, as Doctor Manette and Carton observe. Their remarks parallel those of Defarge and his wife, as they too await the "tempest" and its lightning, in Chapter XVI of the second book:

"It is a long time," repeated his wife; "and when is it not a long time? Vengeance and retribution require a long time; it is the rule."

"It does not take a long time to strike a man with Lightning," said Defarge.

"How long," demanded madame, composedly, "does it take to make and store the lightning? Tell me."

But Defarge has not long to wait, nor does the little group in Soho. The footsteps that echo in the dark room are in a hurry, pounding into their lives. They are the footsteps of the wine-stained feet in St. Antoine, of the blood-stained feet yet to come. Ironically it is Darnay (through whom the others are all involved in the Revolution) who asks whether the footsteps are coming to them as a group or individually. In the end, of course, they are coming not for Lucie or Darnay, but for Carton, and his voluntary acceptance of whatever they may bring exactly forecasts his final acceptance of another's fate. Finally the tempest is upon them. The description looks forward, with its "rush and roar," its "thunder and lightning," to the Revolution scene:

Saint Antoine had been, that morning, a vast dusky mass of scarecrows heaving to and fro, with frequent gleams of light above the billowy heads, where steel blades and bayonets shone in the sun. A tremendous roar arose from the throat of Saint Antoine, and a forest of naked arms struggled in the air like shrivelled branches of trees in a winter wind: all the fingers convulsively clutching at every weapon or semblance of a weapon that was thrown up from the depths below, no matter how far off.

Who gave them out, whence they last came, where they began, through what agency they crookedly quivered and jerked, scores at a time, over the heads of the crowd, like a kind of lightning, no eye in the throng could have told. [2, xxi]

The "crash, and fire, and rain" also match the three chapters that describe the Revolution: "Echoing Footsteps," "The Sea Still Rises," and "Fire Rises." But most precise of all is the foreshadowing "sweep of water" which, in its rush, "stopped" Carton. Compare his last moments on the scaffold:

The murmuring of many voices, the upturning of many faces, the pressing on of many footsteps in the outskirts of the crowd, so that it swells forward in a mass, *like one great heave of water,* all flashes away. [italics mine]

Even Carton's final resurrection is hinted in the rising of the moon which ends the storm. In fact, no major movement of the novel is without its reflection in this scene—the introduction of characters and of the relations between them; the awaiting of the tempest, the listening to approaching footsteps; the breaking of the storm; Carton's sacrifice, his death, his resurrection.

The basis of the elaborate structural synecdoche we have just been examining is to be found in Dickens' use of details, especially details of setting, as means of establishing clusters of meaning and feeling—which, in this novel, finally resolve themselves into two great polar loci, London and Paris, the tales of the little house in Soho and the streets of St. Antoine. *A Tale of Two Cities* displays in its very title this tendency of all Dickens' later work to polarize into two main locales, around one or the other of which all the action centers. This geographical organization is at the heart of each novel's structure,* and on it too depends the powerful sense of atmosphere that is one of Dickens' trademarks. Thus is the "unnecessary detail" of the novels crucially significant in their overall effect. Similarly, the principle of combination and connection that holds these details together in their clusters and larger configurations is contiguity. Metonymically and anaphorically controlled patterns dominate the structure, keeping the materials ordered in what, from one point of view, might seem a rather rigid and artificial rhetorical frame. This same principle may be seen operating on every level of the style, articulating sentence and paragraph, episode and plot; characters are built on it, and setting is everywhere determined by it. Artificial as Dickens' rhetoric may sometimes seem, it allows him to command effects which are out of the question for most writers, at once realistic in kind and in quantity of detail, and almost allegorical in the schematization and intensity of rendering. The blend is dream-

---

*See Chapter 4 for detailed analyses of these larger structural patterns, more properly viewed as elements of plot than of style.

like, hallucinatory, super-real. Dickens seems to have tapped a source of imaginative truth which, although it surely corresponds to modes of perception and feeling in all men, has rarely been exploited for literary purposes with any success, and has still more rarely given rise to so full and elaborate a fictive world.

# 2

# The Vision of Reality

AS we move now from considerations of Dickens' style to a concern with his vision of reality, we meet difficulties that go beyond the usual problems arising in the analysis of an author's literary method or manner. These difficulties are of two sorts, one arising from the question now to be posed—what is the relation, in Dickens, between stylistic features and the world-view?—and the other from the rather unusual answer we are obliged to offer to that question here. The first difficulty is one of methodology, for modern criticism has no well-developed theory of literary manner, though much has been written about particular manners, such as realism, naturalism, and so on. What is especially unclear in the theory of literary manner is the relation between an author's actual world and his fictive world, and how this relation is manifested in his style. This is one of the most tangled questions in contemporary criticism, namely the question of mimesis. And because it is precisely the movement from style to manner that I now want to trace in my analysis of Dickens' novels, I shall begin this chapter with an attempt to set forth some of the primary distinctions necessary for dealing with problems of mimesis.

The second difficulty is one which arises simply because it is Dickens we are studying. The literary manner in which he practiced has never been given a name, and has been only sketchily investigated—even though a number of artists have worked in it, as I intend to suggest in my final chapter on Dickens' place in Victorian culture and society. Because the ground has been so little cultivated, I shall of necessity proceed rather abstractly and theoretically, both in the present chapter and in the one that follows it and develops its themes. I shall draw on a number of the novels for illustration— especially *A Tale of Two Cities,* since the stylistic features already discovered in it are to provide the foundation for much of what we can say about Dickens' literary manner— but there will be no very full or detailed analysis of any single novel in this chapter or the next. The application of what we learn about Dickens' vision of reality must wait until all the theoretical questions have been raised and studied.

## *Mimesis*

The literary manner of an author—his realism, or his naturalism, or his symbolism, and so on into the manners which have no names—is his way of coming to terms with life in the medium of fiction. Men write fiction to make sense of their experience of the world, and to make that experience theirs by saying how it is for them, by formulating for themselves and their readers the facts of life. Thus the novelist Paul Goodman has described some of his early "naturalistic" fiction as the expression of his willingness then "to regard the scene and the society as *my* scene and *my* society, rich in interest, still possessing the potentialities of

life, worth transcribing with fidelity."[14] Or, with a somewhat different focus, Northrop Frye distinguishes modes of
fiction as "romance," "novel," "anatomy," "confession," and
their combinations—all again largely on the basis of the
author's attitude or stance vis-à-vis his world.[15]

Novelists do not tell us *what is* so much as *the way it is.*
Truth to life in fiction is a matter of ways and kinds rather
than of facts and data. When facts do appear in a novel,
they have a function different from the one they have in
history or biography, as the reader of *A Tale of Two Cities*
may see easily enough. Works like the *Tale,* or like *Heart of
Midlothian, The Blithedale Romance,* or *Moby-Dick,* are
full of what might be called "nonfictional fiction," genuine
reports and accounts of real things, events, people, utilized
as integral parts of the imaginative whole. Often it is impossible to decide whether the "facts" a novelist presents have
actual counterparts or not; many a fictional statement could
be a statement of fact, many a novel could be a biography or
an autobiography. But we do distinguish between these cases,
between the factual and the fictional, wherever the author
gives us evidence that permits us to do so. In nonfiction
we are concerned with what actually is or was; considerations of accuracy and veracity come into play. But if an
author presents his work as a fiction, we read it differently, and its factuality is not in question. In *Moby-Dick*
it does not make much difference to know that the sperm
whale is not, contrary to Ishmael's assertion, the largest of
mammals. It is only important that the sperm whale be so
regarded *in the book,* for we have to do with what life is
like, what *sorts* of cases there are or might be, not with what
is *the* case.

Yet some authors, such as Defoe, pretend to relate the true
events of private histories, and arrange their stories accord-

ing to notions of how things happen and how people act in everyday life—with the apparent intent of taking the reader in. Defoe selects extraordinary human beings and extraordinary situations, to be sure; but his aim seems to be to get his reader to believe in his stories as genuine reports of experience, and he goes at it chiefly by paying attention to the commonplace circumstances which give body and content to the unusual as well as to the usual in human affairs. Moll Flanders' career may be incredible when taken as a whole (as, for example, in Defoe's subtitle), but the details as they are worked out, bit by bit, strike the reader as familiar, even tediously so.

Other writers make less pretense to this sort of factuality, yet follow similar principles of selection and ordering; their truth to life consists in mentioning the same things they might mention in recounting something that had actually happened to them or in their presence—but without any protestations that these are indeed the facts, truth *from* life.

A very different sort of writer, Poe, is nonetheless striving like Defoe to come to terms with life by means of language, and the fictive world he presents has its meaning in relation to everyday reality just as much as any author's, though he does not present it "realistically"; Poe is not concerned with the commonplaces of experience or with the ordinary ways of recounting them, and yet the effect of his special vision—its very specialness—depends on there being a familiar reality in the background, habits of belief which we seem to share with Poe in spite of his peculiar imagination. We must have gazed into ordinary mirrors in order to appreciate the effect of a distorting one, and not simply because we need the standard of reference, but also because we need to recognize the principle of relationship between mirrors and reality, the terms of the perceptual event.

When Poe puts his "faith in dreams as in the only realities," he has not changed the conditions of his art, he has simply inverted his terms. To tell a dream one must use the language of the real world, though of course there will be more "as if" constructions than in telling other things. Similarly such a writer as Hawthorne, who likes to refer to his work as dreamy and phantasmagorical, and who is not quite sure whether he believes in the world of solid objects or not, is obliged to mention such objects in order to say anything at all.

In these remarks concerning various sorts of storytellers and their truth to life, two different grounds of verisimilitude may be seen lurking in the theoretic background: that which appeals to our *judgment* of the correspondence between a fiction and life, and that which appeals to our *impression* of the lifelikeness of a fiction. Both these appeals go under the name of verisimilitude, but they are quite different. The first may be termed natural verisimilitude, the second artificial verisimilitude.

The secrets of achieving natural verisimilitude are the secrets of literary art in general: sensitivity to experience, intelligence, knowledge of the conventions of fiction, taste, talent. Such a list might be expanded greatly, but the main elements are these. To say what life is like, one must know something about the way life is and be able to imagine situations, people, and events that will conform to that knowledge.

Artificial verisimilitude, however, is scarcely a matter of fidelity at all, but rather one of appearance or effect. It is the "illusion of reality" spoken of by critics, the "credibility" or "authenticity" or "genuineness" that are often mentioned as virtues of fiction. The methods by which novelists achieve such effects are much more technical and specialized than the means of achieving natural verisimilitude—they include such devices as the simulation of artifacts (letters, diaries, autobiographies, and so on) found in ordinary life; or the choice of familiar materials (ordinary kinds of people and events); or the use of commonplace ways of talking about things (simple diction and syntax). Critics have frequently interested themselves in this sort of verisimilitude, and an inventory of such devices might take up many pages; but the main difference between the two kinds of truth to life ought to be clear from these few illustrations: namely, that artificial verisimilitude is essentially a matter of technique and effect, whereas natural verisimilitude is a matter of fictive truth, displayed and enhanced by method perhaps, but not immediately dependent on it in the way that artificial verisimilitude is.

Now either of these kinds of verisimilitude may be regarded as an important element in an author's literary manner—his realism, naturalism, or whatever. But one must be continually on guard against confusing the two ways of taking the problem of truth to life. For example, when critics talk about Dickens' realism or lack of it, they sometimes fail to distinguish the truth of his perceptions about the way the world is from his means of presenting those perceptions. Thus there arise the quarrels over whether or not Dickens' "flat" characters (E. M. Forster's term[16]) are lifelike. This critical battlefield bristles with as many standards as there are disputants: James thought Dickens "created nothing but figures," a poor substitute for "human character"; Orwell called them "gargoyles," and Mario Praz suggests that they are "more alive than life."[17] George Gissing and Robert Liddell maintain that Dickens was only describing with perfect accuracy the bygone oddities of his day,[18] and George Santayana goes even further in defending him:

When people say Dickens exaggerates, it seems to me they can
have no eyes and no ears. They probably have only *notions* of
what things and people are; they accept them conventionally,
at their diplomatic value. Their minds run on in the region of
discourse, where there are masks only and no faces, ideas and
no facts; they have little sense for those living grimaces that
play from moment to moment upon the countenance of the
world.[19]

With such a view Dickens would substantially have agreed.
In the preface to *Martin Chuzzlewit* he states his case:

What is exaggeration to one class of minds and perceptions, is
plain truth to another. That which is commonly called a long-
sight, perceives in a prospect innumerable features and bearings
non-existent to a short-sighted person. I sometimes ask myself
whether there may occasionally be a difference of this kind
between some writers and some readers; whether it is *always* the
writer who colours highly, or whether it is now and then the
reader whose eye for colour is a little dull?

I doubt whether this controversy really takes us very far
in understanding Dickens' truth to life, for all that he himself seems to offer testimony favoring one side of the question.
The confusion over whether or not he exaggerates arises not
from ambiguous qualities in his characters, but from our own
inability to agree about what is at issue. For although it may
be true that Dickens' characters are in some ultimate sense
very like the people we see around us every day, the means
by which they are presented to us, the way we are told about
them—in short, the author's use of literary devices which
work for or against artificial verisimilitude—do not much
cater to our habits of response, our conventions of lifelikeness. Dickens certainly attains a very high degree of natural
verisimilitude, in that he renders experience in a way that
generations of readers have found deeply meaningful, an

important vision of reality; but he conveys this vision by means of devices which, although sometimes conducive to artificial verisimilitude, are often destructive of it. The special blend of devices working for and against this impression of truth to life determines, to a large extent, the quality or flavor of Dickens' vision of reality, his natural verisimilitude. Furthermore, the conventions of artificial verisimilitude are more than bare literary devices. Thus, for example, in an author's decision to maintain or violate plausibility by the use of a *deus ex machina*, we see something of his attitude toward life—not so much an indication of what he thinks the possibilities of life are, as a hint of the kind of situation that forces him to choose the "impossible" alternative, as opposed to the kind that allows him to remain in the realm of the plausible. It is also significant in an author's view of life whether he seems more comfortable within the range of ordinary probability, or outside it. Such subtle questions cannot be treated without making careful distinctions between the two kinds of verisimilitude.

In the following pages on Dickens' narrative stance, I shall take up several problems of artificial and natural verisimilitude, in an attempt to establish the connections between the features of Dickens' style already examined and his vision of reality. My approach to the problem takes narrative stance as the major fact of literary manner, and the mediating element between style and world-view.

## The Role of the Narrator

In a very provocative essay George Henry Lewes tells us, "Dickens once declared to me that every word said by his characters was distinctly heard by him." In Lewes' view, this boast (or confession?) is to be taken literally and accounted for on psychological grounds:

He was a seer of visions; and his visions were of objects at once familiar and potent. Psychologists will understand both the extent and the limitation of the remark, when I say that in no other perfectly sane mind (Blake, I believe, was not perfectly sane) have I observed vividness of imagination approaching so closely to hallucination.

. . . . .

What seems preposterous, impossible to us, seemed to him simple fact of observation. When he imagined a street, a house, a room, a figure, he saw it not in the vague schematic way of ordinary imagination, but in the sharp definition of actual perception, all the salient details obtruding themselves on his attention. He, seeing it thus vividly, made us also see it; and believing in its reality however fantastic, he communicated something of his belief to us. He presented it in such relief that we ceased to think of it as a picture. So definite and insistent was the image, that even while knowing it was false we could not help, for a moment, being affected, as it were, by his hallucination.[20]

John Forster, in spite of his violent disagreement with Lewes on the nature and origin of Dickens' ability, goes even further in attributing unusual powers of imagination to his friend:

No man had ever so surprising a faculty as Dickens of becoming himself what he was representing; and of entering into mental phases and processes so absolutely, in conditions of life the most varied, as to reproduce them completely in dialogue without the need of an explanatory word.

And he quotes a letter from Dickens, in which the author himself similarly describes the creative act which brings forth his imaginary world: "I don't invent it—really do not—but *see it*, and write it down."[21]

The kind of vision reported by Lewes and Forster and by Dickens himself is probably no less common among artists than among the inmates of mental institutions, although the degree of hallucination (or imaginative vision) is rarely so great in the artist as it is in those touched by madness. But Dickens' imaginative powers were so compelling that he could not only "see," but even "be" the characters he created. I do not mean merely that he identified with them, took sides, and so on; his projection (what Keats called "negative capability") was much more complete than that. A glance at the "Memoranda" book in which he recorded ideas for stories during his later years will indicate just how total that identification was; here are some examples, ranging from the barest hints and snatches of action to ideas for major events and turns of plot:

Bedridden (or room-ridden) twenty—five and twenty—years; any length of time. As to most things, kept at a standstill all the while. Thinking of altered streets as the old streets—changed things as the unchanged things—the youth or girl I quarreled with all those years ago, as the same youth or girl now. Brought out of doors by an unexpected exercise of my latent strength of character, and then how strange!

Done in Mrs. Clennam

The lady *un peu passée*, who is determined to be interesting. No matter how much I love that person—nay, the more so for that very reason—I MUST flatter and bother, and be weak and apprehensive and nervous and what not. If I were well and strong, agreeable and self-denying, my friend might forget me.

I affect to believe that I would do anything myself for a Ten Pound note, and that anybody else would. I affect to be always book-keeping in every man's case and posting up a little account of good and evil with everyone. Thus the greatest rascal becomes "the dearest old fellow," and there is much less difference than you would be inclined to suppose between an honest man and a scoundrel. While I affect to be finding good in most men, I am in reality decrying it where it really is, and setting it up where it is not.

Done in Dorrit [Henry Gowan]

I am a common woman, fallen. Is it devilry in me—is it a wicked comfort—what is it—that induces me to be always tempting other women down, while I hate myself!

The two men to be guarded against, as to their revenge. One, whom I openly hold in some serious animosity, and whom I am at the pains to wound and defy, and estimate as worth wounding and defying; the other, whom I treat as a sort of insect, and contemptuously and pleasantly flick aside with my glove. But it turns out to be the latter who is the really dangerous man; and, when I expect the blow from the other, it comes from *him*.

*We* must emigrate to China.

WE,——together.

I stand by my friends and acquaintances;—not for their sakes, but because they are *my* friends and acquaintances. *I* know them, *I* have licensed them, they have taken out *my* certificate. Ergo, I champion them as myself. [Podsnap]

"If they were great things, I, the untrustworthy man in little things, would do them Earnestly"—But O No, I wouldn't! [Eugene]

As to the question whether I, Eugene, lying ill and sick even unto death, may be consoled by the representation that, coming through this illness, I shall begin a new life, and have energy and purpose and all I have yet wanted: *"I hope I should, but I know I shouldn't. Let me die, my dear."*[22]

It should be pointed out that not all the notebook entries are couched in the first person. I have quoted most of those that are, to show the variety of points of view with which Dickens was able to identify—not merely the major figures such as Eugene, with whom he might be expected to feel and think, but also minor characters—even despicable ones—like Podsnap and Henry Gowan, with whom we would suppose him to have little sympathy. In this sense at least, Dickens seems to be *in* all his characters, to feel with and identify with them, regardless of the formal perspective finally adopted for their presentation in the novels. This identification with all the characters is especially important because it seems to prevent his taking any one role and identifying himself deeply with it. We never have the impression that the author is himself the hero, as we do for instance in *Middlemarch* or *Evelina* or *The Sun Also Rises*. Not even Dickens' first-person novels give us this sense of the author as protagonist. Perhaps the simple fact that readers are less used to this point of view than to the objective third person may account for the artificial, detached effect; at any rate, David, Esther, and Pip are rather thin, distant heroes ("bubbles," E. M. Forster calls them); the use of the "I"-perspective seems strangely to dilute the life of the Dickens hero. No one would argue that Esther's half of *Bleak House* is as vital as the third-person narrator's half, still less that Esther stands for Dickens. David and Pip partly represent him, but only with Pip does the first person seem to make much difference: at least Pip tells his own story; David merely tells a story which sometimes involves him, as in the late picaresque tradition where the hero no longer is allowed to have his own adventures.

According to Morton Zabel, the split point of view in *Bleak House* is a formal indication that Dickens "had come to stand both inside his story and outside of it." The proof, of course, lies in the paradox that in *Bleak House* Dickens seems to be most *in* his story when he is *out* of it (the third-person narrative), and most *out* of it when he is *in* it (the first-person narrative). This Zabel explains as an expression "of his own increasing ambiguity of mind and feeling, the sentimentalist at grips with the radical in his nature, the conformist at odds with the critic and social rebel."[23] One can understand how Zabel's interpretation is right, so far as it

45

goes; certainly it helps explain a number of thematic incon-
sistencies in *Bleak House*. But we need to press the inquiry
further, to ask how this peculiar inside-outside effect is
achieved and how it influences our total impression of Dickens' novelistic world.

There is plenty of evidence in the novels themselves that
Dickens was interested in experimenting with point of view.
At least as early as *The Old Curiosity Shop* he was tinkering
with it. And even in the novels told entirely in the third
person, passages can be found where the perspective suddenly
tilts and the detached narrator is himself plunged into
action. Thus in *A Tale of Two Cities,* during the frantic
flight of the Darnays from Paris, the point of view slips into
the first person, prepared for by a shift into the present tense
at the beginning of the episode—

The same shadows that are falling on the prison, are falling,
in that same hour of the early afternoon, on the Barrier with the
crowd about it, when a coach going out of Paris drives up to
be examined

—and very subtly brought to overt expression by the merging
of dialogue and narrative:

[Lucie cries,] "Look back, look back, and see if we are
pursued."

"The road is clear, my dearest," [Lorry replies]. "So far, we
are not pursued."

Houses in twos and threes pass by us, solitary farms, ruinous
buildings, dye-works, tanneries, and the like, open country,
avenues of leafless trees. The hard uneven pavement is under
us, the soft deep mud is on either side. Sometimes, we strike into
the skirting mud, to avoid the stones that clatter us and shake us;
sometimes we stick in ruts and sloughs there. The agony
of our impatience is then so great, that in our wild alarm and
hurry we are for getting out and running—hiding—doing anything but stopping. [3, xiii]

The strange alternation of dialogue—still presented as if from the third-person point of view—with narrative in the first person, goes on until the end of the chapter, and is evidently intended to heighten the immediacy and suspense of the escape. In fact, whenever Dickens employs this curious device, he seems to count on it to intensify the emotion. In *Our Mutual Friend* he uses it in the scene where Gaffer Hexam's body is found, again in the scene where Rogue Riderhood is revived from apparent drowning, and yet again in Betty Higden's death scene.

A similar device, sometimes termed "represented speech," has been described by students of point of view in Dickens.[24] Knud Sørensen quotes the following passage from *Bleak House* as an example:

He is borne into Mr. Tulkinghorn's great room, and deposited on the Turkey rug before the fire. Mr. Tulkinghorn is not within at the present moment, but will be back directly. The occupant of the pew in the hall, having said thus much, stirs the fire, and leaves the triumvirate to warm themselves. [XXVII]

Both represented speech and the bolder switch to the first person are examples of toying with the point of view for dramatic effect, the latter reserved for particularly demanding cases; yet a sense of labor and contrivance in the sudden changes of person often vitiates the device, destroying rather than enhancing the excitement by putting the reader off—if he notices the trick. The qualification "if he notices" is important, because Dickens also experimented with the shifting point of view at much greater length—in *Bleak House*—and there his success is correspondingly greater because the perspective is maintained for such long passages that the reader ceases to notice, the trick becomes convention and does its work without jarring the reader's expectations.

47

The present interest of Dicken's technique in *Bleak House*, however, does not reside in the shifting point of view, nor does it inhere in the first-person narrative at all; I am concerned rather with the narrative stance implied by Dickens' use of the present tense in the third-person narrative. Ordinarily Dickens reserves the present tense for the first-person framework, and for passages of represented speech. This may be explained as part of the general striving after immediacy in such sections. In *Bleak House* the result of combining an objective point of view with present-tense narration is a remarkable effect of both immediacy and detachment—an effect that is peculiarly Dickensian, though nowhere outside this novel (somewhat of a literary curiosity because of its narrator's nonomniscient omniscience) is the effect quite so striking. The combination of third person and present tense seems to merge narrative and narrator; events simply happen without seeming to be narrated at all. The extreme example is at the very opening of the novel, where the use of participles as main verbs seems to leave the sentences hanging in air, pure reflections of the scene, uncolored by the consciousness of an observer:

London. Michaelmas Term lately over, and the Lord Chancellor sitting in Lincoln's Inn Hall. Implacable November weather. As much mud in the streets, as if the waters had but newly retired from the face of the earth, and it would not be wonderful to meet a Megalosaurus, forty feet long or so, waddling like an elephantine lizard up Holborn Hill. Smoke lowering down from chimney-pots, making a soft black drizzle, with flakes of soot in it as big as full-grown snow-flakes—gone into mourning, one might imagine, for the death of the sun. Dogs, undistinguishable in mire. Horses, scarcely better; splashed to their very blinkers. Foot passengers, jostling one another's umbrellas, in a general infection of ill-temper, and losing their foot-hold at street-corners, where tens of thousands of other foot passengers have been slipping and sliding since the day broke (if this day ever broke), adding new deposits to the crust upon crust of mud, sticking at those points tenaciously to the pavement, and accumulating at compound interest.

The effect of this method has been described by J. Hillis Miller:

. . .it removes the spectator and the narrator from the scene, or at least it seems to reduce him to an anonymous and detached observer, a neutral seeing eye. To say "the fog creeps" much more actively involves the spectator [narrator? reader? both?] in perception and judgment than to say "fog creeping." The latter expression suggests that the activity is happening, but somewhere outside the immediate area of sensation. I know the fog is creeping, but I do not directly and intimately know it. I dissociate myself from the activity and contemplate it from a distance.

This paradoxical combination of detachment and immediacy exists throughout the novel, for when Dickens finally uses verbs they are in the present tense, and the historical present is used throughout the novel in the third-person narration. If the use of participles rather than full verb forms withdraws the narrator from his world, the present tense narration is still far more detached than narration in the more usual past tense.[25]

Miller emphasizes one side of the combination—the detachment; but the style does not simply withdraw "the narrator from his world." The immediacy of which Miller speaks is an opposite effect of the same cause as that which results in detachment. It is not so much that the narrator "dissociate[s himself] from the activity and contemplate[s] it from a distance," as that the narrator peculiarly identifies himself with the activity, gets inside it, lends it his own life, and thereby himself disappears. The narrator *becomes* the narrative. This, of course, is the hallucination theory of Lewes and

Taine carried to its extreme: in the act of projective imagination, Dickens loses himself in the vision he creates. The things, characters, and events described vibrate with immediacy, as if it were our hallucination and not Dickens'.

This identity (stronger than identification) of narrator and narrative is pressing behind all of Dickens' work, not merely this special, paradigm case. It explains the entries in his "Memoranda" book, where Dickens seems to be *in* so many characters, and it explains still another and even more striking entry there, which I have reserved for quotation at this point in the argument:

Open a story by bringing two strongly contrasted places and strongly contrasted sets of people, into the connexion necessary for the story, by means of an electric message. Describe the message—*be* the message—flashing along through space—over the earth, and under the sea.

This is the ultimate blend of immediacy and detachment, of being "both inside his story and outside of it," as Zabel puts it.

Wolfgang Wickardt, in discussing the mode of the third-person narrative in *Bleak House,* refers to it as the "lyrical present,"[26] but this is misleading because the lyric "I" is almost invariably a strong "ego," a presence that is always *there*, defined and somewhat separate, whereas Dickens loses self in the identification with the moment of action, is both there and not there. If this is lyric, it is the very special sort of prose lyric which Roman Jakobson has described in an article on Pasternak:

The first person is...shoved *into the background.* But this is only an apparent minimization—the eternal hero of the lyric is also present here. It is only that the hero is metonymically placed; thus in Chaplin's "A Woman of Paris," the train itself is not seen, but we perceive its arrival by the reflexes of the people photographed, the invisible train moves transparently, as it were, between the screen and the audience. The images of the surroundings in Pasternak's lyrics function, in a similar manner, as contiguous reflections, as expressions of the poet's "I" through metonymy.[27]

As Jakobson hints here, the paradox of the absent narrator is intimately involved in the whole problem of "metonymic style." If we look closely at Dickens' use of metonymy, and at his related habits of focusing on the physical setting, moving his eye along its contiguous surface, and marking off bits of the scene by devices such as anaphora, we can see exactly how the "I" is swallowed up in his presentation of the world.

In one sense, the disappearance of the narrator may be regarded as a natural corollary of allowing the scene to stand alone, to provide its own interpretation of itself. In the Hunger passage quoted earlier, for example, the scene quivers with suppressed fury, not dependent on the narrator's active perception at all, but on the metonymies for hunger which seem to arise automatically from the situation itself. Even as he is enumerating the concomitants of hunger—the desire to take in—Dickens' diction reveals the stronger, opposite urge—to throw up, off, out—to revolt. "Hunger was pushed out of...the tall houses...Hunger...started up from the filthy street...Hunger was shred into atomies...." The "offal," the "bad bread," the "dead-dog preparation"—all make for a general feeling of revulsion and revulsion of feeling. In addition, the sense of danger, the ominous prophecy, resides in the rhetoric itself—the metonymies which grow into menacing personifications, the nightmarish metaphors which promise us that our worst dreams will come true—have already come true. Let me now give the Hunger passage in its entirety:

And now that the cloud settled on Saint Antoine, which a momentary gleam had driven from his sacred countenance, the darkness of it was heavy—cold, dirt, sickness, ignorance, and want, were the lords in waiting on the saintly presence—nobles of great power all of them; but, most especially the last. Samples of a people that had undergone a terrible grinding and re-grinding in the mill, and certainly not in the fabulous mill which ground old people young, shivered at every corner, passed in and out at every doorway, looked from every window, fluttered in every vestige of a garment that the wind shook. The mill which had worked them down, was the mill that grinds young people old; the children had ancient faces and grave voices; and upon them, and upon the grown faces, and ploughed into every furrow of age and coming up afresh, was the sign, Hunger. It was prevalent everywhere. Hunger was pushed out of the tall houses, in the wretched clothing that hung upon poles and lines; Hunger was patched into them with straw and rag and wood and paper; Hunger was repeated in every fragment of the small modicum of firewood that the man sawed off; Hunger stared down from the smokeless chimneys, and started up from the filthy street that had no offal, among its refuse, of anything to eat. Hunger was the inscription on the baker's shelves, written in every small loaf of his scanty stock of bad bread; at the sausage-shop, in every dead-dog preparation that was offered for sale. Hunger rattled its dry bones among the roasting chestnuts in the turned cylinder; Hunger was shred into atomies in every farthing porringer of husky chips of potato, fried with some reluctant drops of oil.

Its abiding place was in all things fitted to it. A narrow wind-ing street, full of offence and stench, with other narrow winding streets diverging, all peopled by rags and nightcaps, and all smelling of rags and nightcaps, and all visible things with a brooding look upon them that looked ill. In the hunted air of the people there was yet some wild-beast thought of the possi-bility of turning at bay. Depressed and slinking though they were, eyes of fire were not wanting among them; nor compressed lips, white with what they suppressed; nor foreheads knitted into the likeness of the gallows-rope they mused about enduring, or inflicting. The trade signs (and they were almost as many as the shops) were, all, grim illustrations of Want. The butcher and the porkman painted up, only the leanest scrags of meat; the baker, the coarsest of meagre loaves. The people rudely pictured as drinking in the wine-shops, croaked over their scanty measures of thin wine and beer, and were gloweringly confidential together. Nothing was represented in a flourishing condition, save tools and weapons; but, the cutler's knives and axes were sharp and bright, the smith's hammers were heavy, and the gunmaker's stock was murderous. The crippling stones of the pavement, with their many little reservoirs of mud and water, had no footways, but broke off abruptly at the doors. The kennel, to make amends, ran down the middle of the street—when it ran at all: which was only after heavy rains, and then it ran, by many eccentric fits, into the houses. Across the streets, at wide intervals, one clumsy lamp was slung by a rope and pulley; at night, when the lamplighter had let these down, and lighted, and hoisted them again, a feeble grove of dim wicks swung in a sickly manner overhead, as if they were at sea. Indeed they were at sea, and the ship and crew were in peril of tempest.

For, the time was to come, when the gaunt scarecrows of that region should have watched the lamplighter, in their idleness and hunger, so long, as to conceive the idea of improving on his method, and hauling up men by those ropes and pulleys, to flare upon the darkness of their condition. But, the time was not come yet; and every wind that blew over France shook the rags of the scarecrows in vain, for the birds, fine of song and feather, took no warning.

Metonymy is the dominating figure; almost everything is controlled by it. The opening personification shows the method (one that is behind much of Dickens' comedy too) of taking a conventional phrase literally—the metonymy of name for thing named—and playing with the unsuspected ironies and incongruities. Saint Antoine, his "saintly presence" attended by the "lords" of poverty and wretchedness, provides a typical instance of the manipulation of names and meanings for satirical effect. But the metonymy is double-edged, for behind the grim irony—the willful word-magic— lies a deeper *belief* in the personification: Saint Antoine in his monstrous collective person does in fact pose a greater threat than the vague starvelings he represents. By the same token, the "rags and nightcaps" (clothes for wearers) are more fearsome when dehumanized still further as scarecrows. And Dickens believes in the dehumanization. What is notable is that, in spite of the direct forewarnings at the end of the passage, most of the burden of prophecy is carried by the scene itself, couched in metonymy; the narrator is not really needed to tell us how to understand the scene, and when he does step before the curtain it comes as something of a superfluous tap with a hammer much too large for the job.

Driving his point home in the final paragraph, Dickens is not content with a retiring role, but the devices he uses in the main body of the passage, more typical of his style, are scarcely those of a self-conscious narrative voice. Again and again metonymy is called upon to represent internal states of mind through external appearances, sometimes in the character's physical aspect, sometimes in the look of his surroundings: "eyes of fire," "compressed lips, white with what they suppressed," "murderous" gunstocks, indeed "all visible things with a brooding look upon them that looked ill." This is the technique of a narrator who wishes to remain strictly in the background, and is therefore unwilling to exercise even his prerogative of omniscience. The physical surface must speak for the inner condition. Pushed to its extremes, this is the opposite of dehumanization; it is animism, another basically metonymic device in its dependence on the contiguity of characters and the objects which surround them. Dickens is continually on the verge of animating his props in the Hunger passage: the wine-shop signs seem more than mere pictures of citizens "gloweringly confidential together," the stones of the pavement are actively "crippling," and the kennel, "to make amends" for the lack of footways, runs designedly and willfully into the houses. We have already seen other animistic states and events in the characterization of the Marquis—his coach expressing his rage, the gargoyle outside his bedroom window assuming his features and life. Animism is found throughout Dickens, so frequently as to be a mark of his style. In *Bleak House*, for example, Tulkinghorn is characterized by reference to his clothes, his books, even his glass of wine:

One peculiarity of his black clothes, and of his black stockings, be they silk or worsted, is, that they never shine. Mute, close, irresponsive to any glancing light, his dress is like himself. [II]

The titles on the backs of his books have retired into the binding; everything that can have a lock has got one; no key is visible. [x]

Mr. Tulkinghorn, sitting in the twilight by the open window, enjoys his wine. As if it whispered to him of its fifty years of silence and seclusion, it shuts him up the closer. [XXII]

The sort of comment which the animism allows here is founded entirely on the contiguity of the character and his appurtenances, the fact that they "go together." The narrator seems to melt into the scene, for he is not needed to make the connection; the objects put themselves forward, make their own meaning.

In such passages the concentration on the *mise en scène* is a familiar device of artificial verisimilitude, but the

55

peculiar life and meaning with which these objects are infused gives everything a dreamlike cast. This characteristically Dickensian combination of factuality and subjectivity (corollary to detachment and immediacy) may be used to foreshadow future events, to suggest present circumstances, to hint at mysteries of the past—all varieties of authorial activity which, if pursued directly, by an omniscient narrator, might crack the novel's façade of independent life. Not that the effects are realistic—on the contrary—but the combination of techniques working for and against the artificial verisimilitude produces a strange impression of a world "supernaturally natural," and true to life as a nightmare seems true to life. The most striking example, which also shows clearly how simple metonymy may be developed into a full-scale animism, is the Stone Face sequence, where, after the death of the Marquis with his stony face and angrily pulsating nose, the stone gargoyle outside his window at the château takes on a kind of life in order to express his "posthumous emotions." To such surrealistic extremes did Dickens' reluctance to enter directly into the minds of his characters lead him. Even Esther Summerson, whose thoughts in *Bleak House* are literally an open book to us, sometimes indulges in animism for the representation of her own state of mind, especially when she is under great emotional strain, as in the scene where she is led to her mother's body:

At the same time I remember, that the poor girl seemed to be yet telling her story audibly and plainly in my hearing; that I could feel her resting on my arm; that the stained house fronts put on human shapes and looked at me; that great water-gates seemed to be opening and closing in my head, or in the air; and that the unreal things were more substantial than the real. [LIX]

Dickens' refusal to let the reader into his characters' minds may seem at odds with his habit of identifying with his characters, thinking their thoughts, as we have seen it in the "Memoranda" book, but if we recall the peculiar combination of immediacy and detachment which informs Dickens' typical narrative stance, we can see that a similar principle is operating in characterization. The immediacy of the characters arises from the apparently objective treatment, the insistence on physical detail and on the visible setting; thus the characters seem firmly placed in the scene, very close to us, while the narrator is at a distance or unnoticed. On the other hand, the narrator is actually manipulating the scene extravagantly, seeing faces on houses, hearing whispers from goblets of wine, and so on. The "realism" is extremely subjective, and to the extent that external circumstances reflect the thoughts of the characters, the narrator (I do not, of course, mean Esther, but the author-narrator, Dickens) *is* identifying with his characters, thinking for them through the *mise en scène*. Yet the narrator seems to shrink into the background, and even the characters dwindle before the fantastic vitality of the setting. As Esther says, "the unreal things," that is, the suddenly vivified, hallucinatory objects of the scene, become "more substantial than the real."

Critics have suggested that the coming to life of inanimate objects reflects Dickens' view of a world gone mad. I should put the emphasis somewhat differently: Dickens' is not the simple gothicism of *The Castle of Otranto* (where animism dominates everything), because his wierd transmutation of inanimate into animate takes place in a world abundantly populated with "real," that is, ordinary physical objects; it invades the familiar, it is our own world—London shrouded in its usual fog—gone mad. The point is that the madness is not merely the madness of fantasy (though it is fantastic), but also the madness of reality. It is the madness, we might say, of a world in which we are required to see everything without benefit of point of view, as if there were no ground underfoot. This, frightening as it is, seems to be the way Dickens took things. The reification of intangibles—mental states, social conditions, future possibilities, and the like—which the animism implements is not simply magical; there is conviction in it, and truth. In the Hunger passage, the "grim illustrations of Want" are simultaneously threats of retaliation. The entire scene is menacingly alive. It is what it seems. The value of the metonymy is that the representing elements are themselves concrete instances of the represented whole. The knitted foreheads, the crippling stones, are there in the scene, to be taken for what they are, as well as for what they stand for; they are the result of what they stand for— brooding, disregard for life and limb, desire for bloody revenge.

Again, what I want to stress is the absence of the narrator from the scene. There is no need for him to draw attention to himself by pointing out the significance of the various symbols, for each symbol stands, as it were, for itself. Metonymic symbols do not suggest comparisons or distract us from the presented scene, as most metaphoric symbols do; thus the narrator, who is the link between the fictional world and the real one, never seems to intrude on our awareness by making allusions or drawing analogies which depend on a reality outside the novel.

But it may be objected that the mere ordering of the scene itself suggests the operation of narrative intelligence; who, after all, is making the innumerable little choices of diction and syntax, who is deciding which detail comes first, which second? Clearly enough, the narrator determines all this. But in Dickens the kinds of choice made, and the kinds of order imposed, contribute as much as anything could to the illusion of a story telling itself, without a narrator. For example, the heavy emphasis on the spatial and physical detail, although it depends ultimately on the narrator's selection of a particular class of referents for his linguistic signs, hardly appears to be a function of the "I," and in fact encourages the opposite illusion, by providing a continuous surface for the attention to follow, unaided by authorial direction, uninterrupted by forced shifting of our gaze.

Of course there *are* shiftings and refocusings, and—still more damaging, one would think, to the illusion of the scene's independent life—these shiftings are marked rather strongly by elaborate rhetorical gestures such as anaphora, which might be expected to remind us of the narrator's controlling presence. But even though such shiftings certainly occur, their disruptive force, so far as it threatens to reveal the narrator's hand, is in fact largely neutralized by the very use of anaphora and similar devices. In a "realistic" novel— say Jane Austen's *Emma*—the selection and ordering of details is what we might call "socially" or "conventionally" determined; many details seem to have been omitted, as irrelevant or uninteresting ("unnecessary" in Orwell's terms); and those actually selected seem to be arranged and presented with a view to expressing a particular attitude, a notion of what is important—all of which gives rise to the reader's feeling that things "add up," that one thing leads to another in an organic way. Thus, appropriate as it may seem to call her method "realism," Jane Austen's contriving intelligence is in evidence at every point, shaping and arranging things with careful artifice. We feel her presence in the abstraction and orientation. It is, in fact, essential to the realistic effect that we be aware of the narrator in reading *Emma* or *Pride and Prejudice*. With Dickens the situation is quite different. There is little apparent abstraction (and thus little apparent choosing), and the ordering is of a very peculiar sort—artificial in such a way as to strike us as even mechanical. The order given in devices such as anaphora is imposed from above, like the grid used in interpreting an aerial photograph, so that the elements do not seem to add up or move in a particular direction, but rather to exist all at once, articulated without being integrated, ordered without being organized. The detail is not presented according to principles that foster a sense of growth and change in time, the essence of realistic plot and character. Instead, the method involves a halting of time, a freezing of the scene to allow "photographic accuracy" in the representation of life-going-on. This is exactly comparable to the timeless quality of the present-tense narrative in *Bleak House,* with its immediacy and detachment, and its impassive camera-eye narrator.

Of course there is some direction and progress in even the most ornamental of Dickens' scenes. But this orientation rarely arises from the rhetorical ordering; it is usually embedded in the details themselves, which only *seem* to be accidental and unchosen. Thus in the Hunger passage, emotional organization is implied in the way the scene develops, first from Hunger "pushed out of the tall houses, in the wretched clothing," to the Hunger "shred into atomies," then from the "wild-beast thought of the possibility of turning at bay" to the "murderous" gunstocks and "crippling stones of the pavement." This movement is not inherent in the scene itself (though it appears to be), but is a movement of the narrator's perception, or of his attitude toward what he perceives, as he reads more and more violence into the details before him. The bias of the narrator's intelligence may thus be exposed to our view, but the emotion works only as an undercurrent, subverting the structure of the rhetoric rather than following it. And in any case, the feeling seems to have less to do with the narrator than with the independent existence of the scene itself, with the objects which present themselves because *there they are,* already quivering with life.

There is no need to press the point too far; no one wants to say that Dickens' stories actually wrote themselves (even though he himself comes close to saying they did), but only that much of their Dickensian effect consists in the detached immediacy of his particular narrative perspective. Not to labor the argument, I shall introduce only one more, somewhat negative observation in its support. It might be assumed, given what has been said about the difference between metonymy and metaphor as manifestations of narrative control, that any use of metaphor brings the "I" prominently into the scene. In metaphorically oriented works—lyrics in particular—the "I" is commonly the center of attention. The fetching of comparisons far and wide contributes to this egocentricity, for it forces upon us an awareness of the authorial intelligence searching out correspondences. How then do we account for Dickens' metaphors?

First of all, it should be emphasized that the complete "absence" of the narrator from the narrative is only a negative impression at the very most, and that it is the author's predilection for metaphor or metonymy, not his total reliance on one or the other, that determines the perspective. When Dickens uses metaphor, we must recognize that he is intruding in the scene. The metaphors of the Hunger passage— the comparison of the street lamps to sea-lamps on a ship, or the comparison of the darkness surrounding the lamps to the darkness of man's condition—clearly show Dickens the narrator stepping in, to comment on the story. Both these metaphors are part of the overt prediction (as distinguished from mere foreshadowing) which Dickens feels so often compelled to introduce in his tales ("For, the time was to come . . ."). It might even be argued that metaphors are invariably to be found in those passages traditionally condemned for their "editorializing" tone, where Dickens sentimentally or angrily or bitterly inserts his own opinion of the world he has created. Such is the basis, for example, of the metaphoric passage in the last chapter of the *Tale:*

Crush humanity out of shape once more, under similar hammers, and it will twist itself into the same tortured forms. Sow the same seed of rapacious licence and oppression over again, and it will surely yield the same fruit according to its kind.

The oratorical tone that is so unpleasant here marks the author's withdrawal from the story in order to grind his own axe, his rather conventional moral indignation, a declaration of authorial intentions.*

And yet, even in metaphor, Dickens' narrative perspective is often maintained in its detachment. The "lamp-light" metaphor in the Hunger passage is a good example, for here the setting—basis of most of his metonymies—predominates as usual, so that the comparison seems less invented than stumbled upon. The motion of the lamps seems like the

---

*The problem of irony is not so easily dealt with as that of metaphor. Does the presence of irony necessarily remind us of the narrator? Take the case of *Moll Flanders,* where we are frequently presented with what must be regarded as "unintentional irony." Instances of this sort surely make us aware of the narrator's (Defoe's, not Moll's) presence; but it is not so obvious that *intended* incongruities between states of affairs "expressed" and "implied" will have this effect. The ironic conception of Doctor Manette's part in the denunciation of his son-in-law does not produce any special awareness of the narrator as we read; on the other hand, the harsh, satirical treatment of Stryver may remind us that we are being told a story, by a narrator who has his own thoughts and opinions. Perhaps we could say that Dickens' detachment (and hence the usual narrative perspective) collapses only when the irony veers toward sarcasm, tantamount to a loss of control much as in Defoe's "unintentional irony."

swaying of ship-lanterns at sea, which in turn reminds us of tempest, ship, and crew (connection by contiguity), and from these we are referred back again metaphorically to the state of France, its being at sea and in danger of tempest. Dickens' tendency is to extend his metaphors, chiefly by metonymic attachment of the related circumstances, until the original comparison becomes almost mythic, often with something like a plot line relating the separate elements of the expanded correspondence. Consider, for example, the further development of this "lamp-light" metaphor, which becomes a full-fledged "sea" metaphor in Dickens' description of the Revolution (2, xxi):

As a whirlpool of boiling waters has a centre point, so, all this raging circled round Defarge's wine-shop, and every human drop in the caldron had a tendency to be sucked towards the vortex. . . .

With a roar that sounded as if all the breath in France had been shaped into the detested word ["Bastille"], the living sea rose, wave on wave, depth on depth, and overflowed the city to that point. Alarm-bells ringing, drums beating, the sea raging and thundering on its new beach, the attack begun.

. . .Suddenly the sea rose immeasurably wider and higher, and swept Defarge of the wine-shop over the lowered drawbridge, past the massive stone outer walls, in among the eight great towers surrendered!

So resistless was the force of the ocean bearing him on, that even to draw his breath or turn his head was as impracticable as if he had been struggling in the surf at the South Sea. . . .

. . .So tremendous was the noise of the living ocean, in its irruption into the Fortress, and its inundation of the courts and passages and staircases. All around outside, too, it beat the walls with a deep, hoarse roar, from which, occasionally, some partial shouts of tumult broke and leaped into the air like spray.

The sea of black and threatening waters, and of destructive upheaving of wave against wave, whose depths were yet unfathomed and whose forces were yet unknown. The remorseless sea of turbulently swaying shapes, voices of vengeance, and faces hardened in the furnaces of suffering until the touch of pity could make no mark on them.

The completeness and inner consistency of the metaphor, as it is extended and expanded to constitute a world in itself, seem to lift the figure out of the realm of metaphor altogether. We believe in the metaphor as though it were not a metaphor at all. The power of such figures to compel belief is beyond rhetoric, as Ernst Cassirer has suggested in *Language and Myth:*

For mythic thinking there is much more in metaphor than a bare "substitution," a mere rhetorical figure of speech; . . . what seems to our subsequent reflection as a sheer transcription is mythically conceived as a genuine and direct identification.[28]

All of Dickens' major metaphors—the widely discussed symbols which lie at the center of his didactic concerns in the novels—have this "mythic" quality. Pestilence and tempest, court and prison, factory and slum, these are more than mere metaphors for aspects of society; they *are* aspects of society. The dust-heaps in *Our Mutual Friend* do not merely represent wealth, nor is their function simply to establish the psychological relation between money and excrement: rather an *identity* is posited—money *is* excrement, "gold-dust." Similarly the sea-mob in *A Tale of Two Cities*, the scarecrow-citizens of Saint Antoine, the blood-wine on the cobblestones—in varying degrees these figures have transcended metaphor to become dreamlike amalgams of object and feeling. The effect is weirdly hallucinatory, rather more like dream than myth. Objects are exhaustively described with the vividness of detail characteristic of dream; the "meanings" of the objects are also dreamlike, so that things count as passions yet remain things too, in a way that is rarely felt in waking life. Taine made the point brilliantly a century ago:

An imagination so lucid and energetic cannot but animate inanimate objects without an effort. It provokes in the mind in which it works extraordinary emotions, and the author pours over the objects which he figures to himself, something of the ever-welling passion which overflows in him. Stones for him take a voice, white walls swell out into big phantoms, black wells yawn hideously and mysteriously in the darkness; legions of strange creatures whirl shuddering over the fantastic landscape; blank nature is peopled, inert matter moves. But the images remain clear; in this madness there is nothing vague or disorderly; imaginary objects are designed with outlines as precise and details as numerous as real objects, and the dream is equal to the reality.[29]

Juggle the last clause and you have it precisely: the reality is that of dream.

# 3

# The Analogy to Dream

EVEN though in saying that the reality in Dickens' novels is that of dream, I intend only an analogy, I do wish to press the analogy beyond mere illustration. The correspondences which allow the analogy to be drawn at all are both so full and so precise that one is tempted to suggest that novel-writing may have amounted for Dickens to the same sort of activity that other men engage in when they recount their dreams. At least it must be admitted that, since the structures of these activities have so much in common, the needs they meet and the goals they serve must also be rather alike. Strictly speaking, of course, it makes no sense to say that Dickens is a "dream-writer," for we know well enough that dreams are not written but had; I shall take up this problem in the first part of this section, under the heading "The Imitation of Dreams." No matter what its difficulties, much of Dickens' style and manner is accounted for by the dream analogy: many peculiarly Dickensian characteristics are thus thrown into new, clarifying perspective, and are shown as cohering parts of a self-consistent system. The various features of Dickens' vision of reality discussed in the previous section—the hallucinatory quality, the strange stance of the narrator, the paradoxes of orderliness-without-organization and immediacy-detachment—all have their interconnected places in dream theory. Similarly, the analogy allows us to understand more clearly the function of Dickens' stylistic devices in simultaneously concealing and revealing his emotionally explosive subject matter, just as in Freudian theory the elements of the dreamwork both hide and display the dream content.

## The Imitation of Dreams

I should emphasize by stating it at the outset that I do not think of Dickens as a surrealist, not at least in the usual sense of that term. Most surrealists *consciously imitate dreams* (or think they do), and Dickens rarely does this, though an interesting passage in the letters muses on the possibility. This distinction is important, because good reasons can be presented for the view that, on purely theoretical grounds, any attempt to imitate dreams is doomed to failure. Dreams themselves, as the best authorities have reiterated, are completely unavailable to conscious thought. Thus Freud's work, as he acknowledged, was based on the *telling* of dreams, not the dreams themselves:

In investigating dreams even the object of research, the dream itself, is indefinite. A delusion, for example, presents clear and definite outlines. "I am the Emperor of China," says your patient plainly. But a dream? For the most part it cannot be related at all. When a man tells a dream, has he any guarantee that he has told it correctly, and not perhaps altered it in the telling or been forced to invent part of it on account of the vagueness of his recollection? Most dreams cannot be remembered at all and are forgotten except for some tiny fragments.... [But] any disadvantage resulting from the uncertain recollection of dreams may be remedied by deciding that exactly what the dreamer tells is to count as the dream, and by ignoring all that he may have forgotten or altered in the process of recollection.[30]

Accordingly, surrealist efforts at imitating dreams are restricted, by the nature of the case, to an indirectness even more defeating than the stubborn inappropriateness of all media used to represent life; the thing-to-be-expressed and the expression are distanced not only by words or paint, but also by the necessarily hypothetical character of any representation (including even mere remembering) of such unconscious experience. To tell a dream truly and fully is as difficult—and for the same reasons—as to describe what it is like to be dreamlessly asleep. But surrealists try to do more than tell their dreams; most often, they want to re-create them. Accordingly, the marked effects of surrealist art reside not so much in the rare successes in producing feelings akin to those we have in dreams, but instead in the failures, which remind us of what dreams are like by a kind of negative implication; the groping work of art seems so strange, so mechanically unreal, rather like our memories of dreams, which never quite suit us though we are at a loss to say why.*

*Compare Julian Symons, *Charles Dickens* (London, 1951), p. 87: "Dickens employs the method of surrealistic painting, by describing the fantastic shapes and figures that occupy his mind in the soberest tones of naturalism: but there is an important difference between his attitude and that of the surrealists. Dickens worked without self-consciousness, in the belief that he was using the real colours of everyday life; the surrealists are highly self-conscious artists, well aware of their own quaintness and queerness. The strangeness of Dickens is natural; that of the surrealists is, however ingeniously, contrived."

An important reason for leaving *David Copperfield* out of the present account of Dickens' dream novels is precisely that, there, Dickens *was* consciously imitating dreams, with disastrous results for the parts of the novel most surrealistically contrived—see, for example, the four "Retrospect" chapters.

What fiction can quite reasonably imitate is the telling of dreams, which is the only conscious experience we have of them anyway (taking "remembering" as a kind of telling to oneself). This is not what surrealism attempts, but it may be—and has often been—the basis of comparison between art and dream. "Telling a dream is telling a kind of story," writes the philosopher Norman Malcolm; it is also "like imagining something" except that "there is no place for inventiveness, for changing one's mind, for having things as one will. One tells a dream under the influence of an impression—*as if* one was faithfully recalling events that one witnessed."[31] Much literary imagining and storytelling seems like dream-telling in a loose way, for both involve the expression, in language, of largely nonlinguistic materials—feelings, events, impressions of the senses—which are better described as "imagined" rather than "experienced," as "recounted" rather than "remembered." But not all literary tellings seem comparable to dream-tellings in other than these broad ways. The details of the tellings differ—in *contents*, in kinds of *relations between elements* of the contents, in *attitude of teller* to the telling. More than most writers, Dickens tells his stories *as if* they were dreams, in all three of these respects.

## Contents

As everyone knows, dreams seem predominantly visual. It is as if we were "seeing things," and in our telling of them we are often hard put to translate into language such visual impressions as remain after waking. Freud finds this visual quality of dreams a crucial factor, and in his theory the "regard for representability," that is, the necessity of "transformation of thoughts into *visual images*," is spoken of as "the most interesting [achievement of the dreamwork] from the psychological point of view."[32] Freud hypothesizes a temporal sequence in this transformation:

Clearly what has to be accomplished by the dream-work is the transformation of the latent thoughts, as expressed in words, into perceptual forms, most commonly into visual images. Now our thoughts originated in such perceptual forms; their earliest material and the first stages in their development consisted of sense-impressions, or, more accurately, of memory-pictures of these. It was later that words were attached to these pictures and then connected so as to form thoughts. So that the dream-work subjects our thoughts to a *regressive* process and retraces the steps in their development; in the course of this REGRESSION all new acquisitions won during this development of memory-pictures into thoughts must necessarily fall away.[33]

If we were to follow out this line of argument, we might say that the telling of the dream constituted a next step, a translation of visual contents back into language—but this would be, in Freud's view, a false step, for a translation "back again" to the original dream thought would have to involve interpretation, that is, psychoanalytic editing. Of course, the notion that the original dream thought ever has a form of words to express it (until the dream itself, or its telling, is interpreted) is at the very least unprovable, and Freud's characterization of the dreamwork perhaps suffers here from too much schematization. Whether or not we agree that the meaning of any particular dream sequence is expressible in language (either in the telling of the dream or in an interpretation of it), it surely does not follow that the meaning has ever been so expressed. To suppose such a phrasing of the dream thoughts leads one, so it seems to me, to treat the dream-telling too much as if it were merely a cloak which must be torn away to reveal the hidden truth. But in fact the only truth we have is in the telling of the dream, and it is that telling which we want to understand; interpretation is better viewed as an understanding than as an unveiling.

The point is worth bothering with because the analogous situation in literature is so easily misconstrued. We must not suppose that the novelist has some formulated thought (conscious or otherwise) which lies behind his telling of the story. Sometimes an author will give us to believe that he works from a premise of this sort (as Hawthorne in the preface to *The House of the Seven Gables* tells us his moral, "that the wrongdoing of one generation lives into the successive ones"), but such pat formulations must always be taken as Hawthorne indeed intends us to take his—only as what he calls a "provided" truth, a summing up of the book, not its meaning. Similarly, when critics offer us formulations for the underlying thought of this book or that, they are offering interpretations which may help us grasp some point in the story, but will by no means explain, let alone stand for it. The telling of the story is what counts, not only for effect on an audience, but for meaning too, and no form of words is an adequate substitute.

Some such misconception of the relation between the telling of a story and its meaning lies behind most discussions of mimetic art which posit a correspondence between the fiction and an imitated reality. Theorists of realism talk about the referential use of language in the novel, or the closeness of its texture to the texture of real life, or the specificity and particularity of mimetic style. But much of this is beside the point. No writer can get along without using many names, which may be said to denote or to refer to things, events, qualities, and so on. The specificity or exclusiveness of denotation (in which clarity largely consists) does not depend on the word itself, but on the total context, both linguistic and social. But then it is misleading to talk about the "closeness" of a text to the reality it reports, for the important relation is not that of sign-to-referent, but of sign-to-sign.* What any author gives us is his notion of reality, the *way* he imagines things, his vocabulary and his syntax, his habits of vision and blindness; and all this can only be experienced or interpreted, not pinned down to some congruent set of external circumstances. If one wants to say—as I do now—that Dickens characteristically chose to record visual impressions of tangible reality, one must not suppose that he was therefore imitating the real world he saw around him, any more than the dreamer imitates his world when he dreams of it or tells his dream. The images in Dickens' fiction, like the images in a dream, are not *of* anything except themselves. To say that Leigh Hunt served as a model for Harold Skimpole tells us no more than to say that my Uncle George served as a model for himself in my dream. Skimpole is Skimpole, the Uncle George in my dream is the Uncle-George-in-my-dream, that and no more. The meaning is in the context, not in the reference outside it. The fact that I recognize Uncle George in my dream is not part of his

*For the realistic novel, at least that in the tradition of Defoe, it is no doubt true that the *object* of reference has a characteristic solidity—tables, teacups, bolts of holland—and this tangibility of things referred to is probably what theorists have in mind when they talk about the semantics of realism, though surely no special relation between sign and referent enlivens Defoe's (or Dickens') telling over the inventory of his imaginary world. The belief that words can correspond to their objects in varying degrees is simple word-magic (this is the point of Swift's satire of the Royal Society's notion of language reform, in *Gulliver's Travels*). It is the choice of a particular class of things as referents which weights the novelist's world down (like the linguistic philosophers of Lagado) and lends it the apparent solidity of the real; and this only incidentally has anything to do with language. If we want a linguistic criterion for realism, we must look for it in the correspondence of an author's syntax and rhetoric, his habits of mind and lines of thought, to those of the audience he writes for.

72

meaning there. Of course I recognize him; I have invented him. Dickens' heavy emphasis on the visual does not mean that he was copying from his experience, but that he took experience visually—as he says in the letter to Forster already quoted, he *saw* the world he imagined.

Here we begin to see more strikingly the appropriateness of the dream analogy. Dickens' hallucinations—for which the testimony is, to my mind, convincing—are like the images of dream, that is, predominantly visual (though aural too, as Lewes reported). Consequently the telling of the story, like the telling of dreams, must be adjusted to such material. The language mentions things that are visible. Objects pile up in the imagination with the same profusion and clarity as in dream, and the reporting of them is as full and vivid as Dickens' astounding verbal abilities will allow. Moreover, the exception which Professor Malcolm appends to his comparison of dream-telling and "imagining something" will not hold in Dickens' case; for it is curiously true of Dickens' imagination that "there is no place for inventiveness, for changing one's mind, for having things as one will," because so much of his material is *given* in a kind of hallucination. One finds it rather absurd to be saying that Dickens was not inventive, but insofar as he regarded himself as merely a passive reporter of his visions, the description is not so misleading. Nothing else quite accounts for the characteristic narrative stance of the novels or for the detached, "camera-eye" mode of expression.

The dangers of distortion in such a view are obvious enough; we have the notorious history of "Kubla Khan" to warn us of them. But caution must not lead us to other distortions or absurdities. The evidence for something close to "automatic writing" in Dickens is quite full. Some of the later manuscripts are rubbed and blotted, true enough, but up until the final years Dickens seems to have worked with the unhesitating and even unreflecting confidence of the inspired. One guesses that the serial form of publication was more an aid than a hindrance to his art; his dullest and, on the evidence of his letters, most laborious pieces were those he had to give a "finish," such as the Christmas tales. No doubt he was ultimately in control of his fantasies—so that he might send his characters off to America or allow them happy endings under the pressure of expedience—but this fact is irrelevant to the question of literary hallucination, for matters of overall composition and plot were outside inspiration in Dickens' case; his imagination was always of the scene, and the larger structure of action never took possession of him in the way that isolated sections of the story did. Recent efforts to buttress Dickens' reputation by attacking the traditional view of him as an "unconscious artist," refreshing and sensible as they have been in some ways, nevertheless have also tended to exaggerate Dickens' conscious control of his art in much the same way that the older criticism exaggerated the lack of it. Neither approach is analytic enough. Both fail to distinguish the kinds of things Dickens did or did not control, or the kinds of control he exercised. I have already discussed Dickens' ordering of individual passages and scenes. Now, in connection with dreams, we shall see that his principles of connection and order do not argue for or against a theory of Dickens as a conscious artist, but rather make the question less important. In Dickens' novels, as in dreams, there is room both for giving oneself up to the hallucinated or imagined reality, and for superimposing on it a logical, commonsense structure of interpretation.

## Ordering

The ordering of dreams may be regarded in three ways: we may notice (1) the kinds of order and connection demanded by the primarily visual contents, or (2) the kinds of underlying relation possible between apparently unconnected (or "accidentally" connected) elements of the contents, or (3) the kinds of superficial ordering imposed on the contents partly to obscure their true import, partly to make the dream seem logical and sane, or simply to allow the dreamer to tell his dream—that is, to make it of this world. These three ways of approaching the ordering of dreams correspond to Freud's categories of dreamwork: (1) plastic representation and regard for representability, (2) displacement and condensation, and (3) secondary elaboration.

(1) *Plastic representation and the regard for representability.* The primarily visual contents are responsible in great part, as Freud points out, for the characteristic arrangement of objects and sequence of events which we find in dreams. Time and space, the coordinates of visual phenomena, behave rather strangely in the dream world. As things "take place" and "come to pass" in dreams, neither dimension can be notched and measured in the normal manner, for we are asleep and unable to take note of what we dream by referring it to memory or knowledge. Upon waking, we tell where things were and how things looked and what happened next, but if we say that some figure resembled an acquaintance of our waking life, we are embroidering or interpreting our dream, not telling it. The connections and movements of the dream proper seem to operate by juxtaposition and contiguity, in either time or space, and not by resemblance and similarity, which demand an act of conscious comparison and classification.

This should remind us of what has already been said about

75

Dickens' use of detail, his fondness for connection by contiguity, his development of meaning by the alternation and juxtaposition of elements in the plot and the setting. We recall, for example, Dickens' anaphoric ordering of detail, where the bits and pieces of the visual scene are, so to speak, suspended in time by the directionless rhetorical pattern, producing a dreamlike "simultaneity" of the separate elements. What movement there is in the scene appears to be an effect of simple scanning, from point to contiguous point, and the relations between elements are mere juxtapositions, formalized in the anaphoric schematization. As in dream, the realism one would expect from constant emphasis on objects familiar to the eyes is strangely modified by this mode of presentation. The combination of *movement by contiguity* and *order without direction or classification* makes the scene appear to present itself, so that the total effect is not realistic at all, but magical, even supernatural. There is no sense of the beholder's attention going out to meet his world in an act of perception. In that event we should find more abstraction, more selection, more emphasis on this or that meaning. Instead, the world merely impinges, and the narrator is queerly detached.

(2) *Displacement and condensation.* Like his use of anaphora, Dickens' metonymies and metaphors are part of a "dream rhetoric." Again the visual world seems to offer up, unbidden, the materials of these figures. Metonymies are not sought after, but seem to present themselves spontaneously, as if one had no choice but to call the citizens of Saint Antoine "rags and nightcaps," such being the visible, "given" aspect of their nature. Metaphors too, in the Dickensian manner, seem to grow out of the scene, without any conscious effort on the part of the narrator to imagine comparisons or analogies. The sea-mob is literally a sea-mob, not a

mob compared to a sea for purposes of clarity or intensification of meaning. The two elements of the metaphor do not bear on each other semantically in the way that they do, for example, in the metaphysical conceit or in the metaphors of Keats, where the juxtaposition of likeness and difference sets a meaning in relief, a meaning really apart from the metaphorical terms themselves, a meaning *designed* by the author; in Dickensian metaphor there is complete identification, as if the narrator "saw" the sea-mob instead of inventing it.

As Dickens uses them, metonymy and metaphor are primarily devices of displacement and condensation, and they operate in much the same way as those distorting mechanisms by which dream meanings are simultaneously concealed and revealed. Thus the attention Dickens lavishes on the Marquis' nose may be said to obscure his total character, so that he appears "flat," a grotesque; but this metonymy also exercises a focusing effect, so that the total character is summed up in the nose, with its pulsations of hatred displaced from the "whole man." But let us take a new set of examples, to consider afresh Dickens' use of metonymy as a device of displacement and condensation.

One classic variety of metonymy is *name for thing named*. Sylvère Monod has catalogued numerous examples of the fascination of the Inimitable (Dickens' name for himself) with names, including the amusing series of transformations which shortened his son's nickname from "Plornishmaroontigoonter" to just plain "Plorn."[34] In the "Memoranda" book are long lists of names, both for novels and for characters, which one might expect to find in the notes of many novelists. It is not merely Dickens' interest in names that is revealing, but the peculiar quality of the names that intrigued him. From samples like Laughley, Crabble, Slyant, Musty, Whelpford, Lightword (whence Lightwood?), Topwash, Lowely,

Wangler, Spessiffer, Readyhuff, Twinn—all found in the "Memoranda" book—we can see that an element of childish word-magic, or some sophisticated version of the same thing, was behind many of his choices of names. Indeed, sometimes the name *is* the character, as with Boots and Brewer in the Society chapters of *Our Mutual Friend*, Bar and Physician in *Little Dorrit*. More often, however, the name of a character directs attention not to the traits evident in the social façade, but to some reality otherwise hidden behind the character's habitual manner. Thus we may discover from his name alone that the reserved, conservatively dressed schoolmaster, Bradley Headstone, is a man to be feared, or that Veneering's rich display is nothing but appearance. Pleasant Riderhood, in spite of her ugly face and coarse manners, possesses virtues sweet enough to stir the finicky Mr. Venus. And her father, Rogue Riderhood, always protesting his hard-working disinterestedness, is no doubt a kind of waterfront wolf vainly trying to hide himself in grandmother's clothes.

Yet Dickens' names are not merely clues to the real qualities of his characters; almost invariably they both hint at and conceal the secret meaning. (Why, otherwise, did he not simply do what Bunyan does, call a bad man a Badman?) Thus Headstone's name may refer both to his cold reserve in the school room ("stone head") and to his uncontrollable rage when Lizzie turns him down ("headstrong"), as well as to the fatal probabilities of his rivalry with Eugene (Headstone = "tombstone"). In this case, or in the more famous one of Merdle in *Little Dorrit*, Dickens surely knew what he meant, and one need not insist that he concealed anything from himself in his name-play, though we certainly could find relevant meanings which he missed but somehow intended. What is interesting is that the metonymic shrinking of a character into his own name is a condensation, and has the typical function of condensation, namely to conceal and reveal, as it were, in the same breath.

Similarly, Dickensian metaphor both disguises and displays its underlying significance, by means of the condensation and identification of the metaphoric elements. Consider the sea-mob metaphor in *A Tale of Two Cities.* Unlike ordinary metaphors, in which the comparison of two elements may be said to broaden meaning by bringing in a whole new range of implications (as, for example, Donne's "gold to ayery thinnesse beate" or Keats' "still unravish'd bride of quietness"), Dickens' sea-mob has a narrowing, condensing effect on the meaning. In this respect, Dickensian metaphor is rather like "dead metaphor" in its lack of comparative or contrastive force. But a dead metaphor, revivified, always shocks us because we have ceased to notice the literal meanings buried there, whereas it is the mark of Dickens' metaphors that, although they must be taken literally, yet somehow we are not asked to notice correspondences and distinctions between the two elements juxtaposed—they fuse in a single, literal meaning. This sort of condensation and identification of the metaphoric elements is antianalytic, antirealistic, and even antilinguistic. Ordinary communication in words depends on our habitual willingness to call a spade "a spade," and most metaphor is not really subversive of this principle, but rather makes capital of it, the assumption being that when a young lady is referred to as "a rose" everybody will understand that she is not a rose but only soft and sweet-smelling, and so on. But suppose that the writer said, "No, I don't mean that at all, I mean she *is* a rose!" In such a case—and it is Dickens' case—we are in the realm of dreams, where one thing may be what is ordinarily thought of as two, or in mythology, where horses have the trunks and heads of men and where many a flower is indeed a young lady. To those of us who put a shaken but stubborn faith in words and language, such talk will be distressing; it will be felt that the meaning, if there is any meaning, must be obscured by such unruliness of denotation and reference. One could hardly say that Dickens' sea-mob is conceived realistically, according to the light of reason or common sense: we have no notion of its composition as a mob, its "rounded" character, because we see only one aspect of it—the "sea" aspect. If the crowd were merely *like* a sea, then it could be like other things too, and its nature could be communicated analytically. There would be many words for it. Being a sea-mob, it can be described only in terms that apply to its character as a sea, and the resulting distortion limits and obscures the "mobness" of the mob. On the other hand, the condensation also produces the very strong feeling which inheres in the mob scenes. Because the condensation squeezes out other meanings, the metaphoric identification of sea and mob intensifies the "boiling," "raging," "thundering," "threatening," and "upheaving" that remain. Like his metonymies, Dickens' metaphors end up as grotesques, distortions for the sake of saying what is hardly sayable at all, and saying it with a weird clarity and power.

(3) *Secondary elaboration.* As we have just seen them operating on the level of rhetoric, in his use of metonymy and metaphor, Dickens' habitual disguise and display may seem simply a necessity of style, given the kind of meaning he has to convey; but on the level of plot, the desire both to court and to divert attention strikes one as almost "frantic," if such a methodical application of control may be so termed. The difference between the concealing-revealing devices of rhetoric and those of plot may be viewed in much the same way as the difference, in Freudian dream theory, between the functions of displacement and condensation and those of

secondary elaboration. In Freud's view, secondary elaboration is a more conscious act than the other operations of the dreamwork. While one dreams, the functioning of displacement and condensation is relatively automatic, spontaneous, just as the regard for visual representability seems to be. But as one awakens, the "irreality" of the dream world must compete with the "reality" of the waking world, and whatever remains of the dream must be integrated into one's waking notion of things. The job of secondary elaboration is to provide the dream with a kind of order and sense which is like that of everyday perception and understanding, even though the dream materials thus regulated are either stubbornly recalcitrant or slippery and illusive, hard for the stiff fingers of the logical waking mind to grasp. This process may be partly unconscious (a continuation of the regard for representability which operates throughout the dream) and partly conscious (as when one says, in telling one's dreams, that it must have been thus-and-so because it happened after such-and-such). Appropriately enough then, the operation of secondary elaboration seems less spontaneous than the rest of the dreamwork, rather like a last-minute effort on the part of the dreamer, a final adjustment of the tie and handkerchief before stepping out into the world. This eleventh-hour grooming has an artificiality about it which even the dreamer himself may detect, so that we are sometimes inclined to say, "But my dream wasn't quite so clear as the way I am telling it."

Characteristically the superimposition of this sort of order is calculated to draw attention away from the true meaning of the dream, since it substitutes "reasonable" formulations for the strange juxtapositions and meanderings of dream thought, where import is largely affective, not "logical." The telling of the dream—its translation into ordinary language—represents the final and most stringent operation of secondary elaboration, for any linguistic structuring necessarily filters out all "unsayable" elements of experience, the kinds and gradations of feeling for which we have no words, the peculiar relations of things for which there is no grammar. Moreover, at this stage the dream has already been "had," so that whatever threatening contents it may have can no longer be neutralized by means of primary distortions—displacement, condensation, and so on—and the tender consciousness can only be protected by forgetting or misunderstanding the meaning. Secondary elaboration produces a map and timetable of events, a formal grid of circumstance that overrides the significance of the dream's juxtapositions and unifications, rather as the proverbial taxi driver negotiates a maze of busy streets to take a helpless stranger to a hotel next door to the railway station where the ride began.

Both the excessive concern for order and sense and the compulsive desire to mystify by sheer multiplication of circumstance are salient features of Dickens' handling of plot. The example that comes most readily to mind is his use of the endlessly complicated double plot, which, as we shall see in the next chapter, is his means of preventing the coming together of certain inflammable elements of his story. Many other Dickensian structural mannerisms work a similar obscuring or distorting influence on his deeper meanings—for instance, the superimposition of symmetrical and cyclical structures on *Little Dorrit* ("Poverty" and "Riches") and *Hard Times* ("Sowing," "Reaping," and "Garnering"), where, although the schematized headings may be justified by some aspects of the plots, one feels that readers have been more often misled than instructed by the oblique light thus thrown on the central actions of the novels. Similarly, certain threads of thematic imagery are insisted upon so single-mindedly that they seem to usurp attention from the plot itself: thus in *A Tale of Two Cities* the resurrection motif (and all its Christian overtones) is accentuated at every opportunity, to prepare us for Carton's sacrifice, but the emphasis on this thematic configuration muddles the crucial problem of the novel, the nature of Darnay's guilt—and this without any compensating growth in the significance of Carton's act, since the resurrectings and resurrections of Doctor Manette, Jerry Cruncher, Roger Cly, Darnay, and Carton himself have nothing in common beyond their denominator, nor even anything in distinction beyond their random dissimilarity.

Too often Dickens' leading strains of repetition and pattern seem only to provide a complex unity of surface, while at the same time they draw the reader's attention away from the important thought and feeling embodied in the action itself. To be sure, some of the threads and clusters of imagery take on the "mythic" status of Dickensian metaphor at its best—for example, the pestilence imagery in *Bleak House*, or in *A Tale of Two Cities* the imagery of blood and wine, or of tempest at sea. In such cases the metaphor is so deeply rooted in the setting and action of the novel that there is no question of its distracting attention from the core of meaning: the imagery is built in, not laid on top of the main line of action. But in other cases the metaphoric elements never fuse; the imagery remains merely imagery, a kind of embroidery on the action rather than an integral part of it. This is especially true of the large-scale patterns, such as the resurrection theme in the *Tale*, the similar drowning and resuscitation theme in *Our Mutual Friend*, or the *fact*ory theme in *Hard Times*. Apparently, the broader the conception Dickens is working with, the more chance of his going wrong by overschematization. But this is exactly what we should expect, according to our analogy with the secondary elaboration of dreams; the straining after order and pattern is most easily satisfied by the imposition of some overall framework which "accounts" for the otherwise "unaccountable" and disparate fragments of meaning. Moreover, since there are hidden meanings to be avoided, the large-scale patterns have a special advantage in their creation of an overriding Gestalt, following the camoufleur's principle that the airborne enemy will not see the "trees" for the "woods."

Of course none of Dickens' multitudinous orderings and patternings works against his meaning altogether. The very schematization produces meaning in its own right, namely the growing sense in each of the novels that everything is intimately (though secretly) related to everything else, that bitterest enemies and long-lost friends are continually rubbing elbows unawares. After all, the intricate relations among characters, places, events, and even things, are part of the story, contributing unity and probability, solidity and homogeneity, to a world which is always verging on the fantastic, fragmented realm of hallucination and dream. It may even be argued that Dickens' genius depends on his need to control his materials by means of these laid-on and patched-up relations and repetitions. It is as though he could "tell his dream" in no other way, as though the sense of control were necessary to the spontaneity, were in some way a part of it (as we may describe a compulsion as both automatic and spontaneous). In any event, Dickens' elaborations of plot and theme play a major role (partly negative, partly positive) in the communication of his message, if only because they take up so much of the time and space of the novels. Following our analogy to dream, we may again notice the appropriateness of such structuring and schematization, for the dream itself never quite survives the telling; it is necessarily supplanted by the dreamwork—the plastic representation, the displacement and condensation, the secondary elaboration—in order to make it safely communicable, or even communicable at all.

## Attitude of the Teller

Constantly pressing behind any discussion of Dickens' ways of ordering his materials is a conception of Dickens himself, as author, narrator, "teller of dreams." Such, for example, is the force of the suggestion that Dickens had a compelling need to control by schematization, to mystify by overcomplication, to conceal and reveal by emphasizing the pattern which hides and at the same time contains the deeper design. I have already devoted many pages to an examination of Dickens' narrative stance, treating the question rather formalistically, with special attention to stylistic indications of his way of apprehending and imagining reality—his handling of person and tense, his ordering of detail by means of anaphora and other repetitive and schematic devices, his use of metonymy and metaphor—all these habits of style being related to his peculiar brand of mimesis, which has its origin in a kind of literary hallucination akin to dream. In arguing for the importance of an adequate conception of Dickens' narrative stance, I have proposed a direct correlation between his literary manner and his attitude toward the reality he imagines for us. Within the framework of an analogy to dream, we may specify the nature of this correlation in psychological terms.

So far as we can know, dreams have always come to most people in pretty much the same way, just as waking mental experiences—noticing, deciding, and so on—ordinarily seem like business as usual. How people take their dreams depends on factors which are largely cultural and social. Thus a man may take his dream as a memory or a meaning, a warning or a wish, a message from the gods or a motion of his own soul, according to the bent of various notions he may hold about himself and his world. Many peoples have believed that dreams are divine, sent from a supernatural realm, and that the dreamer is thus temporarily inspired, much as madmen and poets are thought to be (less fleetingly) touched and sanctified by the hands of the gods. In its essentials such a view needs no elaborate theory of the supernatural to support it; there are plenty of people in modern society who, while disclaiming any belief in magic, nevertheless take their dreams as "coming from without," as visitations *they* never invited and surely do not wish to entertain. Such dreamers may not inquire so frequently as the ancients after the origins of their dreams, but neither are they willing to accept them as of their own making.

It is with dreamers of this sort, who see in their nightly vision no offspring of theirs, that Dickens belongs. And following this line of suggestion, we might call his particular literary manner "super-naturalism"—a term that at once conveys the sense of oracular possession which he seems sometimes to have had and suggests the characteristic blend of immediacy and detachment in his style, with its strangely heightened clarity of detail beyond our ordinary experience of life, detail so uncannily vivid as to seem not quite of this world. "Super-naturalism" is all the more useful a term because it allows us to think of these two attributes—the hallucinated, magical quality of Dickens' vision and the typical "photographic realism" of his style—as aspects of the same literary disposition.

Of course Dickens' world is full of magic—one thinks not only of the striking episodes (Krook's spontaneous combustion, the Marquis' stone incarnation), but also of the whole texture of narration and description, full of strange coincidence, mysterious kinships, fantastic illusions, animistic revulsions of nature, contagion, all the trappings of fairy tale and primitive belief in magic. Dickens' habitual, almost ritualistic use of magical formulae may be seen, for example, in his choice of names for his characters, where a sophisticated version of word-magic operates, or in his reliance on incantatory rhythms in crucial moments of plot or feeling (compare the opening of the *Tale*, for instance, with Whitman's trance-inducing periods). Also relevant here is Dickens' fondness for order and pattern, arising from his need to feel in control of things. The primitive magician works up a body of lore to ease his fears and promote his desires; the dreamer arranges and elaborates his dream-telling in order to make some tolerable sense of his threatening visions; similarly Dickens, having conjured up an imaginative world no less strange and frightening, hastens to bind it with a charm of words. His rhetoric is akin to that of spell and incantation, which serves man's desire to exercise control over the world by organizing experience (as it is the function of science to do) under formulae that ritually name its parts and thus presumably ensure its obedience to law and order.

When the magician seeks to impose an order on his world, he does so knowing that his purpose is control; but when the dreamer imposes sense and logic upon his dream, he knows only that he is telling what seems to have happened to him. The dream has possessed him, and now he is recounting that possession. The telling of the dream is nonetheless a controlling mechanism, operating to make the dream safe and communicable, the alternative being to forget it completely. But the dreamer does not feel this as control. Rather, he supposes that he is still somewhat under the spell of his vision, and that he is merely doing his best to explain what has come to him magically in the night. Something of the same combination of possession and control occurs in a writer like Dickens, who finds himself presented with the world he writes down, as if it were not his world, nor his imagination that created it. In truth, the sense of being possessed is itself a method of control, for the feeling that one's world—imagined or real—is not one's own does not merely reflect alienation; it is also a way of staying safely detached, so that nothing can take one by surprise. This protective refusal to commit oneself is, of course, at the heart of the detachment which we have found to be a major characteristic of Dickens' narrative stance—as most strongly exemplified in the opening passages of *Bleak House,* where the narrator seems so completely uninvolved, a disembodied voice, an impassive camera-eye. The predominance of the physical setting in Dickens may be accounted for in the same way, for it is that world—the world of objects and things—which always absorbs the attention of the *detached* observer. When the tendency is carried to the extreme, as it is in Dickens, the characters themselves are viewed as objects rather than as people (the Marquis' nose, Jerry Cruncher's hair, Madame Defarge's knitting), while the affective life thus squeezed out of the characters turns up in the scene itself, producing the pervasive animism we find throughout Dickens.

Here we see just how intimately the detachment in these novels is connected with the immediacy. The fragmentation of perception and the displacement of feeling to the isolated, inanimate parts has a leveling effect, so that everything is somehow of equal emotional weight; thus, as in dream or magic, the smallest irrelevancy has talismanic force. In psychological terms Dickens' detachment, his failure to identify with any particular character (and thus to put himself into the story), results in his identifying with every character, with every object, with every insignificant detail of the action and scene. Like the dreamer—who is everywhere present in his own dream, playing all the roles and even providing the setting by a projection of his own body image—Dickens manages, through his detachment, to lend vitality to every element of his story. He is unable or unwilling to make the sort of contact with the world which, in Gestalt theory, gives rise to a strong figure against an empty background. In his perceptions the background usurps all the attention, vibrating with random life. The effect is that often experienced in walking the streets of an unfamiliar city: the walker, attentive but somewhat uneasy and defensive, notices more than he usually does (for the cues which produce habitual perceptions are missing); having nothing to focus on (being unwilling to give himself to the unknown), the observer does not become involved in the scene as a participant, and thus sees everything as slightly queer—as more real than real, but at a distance, alienated. And people look like Dickensian grotesques.

To sum up, then, Dickens' narrative stance and that of the dreamer may be said to have the following distinguishing marks in common: the apparent absence of control (viewed by the narrator-dreamer as a sort of possession which seizes upon him, or by the critic-analyst as a sort of hallucination chosen by him) entails a vision of the world as fragmented, mysterious, magically and grotesquely alive in every detail; while in truth a great deal of control is constantly being exercised in the perception of this fragmented world, bringing it under the rule of formula and ritual, every separate piece being ultimately accounted for, every mystery solved, and the threatening reality systematized and thus kept at a distance. As may be seen here, any description of the dream-narrative stance also involves a description of the world in which the stance is taken; one does not exist without the other. The total amalgam—a consciousness embracing its reality—determines the literary manner of an author: it gives rise to all the peculiarities of subject and approach which we call as a body "realism" or "naturalism" or "symbolism," or whatever; most important, it is chiefly by reference to the original stance of the author vis-à-vis his reality that we can understand how the parts cohere, and why these and only these are the elements that occur. We have seen this referral value quite thoroughly illustrated in Dickens: a number of paradoxical features in his manner are not at all paradoxical when viewed in the light of his dreamer's stance—the immediacy and detachment, the disguise and display, the refusal to identify with any single character and the identification with all the characters, the fragmentation and the superimposed coherence, the necessary-unnecessary details, the order without organization, the mystification and the need to provide solutions for everything, the sense of being possessed and the desire to control—all of these seemingly contradictory habits and motives prove to be perfectly regular and compatible outgrowths of the dreamer's stance in Dickens.

# 4

# The Novel as Dream

IT follows from a theory of Dickens' literary manner as a "dream manner" that his novels may be analyzed or interpreted in the way dreams are analyzed and interpreted—that is, at once formally and symbolically, as though the incidents of fiction comprised, like those of dreams, a special kind of language, with its own lexicon and grammar.

Up to this point I have been concerned with questions of style and stance, for it is to the texture of details and their ordering, and to the handling of narrative perspective, that one must look for indications of literary manner. These features tell us what sort of art it was that Dickens practiced, and also—as we shall see in the final chapter of this book—something about the problems and attitudes of the age in which he wrote. No doubt such insights, if achieved, are worth our attention, but however interesting Dickens' literary manner may be in itself or as a characteristic mode of dealing with experience in the nineteenth century, there still remains the job of practical criticism to show how individual novels bear the mark of Dickens' dream manner. This is not merely a matter of rehearsing once again the evidences of dreamlike technique in Dickens. Readings of particular novels may sometimes concern themselves with problems of technique and manner, but only as a means of arriving at a fuller understanding of what the novel says, of the story it tells and the experience of life it renders. In studying Dickens the recognition of the affinity of his literary manner with dreams is especially useful, because it gives the clue to the methodology of practical criticism, it tells us how to read the novels; but it is not the same thing as reading them.

In this chapter I shall continue to emphasize the dreamlike effects in Dickens, but with a shift from the theoretical to the practical, and thus from problems of style and perspective to those of structure and content. This is exactly the adjustment a psychoanalyst makes when he moves from theoretical considerations of dreams and dreaming to practical analysis of the particular dreams of particular patients. Bearing in mind the principles according to which dreams are shaped, the analyst looks for the structural elements that convey the content; he studies the parts and their interrelations; he interprets the meaning of the dream on the basis of these patterns and configurations. In proposing a reading of Dickens' later novels as if they were dreams, I shall rely on similar procedures. The analysis that has gone before will provide rationale and orientation for what follows, but the method and results will differ along with the aim. I hope to trace the main lines of structure in each of these novels, to explain what the actions and events mean and why they appear in the order and combinations that they do. I hope to sort out the chief meaning-bearing elements from various false leads and secondary elaborations which complicate and obscure the structure. Once this Gestalt is clear and sharp, I believe we shall be able to understand Dickens' novels more fully, not only as separate works but also as a progressive reiteration of a single developing meaning—like the meaning of a recurrent dream, which, as it comes closer and closer to the surface of the dream events, becomes more clearly structured and more directly represented by the structure, and thus serves as a paradigm through which the earlier versions may be better understood. Thus the analogy to dream provides the basis both for readings of individual novels and for an account of Dickens' development. In pursuing these readings and this account, I shall often speak of Dickens as a psychotherapist might speak of a patient whose dreams he is analyzing; however, it should already be clear that my main interest is not in Dickens' psyche but in his artistry. The point of interpreting Dickens' novels as if they were his dreams is to understand them, not him; and here the analogy to dream breaks down, since the intention is not to help the dreamer to health, but only to take greater pleasure, ourselves, in the dreams.

## The Dark Novels

When Dickens was twelve years old, his father was imprisoned for debt. So that the young Charles would be less of a burden, friends of the family found him a job pasting labels on bottles of shoe-blacking, in a corner of a dingy warehouse. This episode, which continued several months after his father's release from the Marshalsea, was for Dickens the most dismal and indelible of his life. He finally brought himself to mention it to his closest friend, John Forster, but to no one else, not even his wife. The memory was so painful that he found it easier to write about it than to speak of it, and thus we fortunately have his own account, preserved by Forster in his *Life of Charles Dickens*:

"No words can express," Dickens wrote..., "the secret agony of my soul as I sunk into this companionship; compared these every day associates with those of my happier childhood; and felt my early hopes of growing up to be a learned and distinguished man crushed in my breast. The deep remembrance of the sense I had of being utterly neglected and hopeless; of the shame I felt in my position; of the misery it was to my young heart to believe that, day by day, what I had learned, and thought, and delighted in, and raised my fancy and my emulation up by, was passing away from me, never to be brought back any more; cannot be written. My whole nature was so penetrated with the grief and humiliation of such considerations, that even now, famous and caressed and happy, I often forget in my dreams that I have a dear wife and children; even that I am a man; and wander desolately back to that time of my life."[35]

The agony, still felt, is apparent even in the syntax. The importance of the blacking-warehouse episode in forming the emotional subject matter of the novels can hardly be overestimated, and has been recognized by nearly every critic who has written since Edmund Wilson's ground-breaking essay on the subject, "Dickens: The Two Scrooges." As Wilson points out, "the work of Dickens' whole career was an attempt to digest these early shocks and hardships, to explain them to himself, to justify himself in relation to them, to give an intelligible and tolerable picture of a world in which such things could occur."[36] Dickens' full account of the episode (which may be found in both Forster and Wilson) is evidence enough that its effect on him was all-powerful. But in such a case, his memory of the facts is almost certain to have been highly censored and is not to be trusted on the surface. For instance, we hear nothing of sexual experiences at this time (nor would we expect to, even if he could remember them), but surely a boy of twelve, thrown in with the older, more worldly-wise Bob Fagin and "Poll" Green, wandering about the streets every night and on holidays, must have picked up frightening new knowledge and nonsense, to muddle his own growing self-consciousness. What we can be sure of is that the combination of circumstances (his father's imprisonment, his own supposed degradation, his proletarian friends and occupation) presented him with problems of class, sex, and "crime," which he was unable to solve at the time, and which haunted him long afterward. This nucleus of pain forms the content of Dickens' literary dream world, to which he repeatedly "wander[ed]" back.

The question of content is not an easy one in Dickens, for there are a number of levels of subject matter to be distinguished in his novels, and the critics' traditional interest in topical and historical themes—for instance, the concern with the Court of Chancery in *Bleak House*, or the French Revolution in *A Tale of Two Cities*—tends to obscure other matters which are much more important in determining the total effect of the books, even though they may take up less of the total space.

One must dig a bit in order to discover the deepest level of subject matter, the kernel of excitement that lies beneath everything else in these novels. The obvious way is the quickest; we must simply ask what incident gives rise to the series of events which the novel portrays. In *Bleak House* it is the unseemly liaison between Lady Dedlock, the representative of the highest society, and Captain Hawdon, sunk by the opening of the novel to the lowest of the low. In *Hard Times* it is the wicked, loveless marriages in two contrasting classes (Bounderby and Louisa, Blackpool and his debauched wife), the "sanctity" of each union threatened by a third person (Harthouse and Rachael). In *Little Dorrit* it is Arthur

Clennam's illegitimate origin in the sordid affair between his respectable father and a "singing-girl." In *A Tale of Two Cities* it is the rape of a peasant girl and murder of her husband and brother by Darnay's evil aristocratic uncle. In *Great Expectations* Estella, the illegitimate child of a convict, has been raised by Miss Havisham to be a lady, and tempts the working-class boy Pip to aspire above his station. In *Our Mutual Friend* Lizzie, the daughter of a wharf-rat, refuses to be seduced by the elegant but shiftless young barrister Eugene Wrayburn. At the root of each novel the same sore rankles: a sexual transgression somehow related to the overstepping (or the inability to overstep) class boundaries.

Furthermore, each of the novels includes as a part of its overt circumstances some violent death, often but not always that of the villain, which constitutes punishment and atonement for all the sin and guilt presented in the novel: Tulkinghorn, Stephen Blackpool, Rigaud, Carton, Magwitch, Headstone, and Riderhood. The connection between the social-sexual trangression and the violent ends of these characters is not spelled out very clearly in any of the novels, but we can sense the purgative effects merely by attending to the consequences of death, namely the cleansing of the hero and his return to innocence after the climactic scenes of violence and destruction. Thus in addition to problems of sex and class, we must regard guilt and its violent punishment as part of the central subject matter of the novels.

Sex, class, and sin are, of course, the staples of the novel from Defoe and Richardson onward, so we should hardly be surprised to find them in Dickens. Then too, it is easy enough to discover in Dickens' own life—most importantly in the blacking-warehouse episode—the psychic sources of his fascination with and fear of these subjects, and his simultaneous desire and reluctance to bring them together in his novels.

The point of special interest to us is not the origin of these forbidden contents, but their effect on the novels.

Beginning with *Bleak House*, the first of the "dark" novels, and after that in every novel up to *Great Expectations*, the energizing event at the core of the story involves a combination of sexual and social transgression. But when we come to look at the surface of the action, we discover that the sexual and the class content have somehow been quarantined from each other. One strand of plot is given to the "high" characters and one to the "low," as in Dickens' favorite Elizabethan plays. In *Bleak House* Esther and the society of Bleak House and Chesney Wold are contrasted with Richard and his falling in with the low society of Chancery Lane. Similar oppositions include, in *Hard Times*, the moneyed and proper society of Gradgrind and Bounderby and the oppressed and degraded world of Blackpool; in *Little Dorrit*, the respectable, middle-class world of Arthur Clennam and the prison and *nouveau riche* societies of the Dorrits; in *A Tale of Two Cities*, the bourgeois world of the family Manette, adopted by the aristocrat Darnay, and the proletarian world of the Jacquerie. The extremes are held at their distance by the dual structure. Although Dickens does in fact treat both the sexual and social aspects of his subject, he treats them "safely" in isolation from each other. Lovers are rarely allowed to come face to face unless they belong to the same class: this is why, in *A Tale of Two Cities*, Darnay's aristocratic connections are discussed only in the Paris plot until the discovery scene when Doctor Manette's secret diary is brought to light. And of course it is precisely this social emasculation of Darnay in his relations with Lucie and her father that makes him so dull a lover and so characterless a son-in-law.

The apparent exception, *Little Dorrit*, offers perhaps the strongest evidence of the divisive function of the dual plots, for it is exactly the split in the narrative which keeps the lovers apart, sending Amy off to Italy for half the novel, where she must sit and pine for Arthur until the "luck" of Merdle's swindle and her father's death lower her station sufficiently for her to be approached by her suitor. In all of these novels *connection* between characters from the two plots is always abundant (though complicated and indirect), whereas *confrontation* between them is kept at an absolute minimum. Because the impact of one world upon another is not felt, there can be no final integration for these novels, but only a trumped-up ending.

Contrary to what we might expect, the emphasis on circumstantial connections is a powerful means of keeping the strands of action separate. The concentration on superficial unity of plot merely intensifies the split, by drawing attention to connections which could not be made were there no gap to be bridged. Since no joining of the action is allowed to grow from the characters themselves, organically, a unifying web must be laid on artificially, as it were from above.

In *Great Expectations*, however, the sexual and social elements are finally permitted to collide, to be the ostensible as well as hidden subject matter of the novel—because (therefore?) Dickens finally uses a single plot line. Two strands of action can still be traced (a Satis House strand and a Newgate strand), but they come together and are integrated, upon Pip's discovery of his true benefactor, Magwitch, and the corollary facts—that Estella is Magwitch's daughter, that Compeyson is Miss Havisham's former lover, and so on. Here is Dickens' best novel (excepting the unfinished *Edwin Drood,* a more impressive work even as it stands than anything he had done before), and it is his best because he has at last allowed or forced himself to address openly his true subject. The novels written immediately before and after *Great Expectations* are especially interesting because they show Dickens first—in *A Tale of Two Cities*—trying to transform the double plot into a single or integrated plot, and then—in *Our Mutual Friend*—once again trying to utilize the double plot when it had lost its usefulness. *Our Mutual Friend* is really two novels, not a novel with a double plot like *Bleak House* or *Hard Times*. All the interesting subject matter, not just part of it, has been put into the Wrayburn half of the story (so that it turns out, on close examination, to be a lively reworking of the plot and subject matter of *Great Expectations*), and consequently there is nothing left for the Harmon story to be about (not surprisingly, then, it is an utter bore). This of course accounts for the exactly opposed views of the quality of the novel, some critics praising it beyond its deserts, others damning it as Dickens' worst, all according to which novel they have in mind. Dickens seems to have understood the problem, for in *Drood* he has invented a new form in which to treat his characteristic concerns.

The development sketched here, which shows Dickens finally allowing the sexual and the social themes to merge in a single action, is paralleled by a progression in the function of the third element of his basic subject matter—guilt and violent punishment. In *Bleak House* the main act of violence, the murder of Tulkinghorn, is only tangentially related to the sexual and social questions (Tulkinghorn has meant to reveal Lady Dedlock's guilty secret). In *Hard Times* Stephen's death clears him of the criminal charges against him and frees him forever from his miserable wife, but there is no apparent link between his death and Louisa's marriage or Harthouse's attempted seduction. Rigaud's death in *Little*

*Dorrit* seems deserved enough, but not as atonement for the sins of Arthur or his father. In *A Tale of Two Cities* the connection begins to be made: Carton literally dies for Darnay, who bears the inherited guilt of his family. In *Great Expectations* the violence is visited on the hero himself (Orlick's attack on Pip) and only the atoning death is suffered by a surrogate. Similarly in *Our Mutual Friend*, Eugene is violently beaten and almost dies the death that Headstone and Riderhood undergo in his place. Thus it appears that as the sexual and social elements of the hidden contents are brought to the surface and allowed to combine in a single action, the guilt becomes more and more localized in the hero who enacts the sexual-social transgression, and the violent punishment is accordingly reserved for him instead of being displaced to some surrogate.

These then are the centers of feeling in Dickens' dream novels—sex, society, and violent punishment of sin—three topics to which he kept returning until he managed to bring them together in a single line of action. The origin of his concern with them may have been his humiliating service in the blacking warehouse, though we shall never know enough about that period of his life to assay the emotional ingredients of the novels very accurately. What we can know is how Dickens finally came to terms with these haunting preoccupations, for the novels themselves are the record of his struggle with them. To put that struggle in its clearest light, we must begin at the end, or near the end, with *Great Expectations*, the first of the dream novels in which the three problems are brought into clear relation with each other in a single plot. After analyzing this paradigm case, we can go back to *Bleak House* and study the elements of secondary elaboration which hindered and obscured the confrontation of these themes in the earlier dark novels, and the development of various other dreamlike techniques which brought them to more and more direct expression up to and beyond *Great Expectations.*

## Great Expectations

In constructing his novels Dickens consistently took his own advice, as he once offered it to an amateur who wanted to write for his magazine:

Also, taking the pains to sit down and recall the principal landmarks in your story, you should then make them far more elaborate and conspicuous than the rest.[37]

The diction here is appropriate, for Dickens' landmarks are what stick in the memory. The lively and almost universal interest in the Dickens landscape is not to be dismissed as a mere hobbyhorse of the Dickens Fellowship, and although the identification of particular places (so that taverns, houses, streets can become shrines with little brass plates) is largely irrelevant to the critical appreciation of the novels, still the fact that Dickens gave such emphasis to places in his titles and in his arrangements of characters and events must be taken into account. We are able to refer to a London tale and a Paris tale in *A Tale of Two Cities,* just as in *Bleak House* we talk about Esther's narrative and the third-person narrative, each of which likewise centers about a particular locale. The literal landmarks in the story are landmarks of structure much as they are in dreams. The spatial dimension dominates Dickens' novels, providing his usual montage of alternating narrative lines with substance and orientation, just as on the level of style it furnishes the medium for ordering and connecting details. To be sure, the action of any novel must *take place,* but in Dickens place has an organizing function beyond that of mere background.

There are two main strands\* of action in *Great Expectations*: one concerned with Pip's relations to Miss Havisham and Estella and their symbolic place of residence, Satis House; the other centered around the transported felon Abel Magwitch and his symbolic place, Newgate prison. These two strains, filtered through Pip's consciousness, not only give us the content of his life (the events that occur, the people he meets), but also reflect in their emotional tone the inner conflict of his character, which is the central dilemma of the novel. A third set of characters, Joe and Biddy, and their symbolic place, the Forge, seems at the beginning to furnish the major alternative to the world of Satis House, and through the first third of the novel the conflict seems to be between these two worlds alone; but after Pip's departure for London the Forge fades out of the picture, and Newgate takes its place in opposition to Satis House.

The conflict between the worlds of Newgate (or the Forge) and Satis House is a conflict in Pip's soul. Thus it is given in the structure of the novel as the working out of his conflicting interpretations of the things that happen to him, which are the events of the novel itself. Pip's expectations may derive, as he first supposes, from Miss Havisham, because she has taken a fancy to him; or their source may be, as he finally discovers, the convict Magwitch, grateful for Pip's childhood kindness to him on the marshes. Each possibility has full-fledged formal status, in that it involves a set of characters and incidents structurally interrelated; but only one presents a temporal, logically interconnected sequence in which Pip can believe, and thus it represents, until the discovery and reversal, *the action* of the narrative. For the

---

\*I borrow the terminology from Paul Goodman, to whose book, *The Structure of Literature* (Chicago, 1954), I am heavily indebted here; see especially his chapter on "Oedipus Rex," pp. 26–49.

plot of *Great Expectations* this means that the Havisham strand fills the surface of the narrative, while the Magwitch strand lies mysteriously in the background, seemingly unrelated to the progress of the action. In the opening episode (Chapters I to VI), Magwitch jerks Pip up bodily and symbolically into the hidden strand, when, in a scene that is nightmarish in its blend of comedy and terror, he turns him upside down to shake his pockets empty. But Pip has not yet rejected the Forge, and Magwitch fades into the background while the narrative chiefly recounts Pip's fall from grace, his growing bedazzlement with the mirage of Satis House (begun in Chapter VII). Regularly interspersed, however, are incidents which stem, as even Pip can see, from the first scenes with the convict on the marshes. Thus in Chapter X, Pip meets a stranger who stirs his rum-and-water with Joe's stolen file and gives Pip a shilling wrapped up in a pair of pound notes—a gift from Magwitch. That night, in Pip's guilty slumbers,

I saw the file coming at me out of a door, without seeing who held it, and I screamed myself awake.

Following a few more scenes with Miss Havisham, Chapter XV deals with two more convicts escaped from the hulks, and with an act of violence for which Pip feels partly responsible—the savage attack on Mrs. Joe. As Pip says at the beginning of Chapter XVI,

With my head full of George Barnwell [an amateur reading had been forced on Pip by the stage-struck Wopsle], I was at first disposed to believe that *I* must have had some hand in the attack upon my sister, or at all events that as her near relation, popularly known to be under obligations to her, I was a more legitimate object of suspicion than any one else.

Pip conjectures that "either Orlick, or the strange man who had shown me the file" is the culprit. He knows that he himself was the cause of a violent squabble that very day between his sister and Orlick; and, worst of all, Mrs. Joe was beaten with a convict's iron—the very one that Pip had watched Magwitch file from his leg years before:

It was horrible to think that I had provided the weapon, however undesignedly, but I could hardly think otherwise.

Thus, mingling with Pip's swelling ambitions are his growing feelings of guilt; Magwitch and the Newgate strand are slowly beginning to replace the Forge and to present an alternative version of the facts as Pip sees them, although he cannot yet recognize this alternative.

Perhaps there is little need to emphasize the dreamlike cast of places and events in this opening sequence. Critics have often drawn attention to it, especially to the bizarre extravagance of the scenes laid at Satis House. It may be worth pointing out, however, that the carefully paced glimpses we have of the Newgate strand depend heavily for their threatening power on this eerie quality—which so pervades the atmosphere whenever the Magwitch cluster reappears that Pip's dream of "the file coming at me out of a door" seems hardly hallucinated at all. Compare it, for example, with the immediately preceding encounter with the convict who stirs his rum-and-water with that same file. And Pip later says that the two pound notes the convict had given him, "sealed...[by Mrs. Joe] in a piece of paper, and put...under some dried rose-leaves in an ornamental tea-pot,...remained a nightmare to me many and many a night and day." Or consider Pip's hallucinatory identification with George Barnwell, another Newgate figure:

What stung me, was the identification of the whole affair with my unoffending self. When Barnwell began to go wrong, I declare I felt positively apologetic, Pumblechook's indignant stare so

taxed me with it. . . . At once ferocious and maudlin, I was made
to murder my uncle with no extenuating circumstances whatever. . . . Even after I was happily hanged and Wopsle had closed
the book, Pumblechook sat staring at me, and shaking his head,
and saying, "Take warning, boy, take warning!" as if it were
a well-known fact that I contemplated murdering a near relation,
provided I could only induce one to have the weakness to become
my benefactor. [xv]

This passage is a particularly revealing example of how dreamlike effects function in the structure of the novel. From one
point of view, the scene may be regarded merely as a comic
interlude which makes entertaining capital of the Dickensian bumpkins Wopsle and Pumblechook. Yet that it is more
than this is evident even on the surface. Wopsle and Pumblechook—and even Pip—become so caught up in the story of
George Barnwell that they begin to treat Pip as if he were
that ungrateful character. It is typical of Pip's life, as a child
and as an adult, that things are rarely what they seem, or that
their aspect is always on the verge of changing from benign
to menacing. Appearances become apparitions; the "as if"
constructions which are used fancifully to describe occurrences have a mysterious tendency to prove no fancy at all,
but the nightmarish actual truth. In this scene Pip is made
to feel "as if" he were guilty of George Barnwell's sins, and,
as elsewhere in the novel, it turns out that there actually is
something either in Pip's circumstances or in his future com-
mensurate with the feelings raised by the imaginary situation. This is precisely the mechanism of dreams, where the
feelings are always the first and most direct clue to the meaning of the events and images by which they seem to have been
evoked. Pumblechook's absurd warning is perfectly appropriate to the true circumstances of Pip's life, though there
is no way yet for any of the characters or for the reader him-

self to know this. Only when we come to the next scene, the discovery of the attack on Mrs. Joe, do we remember with Pip the warning of the example of George Barnwell. Then we may see how Pip has been the occasion of the murderous assault on his "benefactor" (as she at least had regarded herself), who is also a near relation, his sister as well as his foster mother. This event may be considered the fulfillment of Pip's prophetic dream, in that it provides actual circumstances which account for his previous feelings of guilt. Or, to carry the interpretation a little further, it may be regarded as the fulfillment of Pip's unspoken wish, that the cruel foster mother who has "brought him up by hand" should be punished just as she has offended. Such a view, little as it is supported by the objective facts, has in its favor that it accounts not only for Pip's wish-premonition but also for Mrs. Joe's later repentance—as if she understood the reason for her punishment—and even for her strangely abject and fawning behavior in the presence of Orlick, her attacker, which hardly seems explicable on any other grounds than as a projection by Pip of a childish wish: if she were beaten too, then perhaps she'd think of being nice to me for a change.

All this, however, only explains Pip's strange experience as a dream of his own. There is still more to it, for the dreams in Dickens are not simply part of the story, as dreams of particular characters, but the chief narrative means of the story, the medium of its telling. The Barnwell episode, for example, works as one of many small nodes of meaning that occur throughout the novel, connecting various symbolic patterns which seem unrelated unless viewed as parts of a dreamlike system. Thus Pip's identification with George Barnwell is a dreamlike event which expresses the relations of all of the following occurrences in the novel:

Pip's aid to Magwitch, including his guilt at stealing Joe's file and Mrs. Joe's food.

The reappearance of the file.

Orlick's argument with Mrs. Joe and his subsequent attack on her with Magwitch's filed leg-iron; Pip's sense of guilt.

Pip's suggestion to Miss Havisham that she discharge Orlick from his job as her door-porter.

Magwitch's return and masquerade as Pip's Uncle Provis.

Miss Havisham's death by fire.

Orlick's attack on Pip, after having lured him to the old sluice-house by a note threatening his "uncle."

Magwitch's capture and death in Newgate.

This list reads like a résumé of the whole novel, yet there is a sense in which all these events are entailed by the brief passage under consideration. As Barnwell, Pip is warned that he is "contemplat[ing] murdering a near relation [his uncle], provided I could only induce one to have the weakness to become my benefactor." The immediate event which this curiously literary hallucination foreshadows is the attack on Mrs. Joe, and this in turn brings Orlick and Magwitch together as figures of violence and death (it is Magwitch's leg-iron that has furnished the weapon), and Pip as the ultimate cause of the violence, since he had first stolen the file and had been the origin of the quarrel between Mrs. Joe and Orlick. Thus is Pip's first benefactor brought low through his indirect agency.

Pip's second benefactor (supposed and real) is Miss Havisham. He later comes between her and Orlick, just as he had occasioned the squabble between Mrs. Joe and Orlick, but although Miss Havisham dies a horrible death, Orlick is not involved in it (he revenges himself directly on Pip for this interference, in the scene at the sluice-house). However, Pip is implicated in the death of Miss Havisham, much as he is in the attack on Mrs. Joe. Just as Mrs. Joe had been cruel to Pip, so Miss Havisham was not altogether a kindly benefactor. The moment of her affliction is also the moment of her relenting and asking forgiveness—though in her case this moment comes just before, not after her downfall. Again Pip is forewarned of the disaster by a hallucination, that is, another unacknowledged dream wish, in which he sees her hanging. He returns to her room just in time to see her go up in flames, and in his attempts to extinguish the fire he describes himself and her "on the ground, struggling like desperate enemies, and . . . the closer I covered her, the more wildly she shrieked and tried to free herself" (XLIX). Another benefactor has turned out to be an antagonist, and has paid for it with her life.

Pip's third benefactor is Abel Magwitch, the convict whose leg-iron downs Mrs. Joe and whose daughter finally breaks Miss Havisham's heart as well as Pip's. On the surface, Magwitch's intention to benefit Pip is somewhat less mixed with self-indulgence than the motives of his female counterparts, but behind his actions lurks the same selfish purpose— to manipulate, to *own* Pip: "Yes, Pip, dear boy, I've made a gentleman on you!" — "I says to myself, 'If I ain't a gentleman, nor yet ain't got no learning, I'm the owner of such. All on you owns stock and land; which on you owns a brought-up London gentleman?'" (XXXIX). Pip's response to his third benefactor is immediate hostility, not slowly developing or latent as it was in the earlier cases. Nevertheless, Pip assumes responsibility for Magwitch's safety from the start, even though he associates with him all the guilt and violence which have dogged him throughout the novel; Magwitch informs Pip that as a returned transport he is liable to hanging for his crimes:

Nothing was needed but this; the wretched man, after loading me with his wretched gold and silver chains for years, had risked his life to come to me, and I held it there in my keeping! If I had loved him instead of abhorring him; if I had been attracted to him by the strongest admiration and affection, instead of shrinking from him with the strongest repugnance; it could have been no worse. On the contrary, it would have been better, for his preservation would then have naturally and tenderly addressed my heart. [xxxix]

Later, after their adventures together, Pip softens toward his benefactor and ultimately nurses him in his final hours; but regardless of this change of heart, Pip is quite clearly the unwitting cause of his third patron's death in Newgate. Pumblechook's "Take warning, boy" in the Barnwell scene is justified when Pip's Uncle Provis dies because he has had "the weakness to become my benefactor."

One might go on, and point out the symbolic relations between the scenes in which Pip's benefactors are destroyed and that in which he himself is nearly murdered by Orlick; or one might show how the violence of the novel, associated with crime and guilt and punishment, is regularly expressed in the imagery of prison—leg-irons and chains and convicts—and how all this is part of a larger theme of law, order, and legitimacy versus crime, disorder, and illegitimacy. Such relations and connections are also part of the implied meaning of the Barnwell passage, for they are the principles according to which the various more direct implications of the episode are joined. But further analysis of this sort must wait until we have seen more of the characteristic structures and themes of the dream novel. For the moment, our interest must be confined to the method and effect of the dreamlike Barnwell passage.

What is perhaps most curious is the queer sort of foreshadowing embodied by the episode. The warning to Pip is immediately applicable in the discovery of the assault on Mrs. Joe, but its far-reaching implications cannot be known by any of the characters or by the reader himself—except on a second reading of the novel. Much foreshadowing in Dickens does not function as prediction, but as preparation, so that when the events foreshadowed finally occur the reader may think back (as the characters themselves sometimes do) to the earlier indications, and sense the "rightness" and integrity of the plot. This is a sort of echo effect on which probability in Dickens frequently hinges. But in the Barnwell episode, we scarcely have even this sort of foreshadowing, for when most of the incidents it carries in embryo finally occur, the reader is not reminded of the earlier scene; it is too brief and minor a part of the narrative for him to have paid it such close attention, and he is more likely to have absorbed only its surface meaning—along with its immediate significance as a warning of the attack on Mrs. Joe, which is made explicit by Pip himself in the following scene.

But if the episode is not an ordinary instance of foreshadowing, how then does it function? As I have already suggested, it is one of many such nodes of meaning growing out of the dream manner. Its effect is a combined one, working in conjunction with similar episodes, to produce a general atmosphere in the novel like the atmosphere of dreams. In Pip's world any chance occurrence is likely to have a predictive meaning behind its superficial significance— although Pip cannot see such meanings, or do anything about them—and all these meanings add up to an expression of his real story, the truth of his existence which he cannot know or recognize, but which he nevertheless is constantly shaping for himself by his actions. Everything and everyone is constantly telling him to take warning, and at the same time advising him, as Jaggers does, "Of course you'll go wrong somehow, but that's no fault of mine" (xx). Although not even the reader can tell precisely what threatens Pip until the threat is realized, the dreamlike premonitions and warnings make it clear that he is in danger from hidden, unknown forces which, just as in a dream, seem to exist outside him and his control but which actually express his own deepest feelings and inclinations, the fate he makes for himself. It is not important that the reader detect the significance of such pressures and premonitions before it is revealed (if he could, *The Mystery of Edwin Drood* would not be such a mystery), for Dickens is not a suspense novelist, who must inform the reader what to expect and fear, but a dream novelist, who achieves his tensions between the apparent and the hidden, the dual meaning of events. And exactly as in dreams, the apparent and hidden meanings need not—must not—be clearly distinguished at first, for the essence of the dream symbol is its ability to express many things at once, to combine and condense these in a single image. The threatening aspect of such images, symbols, episodes, comes from this very ambiguity and condensation, for as in dreams so in Pip's world, anything may prove to be something else, and there is no trusting either the ground underfoot or the ceiling overhead. At the catastrophe, it is precisely the image of a falling roof that Pip uses to describe the sudden turning of his fortunes from dream to nightmare.

"The Second Stage of Pip's Expectations" takes place in London, where the Newgate strand completely supplants that of the Forge. Pip is now entirely in the throes of moral conflict. At one moment he is full of vanity and self-importance, hiring a servant, joining the Finches of the Grove, sinking himself and Herbert into debt, and generally behaving like a "gentleman"; in the next, he is guiltily brooding over his past associations with convicts and other "low" persons, Joe included. His single good act comes when he secretly provides the money to make Herbert a success in business. Meanwhile the Newgate and Satis House strands continue to parallel this inner struggle. Pip's sense of guilt, the vagueness and intensity of which make it seem almost like original sin, is symbolized by the Newgate motif of crime and punishment; his pride and ambition are reflected in the Estella–Miss Havisham configuration of jeweled elegance grounded in decay and hurt vanity. In one scene Pip is at Satis House, priding himself on his expectations; in another he is in front of Newgate prison, feeling inexplicable guilt.

In this section Dickens begins to draw the two strands together, in order to prepare for the revelation of Magwitch as Pip's benefactor at the end of Part Two. In a regular pattern, the Magwitch strand presses more and more into the foreground (every fourth chapter now instead of every fifth), working toward its emergence into the surface of the novel. In Chapter xx Pip first feels the oppressive horror of Newgate; in Chapter xxiv he watches Jaggers at work in court, among felons and convicts; in Chapter xxviii he meets the convict with the aiming eye again; in Chapter xxxii, after touring Newgate, he feels himself contaminated by the convicts and their crimes, and recalling earlier experiences of the same sort, he begins intuitively to connect Estella with his guilt; in Chapter xxxvi he comes of age and recklessly presses Jaggers for information about his benefactor; finally, in Chapter xxxix, when Magwitch reveals himself as Pip's benefactor, the hidden strand emerges and the illusion of the apparent strand crumbles away:

All the work, near and afar, that tended to the end, had been accomplished; and in an instant the blow was struck, and the roof of my stronghold dropped upon me. [xxxviii]

This is the discovery and reversal.

Because Dickens' novels present their meanings as dreams do, by symbols and patterns which have hidden implications and interconnections, the most feared and desired confrontations—between the elements of sex, class, and violent punishment of sin—are staved off until at least halfway through the story. Among the results of this avoidance and delay is an intensified pressure toward discovery: the brittle framework of the apparent structure of meanings finally collapses in an explosion of pent-up energy. This, in addition to the qualities naturally associated with Magwitch, accounts for the violence of the scene in which the discovery emerges.

So furious had been the gusts, that high buildings in town had had the lead stripped off their roofs; and in the country, trees had been torn up, and sails of windmills carried away; and gloomy accounts had come in from the coast, of shipwreck and death.

.  .  .  .  .

The wind rushing up the river shook the house that night, like discharges of cannon, or breakings of a sea. When the rain came with it and dashed against the windows, I thought, raising my eyes to them as they rocked, that I might have fancied myself in a storm-beaten light-house. [xxxix]

One may notice by the way how this passage, with its references to "discharges of cannon" and "gloomy accounts...of shipwreck and death," is another instance of dreamlike condensation of events and motifs scattered throughout the novel, here pulling together Magwitch's past and future while heralding his disclosure as Pip's benefactor. But the main thing to understand about these preliminaries to the discovery scene is how the violence is directed at Pip—"I might have fancied myself in a storm-beaten light-house." The emerging hidden strand of events and the apparent strand it displaces are reflections of Pip's inner self, and with discovery and reversal in the plot also begins a similar violent turning about within the character of the hero. But this "character recognition" comes slowly and painfully, for the very reason that it involves giving up so much. Not only Pip, but Dickens himself holds back from the true meaning of the dream, because it contains his own fears and desires as well as his hero's. Still, simply because it contains them, the meaning must be worked out; something must be imagined to bring them to a temporary resolution. After the explosive scene of discovery, the pieces of Pip's world must be picked up and put back together in a new configuration. When the hidden strand emerges in the discovery, it becomes the dominant sequence of action in the dream structure, and takes over the surface of the narrative from the apparent strand it has "reversed." However, some threads of the displaced pattern, although they no longer function as they once did, remain to be accounted for and woven into the new structure of meaning. The gathering up of these broken threads constitutes the resolution, and the end comes when the possibilities of integration have been used up.

The method by which Dickens weaves the frayed ends of the Satis House strand into the fabric of the whole consists of a series of what must be called "secondary discoveries"— of secret family relationships, hidden motives, the buried past. These secondary discoveries are not merely melodramatic devices to wind up the story somehow, nor are they simply adjuncts to the primary discovery; because they represent Pip's world, the avoided and delayed recognition of the truth of his own feelings and actions, they have their own special function in freeing the hero to act out his destiny. Moreover, we shall see how the new integration of plot and character forces Dickens to work out the imaginative consequences of the confrontation of sex, class, and violence as well.

The major movement of the resolution is a single sequence (no longer a double-stranded one, as before the discovery). This sequence begins with Magwitch's appearance and ends with his death:

1. Magwitch reveals himself.
2. Pip confirms with Jaggers the identity of Magwitch as his benefactor.
3. Herbert returns; he and Pip determine to spirit Magwitch away.
4. Magwitch tells his story (connecting Miss Havisham and Magwitch as dupes of Compeyson).
5. Pip bids farewell to Estella, who is to be married to Drummle.
6. Wemmick warns Pip of Compeyson's presence in London.
7. Magwitch is moved to Mill Pond Bank; Pip tells him the escape plan.
8. Pip discovers that Compeyson is following him.
9. Pip recognizes Jaggers' housekeeper as Estella's mother.
10. He questions Miss Havisham about Estella's history.
11. Miss Havisham is burned (shortly to die).
12. Pip discovers that Magwitch is Estella's father.
13. He goes to Jaggers for confirmation of his new discoveries.
14. Wemmick signifies that the time is right to flee.
15. Pip is lured to the marshes by Orlick; Herbert rescues him.
16. Flight.
17. Capture; Compeyson drowned, Magwitch injured.
18. Pip nurses Magwitch in Newgate. (Herbert leaves; Wemmick marries.)
19. Magwitch is tried and condemned, then dies.

Three secondary discoveries are worked into this framework of resolution: (1) the discovery of Compeyson's deceit,
(2) the discovery of Estella's parentage, and (3) the discovery
of Orlick's symbolic meaning. These deal respectively with
the problems of class and society, the problem of sex, and the
problem of crime, guilt and violent punishment.

(1) *Compeyson.* As one by one the tangled knots of plot
are unraveled—Magwitch's imprisonment on the Hulks, Miss
Havisham's betrayal by her lover, even the mysterious figure
skulking about Barnard's Inn—Compeyson's malign influence appears behind the earliest snarling of each thread. And
what is worse, in his career of trickery and fraud Compeyson
has had at least the passive aid of a snobbish and heartless
society. Magwitch tells the story of their trial:

"And when it come to character, warn't it Compeyson as had been
to school, and warn't it his schoolfellows as was in this position
and in that, and warn't it him as had been know'd by witnesses
in such clubs and societies, and nowt to his disadvantage? And
warn't it me as had been tried afore, and as had been know'd
up hill and down dale in Bridewells and Lock-Ups? And when it
come to speech-making, warn't it Compeyson as could speak to
'em wi' his face dropping every now and then into his white
pocket-handkercher—ah! and wi' verses in his speech, too—and
warn't it me as could only say, 'Gentlemen, this man at my side
is a most precious rascal'? And when the verdict come, warn't it
Compeyson as was recommended to mercy on account of good
character and bad company, and giving up all the information
he could agen me, and warn't it me as got never a word but
Guilty?" [XLII]

In this and other passages, it becomes clear that Compeyson
and society are to be regarded as identical in their conscious
and malicious deception of the vulnerable individual. This
is Pip's first lesson—that the system is rotten and treacherous;
but true as the recognition may be, it has none of the quality

THE NOVEL AS DREAM

of self-discovery. Compeyson and what he represents in society are evil; Pip still has no sense of his own involvement in the social guilt, and his attitude toward Magwitch, though somewhat softened, is not yet transformed:

He regarded me with a look of affection that made him almost abhorrent to me again, though I had felt great pity for him. [XLII]

(2) *Estella.* The next discovery is a more profound one, and strikes nearer home to Pip. Because the revelation of Estella's connection with Magwitch involves linking the most desirable thing in his world with the most repellent, Pip's discovery has to be forced upon him by the plot, rather than merely offered to him as information (as in Magwitch's account of Compeyson). The preparation for the discovery of Estella's parentage is therefore begun even before the reversal. In chapters XXVI, XXIX, and XXXII (a sequence regular as clockwork) the ground is laid for the disclosure that Estella is the daughter of Abel and Molly Magwitch: Pip's attention is first directed to Jaggers' housekeeper's hands; then, with his sudden awareness of Estella's hands in Chapter XXIX, a quasi-hallucinatory scene takes place:

As my eyes followed her white hand, again the same dim suggestion that I could not possibly grasp, crossed me. My involuntary start occasioned her to lay her hand upon my arm. Instantly the ghost passed once more and was gone. What *was* it?

A second "What was it?" scene occurs when, standing outside Newgate, he sees Estella's white arm waving to him from the coach. Finally, in Chapter XLVIII of the resolution, Pip consciously compares Molly, Jaggers' housekeeper, and Estella:

I looked at those hands, I looked at those eyes, I looked at that flowing hair; and I compared them with other hands, other eyes, other hair, that I knew of, and with what those might be after twenty years of a brutal husband and a stormy life. I looked again at those hands and eyes of the housekeeper, and thought of the inexplicable feeling that had come over me when I last walked—not alone—in the ruined garden, and through the deserted brewery. I thought how the same feeling had come back when I saw a face looking at me, and a hand waving to me, from a stage-coach window; and how it had come back again and had flashed about me like lightning, when I had passed in a carriage— not alone—through a sudden glare of light in a dark street. I thought how one link of association had helped that identifica- tion [of Compeyson] in the theatre, and how such a link, wanting before, had been riveted for me now, when I had passed by a chance swift from Estella's name to the fingers with their knitting action, and the attentive eyes. And I felt absolutely certain that this woman was Estella's mother.

From here it is an easy step to match Wemmick's history of Molly with Magwitch's tale of his estranged wife and child. Thus one more shred of the apparent strand is woven back into the new pattern; Pip's false expectations—both fortune and Estella—turn out to be derived from Magwitch.

The meaning of this discovery only slowly dawns on Pip. He says, at the beginning of Chapter LI:

What purpose I had in view when I was hot on tracing out and proving Estella's parentage, I cannot say. . . .

. . . I was seized with a feverish conviction that I ought to hunt the matter down—that I ought not to let it rest, but that I ought to see Mr. Jaggers, and come at the bare truth. I really do not know whether I felt that I did this for Estella's sake, or whether I was glad to transfer to the man, in whose preservation I was so much concerned, some rays of the romantic interest that had so long surrounded me. Perhaps the latter possibility may be the nearer to the truth.

The clue to the meaning of the discovery is not in either of Pip's hypotheses, but rather in the very ambiguity which he feels in his motives. It is striking, for instance, that after confirming the story with Jaggers, Pip has absolutely nothing to say about the effect of the discovery on him. After all the "feverish" effort "to hunt the matter down," Pip drops the subject without a word. No doubt he does learn something that changes him, for his attitude toward Magwitch is much more one of acceptance after the discovery, though still dutiful rather than truly loving. But it can hardly be, as he suggests, that some of the romance has rubbed off on Magwitch. Instead, some of the guilt he has felt in connection with Magwitch has been communicated to his feeling about Estella. And more important, the neurotic split between the gentility represented by Estella and the lowness that Magwitch stands for, is partially healed by the revelation of their blood relationship.

The fact that Estella turns out to have been a deserted child is even more significant. The motif of the deserted or illegitimate (and therefore disinherited) child is very frequent in Dickens, of course, and, as so many critics have observed, this preoccupation undoubtedly goes back to his own sense of neglect during the blacking-warehouse days. Magwitch is a father figure for Pip—his *Uncle* Provis, his benefactor, "the creature who had made me" (xl), who calls him "dear boy" and says, "Look'ee here, Pip. I'm your second father. You're my son—more to me nor any son" (xxxix). Pip is himself a deserted child, whose parents have died before he knew them ("I never saw my father or my mother," he says in Chapter i), and his unwillingness to accept a second father is perhaps due in part to his resentment of the original deprivation. The discovery that Estella was also a deserted child, and at the same time that she was not willingly abandoned, makes it possible for Pip slowly to accept Magwitch's love; Estella's story brings his own resentment into the open, as it were, and also exonerates the "father" of them both.

Perhaps this account of Pip's discoveries in regard to Estella does not seem very relevant to the problem of sex in the novel. But it is a peculiarity of Dickens' treatment of the sexual theme that there is very little concern with its usual elements. Instead, the interest resides primarily in the blockage of sexual desire, the reasons for the blockage, and its eventual dissolution. Despite much critical nonsense that has been written about Dickens' "deeply sensitive" portrayal of Pip's love-agonies, the treatment of Pip's desire for Estella is in fact strangely flat and mechanical, just as the love affairs in all the novels have something rather wooden and lifeless about them. What is intense is Pip's expectation and its frustration. As far as Estella goes, there is little expectation and much frustration, and this is again typical of Dickens. The discovery to be made is the cause of this frustration. We are at first led to believe that Estella's inability to love is to blame, but in fact the hindrance to his sexual satisfaction is Pip's own inability to love: Estella is not really the worthy heroine at all—rather, Biddy is—and Pip does not recognize this until too late, although the reader sees all along that she is more desirable than Estella, and that Pip chooses Estella instead partly in order to fail at love, partly because at this point he can love only himself. The touchstone that tells us he has learned his lesson is the freeing of his love for Magwitch, which results from his discovery that Estella is his daughter. Learning the truth about the connections between his apparent and real expectations frees him from his constricted view of himself. He begins to see that the objects he has desired were only delusions, that to be a gentleman is to be like Compeyson and that to love Estella is to be like Drummle; that the only value in these goods is the value originating in the antisocial, sexually loose, violently threatening figure of Magwitch. As he comes to terms with this sort of reality, Pip's stiffness and stuffiness drop away, and he ultimately becomes the gentleman and the lover Magwitch had hoped.

(3) *Orlick*. The third discovery of the resolution follows on the heels of Pip's talk with Jaggers. Of the three revelations, this seems least connected with the natural progress of the action; yet it too has a structural purpose. In Dickens' notes for the resolution of *Great Expectations* he gave the Orlick episode major status:

Miss Havisham and Pip, and the Money for Herbert. So Herbert made a partner in Clarriker's.
Compeyson. How brought in? [First Discovery]
Estella. Magwitch's daughter. [Second Discovery]
Orlick and Pip's entrapment—and escape [Third Discovery]
   —To the flight
     Start
      Pursuit
       Struggle—Both on board
       together—Compeyson drownd [*sic*]—
       Magwitch rescued by Pip. And
       taken—
Then:
   Magwitch tried, found guilty, & left for
                 DEATH[38]

With the discovery of Compeyson's (society's) duplicity and of Estella's parentage, the ensuing acceptance of Magwitch as a "good" father-figure leaves a gap in Pip's defenses. Accepting the good in Magwitch means that Pip will somehow have to face the evil as well, and it comes all in a rush with Orlick's attack. The connection with Magwitch is made explicit in the novel. When Pip answers the suspicious summons to the sluice-house, he knows that he endangers himself if he goes, but jeopardizes Magwitch if he does not:

If I had had ample time for consideration, I believe I should still have gone. Having hardly any time for consideration—my watch showing me that the coach started within half an hour—I resolved to go. I should certainly not have gone, but for the reference to my Uncle Provis.

.   .   .   .   .

Still, the reference to Provis by name mastered everything. I reasoned as I had reasoned already without knowing it—if that be reasoning—in case any harm should befall him through my not going, how could I ever forgive myself! [LII]

Not that he goes merely for Magwitch's sake; rather, because he now accepts Magwitch, all the violence which has been storing up in the novel is suddenly released. Logically, of course, the violence should come from Magwitch, who has seemed to threaten it all along, or from Pip himself; but Dickens cannot allow a character now turned "good" to strike such a blow. The good characters rarely get into fist fights, but are attacked "from behind," as Wrayburn is in *Our Mutual Friend*. Orlick is at hand for the violence, and his superficial unrelatedness to the rest of the action makes it easier for Dickens to open all the stops and revel in the danger and hatred. "Oh you enemy, you enemy!" Orlick exclaims with gruesome delight:

His enjoyment of the spectacle I furnished, as he sat with his arms folded on the table, shaking his head at me and hugging himself, had a malignity in it that made me tremble. [LIII]

Even Pip, bound tight to the ladder, can allow his passion to show: "If I could have killed him, even in dying, I would have done it."

Having faced the violence, which constitutes his punishment for his crimes—comparable to the punishments of Mrs. Joe and Miss Havisham, and later of Magwitch himself—Pip is freed from the third of his problems. His sense of guilt, which has been a major theme throughout the novel, is at last dispelled, and he is now able to love Magwitch without fear of the taint of evil and crime that haunted him before. In accepting the violent punishment, he also accepts the guilt he has been avoiding, and becomes like Magwitch a fugitive from society. After Magwitch's death, he is himself arrested for debt, falls ill, and thus by going through a milder version of Magwitch's own suffering, expiates his own sins and purges his character. There follows a sort of epilogue of rebirth, which is perhaps the weakest part of the typical Dickensian structure, a consequence of Dickens' having never quite managed to resolve all of his hero's problems. As can be seen from the brief sketches of Pip's secondary discoveries, Dickens' way of dealing with the issues of class and sex and guilt does not show him to be very much aware of the implications of the material. He is like the dreamer, who attends only to the surface of events presented because it is precisely their hidden meanings and emotional implications that he fears to admit. To understand this failure of the Dickensian happy ending, and how it relates to his dream manner, we must now consider more elaborately the meaning of the three secondary discoveries, especially as they are emotionally joined as the resolution to Pip's (and Dickens') problems—that is to say, in the light of the whole novel.

Like Dickens' other heroes, Pip escapes death partly because he has not quite deserved it, but mainly because in a sense others have died for his sins. It is an easy matter to show that the sins of Compeyson and Magwitch are only exaggerated versions of Pip's own. His treatment of Joe, his disregard for his old friend's rights and feelings, corresponds to Compeyson's cruel toying with Miss Havisham's affections, and to Magwitch's fundamentally selfish manipulation of Pip's own fortunes. In fact, a certain chain of evil runs through these three characters: Compeyson, like Rigaud in *Little Dorrit*, "sell[s] Society," in that he uses people for his own gain; Magwitch, one of Compeyson's victims, in his turn manipulates Pip's life and boasts of the fact that he "owns a brought-up London gentleman" (xxxix); Pip, Magwitch's victim, is seduced by his false expectations into unfeeling actions toward Joe—actions so like Magwitch's that Pip even considers the possibility of making a sort of gentleman out of his former master and companion in the Forge:

When I came into my property and was able to do something for Joe, it would have been much more agreeable if he had been better qualified for a rise in station.

. . . . .

"If I were to remove Joe into a higher sphere, as I shall hope to remove him when I fully come into my property, [his learning and manners] would hardly do him justice." [xix]

The evil represented by Pip's lack of feeling may be no deadly sin, but in Compeyson the same evil is particularly poisonous because it seems to infect others, not only Magwitch—and, through him, Pip—but also Miss Havisham, another victim who quickly learns how to use people for the gratification of her own spiteful desires. Furthermore, it seems that anyone infected with the moral disorder represented by Compeyson assumes a full share of the guilt, regardless of the degree to which the sin is indulged.

Although not so evident in *Great Expectations* as in the longer novels such as *Bleak House* and *Little Dorrit*, where social institutions (Chancery, the Circumlocution Office, and the rest) play a major part, even here it is clear that the sin and guilt which bring on the catastrophe are rooted not in the individual but in the society itself—public sin, public guilt. Pip's worship of gentility is fostered by social pressures, and Magwitch's first trial and punishment are influenced by class prejudice. Society—or the part of society that exercises power—manipulates the individual, through deliberate mystification and deceit, in order to perpetuate the existing social order. Dickens' view of society is based on the assumption that everyone is implicated in the general guilt. Thus only one resolution is possible for the novels: a losing (though not necessarily fatal) struggle with evil, after which, if he survives, the hero must somehow be removed from the deceitful world to a haven of rest. This is the typical Dickens ending. The moral victory of the hero, represented by his rebirth, always takes the form of a symbolic return to the state of childhood innocence, where actions are direct and undisguised, without the overtones of motive or practice. The character who has achieved this state is commonly shown in some revisiting, as Pip returns to the Forge, scene of his childhood, or as Esther Summerson goes to the new Bleak House, an exact replica of the old. This haven is always separate, secluded, away from society; for although the representatives of evil (Compeyson, Orlick, Miss Havisham) have been isolated and destroyed, the institutional evils of society persist, and the place of innocence must be topographically as well as morally outside their influence.

In *Great Expectations* the return to innocence is qualified by the implication that Pip, through his suffering, not only has been purged of guilt but also has become a true gentleman. Thus his return to childhood is possible only in a symbolic sense. The refuge of innocence is not quite the same place as it was before; or, if it remains unchanged, the hero is different, older and wiser. Pip has hoped to settle down and marry Biddy, but he finds her already married to Joe. He now realizes that he cannot return to the innocent state of his childhood, even though that is what he wants to do, and instead he goes off to the Eastern Branch of Clarriker and Co., where Herbert and Clara will mother him. Dickens' decision not to allow Pip a full return to innocence was no doubt the right one, dictated by the probabilities of his character already set up in the novel. All the same, the final scenes at the Forge leave something to be desired. As Humphry House puts it in *The Dickens World,*

[Dickens] shirks the implications of the reconciliation with Joe and Biddy: there is one emotional scene with friendliness all around, which shows that in spite of his new accent and new manner Pip is the same decent little fellow after all: but what if he had had no Herbert to fall back on, and had been forced to build his fortunes again from scratch in the old village with the Gargerys and Wopsles? Dickens does not face this: he takes Pip's new class position as established, and whisks him off to the East, where gentlemen grow like mushrooms.[39]

This avoidance of the class problem runs all through *Great Expectations*; it is behind the obscure symbolism and strange power in the figure of Orlick; it explains Pip's revulsion from Magwitch, his flight from the discovery; it even tells us why it is that Magwitch must die in prison, rather than live to be pardoned and thus embarrass Pip with his company.

At the beginning of the novel, the choice seems to be between Biddy and Estella, Joe and Miss Havisham, the careers of blacksmith and of "walking-gentleman." Pip the narrator conveys to the reader a feeling that Biddy and the Forge are much more desirable than Estella and Satis House, even though Pip the character is convinced of quite the opposite:

My young mind was in that disturbed and unthankful state, that I thought long after I laid me down, how common Estella would consider Joe, a mere blacksmith: how thick his boots, and how coarse his hands. I thought how Joe and my sister were then sitting in the kitchen, and how I had come up to bed from the kitchen, and how Miss Havisham and Estella never sat in a kitchen, but were far above the level of such common doings. [IX]

If there are no real goods to be had from Satis House, one wonders why Pip is so greatly attracted. Leaving out the question of Estella's sexual desirability (which Dickens characteristically avoids), it will be useful to examine the gentleman's life he aspires to and the blacksmith's life he flees. Even on the face of it, the gentleman's life is certainly no life at all. Pip's education fits him for no manly pursuit; his money buys him no honest pleasures; and the hopelessly inept Herbert and the surly clod Drummle represent the range of quality in his genteel friends and enemies. This picture is drawn with the power of deep conviction, and there is no hint of values hidden beneath the surface. Still, the gentleman's role has some negative virtues, which we can see only by looking at its alternative, the blacksmith's life. Here we find everything pictured as good, beautiful, and true—too much so. Joe is the ideal blacksmith, Biddy the paragon of village schoolmistresses, and so forth. Even the "bad" characters in this pastoral world are not allowed to be really evil—merely comic like Pumblechook and Wopsle. The sole exception is Orlick, who is a slouching beast, a "Cain" (XV), moody, vicious, endowed with cruel cunning. The characterization of Orlick gives the whole pastoral show away, for he is a blacksmith, a journeyman at the Forge, just as Pip is to be. One has the feeling that Orlick got into *Great Expectations* in spite of Dickens, and that his shadow, looming over the Forge and its life, grew large in Dickens' imagination almost without his willing it. His minor place in the action is out of all proportion to the fearful power with which he is delineated, and one feels the excess of crude violence in Orlick as a kind of leftover from the idyllic characterization of Joe and the Forge—an aspect of the actual condition of the poor which Dickens, suppressing it in the others, found himself as it were involuntarily intensifying in this one brutalized and degraded rural figure.

One effect of Dickens' early brush with poverty was his inability to face squarely the conditions of life in the lower classes. As Humphry House again points out,

In much of his description of what he considered to be the grosser kind of social evil there seems to be a contest between a frank acceptance of it as an unwelcome fact and the desire to minimize it because it was unwelcome. There is an open sincerity in his manner when he is attacking injustice, cruelty, humbug, and so on, which is lacking when he attacks the cruder consequences in sex, drink, and dirt, of bad social conditions. . . . In class and habits of feeling Dickens was too far removed from such things to assimilate them fully (he was ashamed when he thought he had become a manual worker), but not removed enough to treat them with detachment. The process of censorship which made him conceal for years the proletarian episode in his own boyhood was similar to that which was constantly at work in his fiction.[40]

An example of this repression is the idyllic picture we get of Joe in *Great Expectations*: Dickens tries to show Pip's earliest choice as the simple one of being either a genteel snob or an honest blacksmith, but the choice of poverty—even idealized poverty—was not so easy for him to make. Orlick shows us the other side of the coin, for in him appear the fearful brutality and depravity which are repressed in the characterization of Joe, but which nevertheless lie at the very heart of Dickens' feelings about the proletariat. The attempt to simplify the contrast between the roles of good-for-nothing gentleman and hard-working, productive laborer—to make the choice between them a matter of black and white—issues in the uncontrollable development of the Orlick figure in the background. This other side must be taken into consideration, for it is the source of Pip's revulsion from his coarse and common existence at the Forge.

Because Dickens does not really believe in the Forge and what it stands for as a desirable way of life, it is dropped from the narrative at the end of Book One (to be revived only as a kind of last resort at the end of the novel). The Satis House and Newgate strands now comprise the dominant line of action, completely overshadowing Joe's part of the story.

In the world of Satis House everything glitters at the surface, cold, bright, and hard as Estella's jewels; but there is no action, and what lies underneath that surface is rotting away. Miss Havisham has not stirred out since her wedding day; it is the world of an aged, self-imprisoned child. In her symbolic death by fire Miss Havisham is consumed by her own inward decay. She has destroyed herself, as Pip's hallucination, when he sees her hanging, must imply. The desiccated wedding garments, symbols of her vanity, are all that is left of her; and they explode almost spontaneously, so that we are reminded of Krook's fate in *Bleak House*. Opposed to this world is the Magwitch strand of the plot, where everything is done in the warmth of affection or the heat of passion; everything is action; it is the uncalculating world of childhood. Magwitch dies thinking of his own child, himself a kind of child about to be delivered from the sternly parental authority of Newgate to that of a Father above. Seen in this way, Newgate becomes merely another version of the Forge.

Such is the structural expression given to the forces that battle within Pip through the major part of the novel. The choice between these worlds would seem to be an easy one; but it is complicated by a powerful ambivalence in Pip's attitude toward Magwitch. In spite of—and partly because of—all that Magwitch has done for him, Pip is terrified and repelled by his benefactor:

The abhorrence in which I held the man, the dread I had of him, the repugnance with which I shrank from him, could not have been exceeded if he had been some terrible beast. [xxxix]

This repugnance is explained on the surface by the fact that Pip's relations with society—first with Mrs. Joe, Pumblechook, and Wopsle, then with Estella and Miss Havisham—have infected him with a self-important worship of gentility and a snobbish revulsion from what is "low." Pip's childhood sleep is disturbed "through thinking...of the guiltily coarse and common thing it was, to be on secret terms of conspiracy with convicts" (x). He supposes that his compassionate action—feeding and sympathizing with the starving convict on the marshes—is a loathsome and shameful crime. This is simple enough, and true to the facts of Victorian respectability-worship; but the power with which this guilt and loathing clings to the Newgate plot, in each of its mysterious eruptions into the superficial progress of the action, makes the explanation of it as mere snobbery seem inadequate. After Pip has coincidentally shared a coach with Magwitch's convict emissary of the "aiming eye," he says:

I could not have said what I was afraid of, for my fear was altogether undefined and vague, but there was great fear upon me. As I walked on to the hotel, I felt that a dread, much exceeding the mere apprehension of a painful or disagreeable recognition, made me tremble. [xxviii]

Again, after Wemmick has given him a tour of Newgate, Pip muses over the strange circumstance

...that I should be encompassed by all this taint of prison and crime; that, in my childhood out on our lonely marshes on a winter evening I should have first encountered it; that, it should have reappeared on two occasions, starting out like a stain that was faded but not gone; that, it should in this new way pervade my fortune and advancement. While my mind was thus engaged, I thought of the beautiful young Estella, proud and refined, coming towards me, and I thought with absolute abhorrence of the contrast between the jail and her. I wished that Wemmick had not met me, or that I had not yielded to him and gone with him, so that, of all days in the year on this day, I might not have had Newgate in my breath and on my clothes. I beat the prison dust off my feet as I sauntered to and fro, and I shook it out of my dress, and I exhaled its air from my lungs. So contaminated did I feel, remembering who was coming, that the coach came quickly after all, and I was not yet free from the soiling consciousness of Mr. Wemmick's conservatory, when I saw her face at the coach window and her hand waving to me. [XXXII]

This sense of contamination must have a deeper cause than Pip's genteel sensitivity. We can understand it better if we study the connection between Magwitch and Joe, between Newgate and the Forge. The whitewashing of the world of the Forge has resulted in a compensatory blackening of the other proletarian scene—which is infused with the depraved animality seen in Orlick, no less a "beast" than Magwitch. (It is perfect that Orlick should be compared to Cain while Magwitch is named "Abel.") The warmth and affection of the Forge, as against the icy rigidity of Estella and Satis House, are now raised to the heat of passion, brutality, and guilty terror.

Of course this double view of the proletariat, which runs through all of Dickens, is compounded of his sympathy for its plight and his fear of its brutality and violence. It goes back again to his early experience in the blacking warehouse. In that trauma his notions of poverty seem to have become inextricably associated with powerful fantasies of sex and crime, and no later growth in him of humanitarian principles ever eased the burden of the poor which the blacking-warehouse episode seems to have laid upon him. So in *Great Expectations* crime and wealth and sex are guiltily entangled, and one purpose of the novel is to make sense of them.

To put things rather schematically, one may interpret the relations between the Forge, Newgate, and Satis House as follows: once Pip allows himself to be tempted by Estella, the sexual-social lure offered by the genteel world, the pastoral scene of his childhood is suddenly transformed into the threatening, violent world of Newgate. Joe becomes Magwitch, good becomes evil, innocence becomes guilt; Newgate is found to be opposed to Satis House, just as the Forge had originally been. Only after the disintegration of the Satis House world does the Forge slowly come back into the picture and Newgate slowly fade into the background.

Although Pip is ultimately purged of his guilt, the expiation and punishment are represented largely in symbolic terms, and Pip is never allowed to come to grips with his problem in a "real" situation (as he might have, for instance, in his return to the Forge). This failing in the novel—and, unhappily, in all Dickens' other novels of this period—is what produces the notorious lack of conviction that so vitiates the little epilogues predicting the hero's future happiness which Dickens commonly adds at the end. In *Great Expectations* the equivocation is made all the more obvious by the famous alternative endings. The original ending, in which Pip and Estella are shown going their separate ways, was canceled by Dickens in favor of a "happier" one, at the instigation of Bulwer-Lytton. The debate over which ending is the more appropriate to the story has preoccupied critics ever since. Notable among the preponderant unhappy-endians are John Forster and George Bernard Shaw. More recently it has become fashionable to agree with Dickens' final choice, and a multitude of critics, on various grounds, have plumped for matrimony. Actually, there is little difference between the versions. What is important in both endings is not the reconciliation of lovers, but the comparison of fates and the final statement of hope—the possibility of understanding through suffering. It is significant that the only passages that resemble each other in the two endings are the following:

*First Version*

...she gave me the assurance, that suffering had been stronger than Miss Havisham's teaching, and had given her a heart to understand what my heart used to be.

*Second Version*

"But you said to me," returned Estella, very earnestly, "'God bless you, God forgive you!' And if you could say that to me then, you will not hesitate to say that to me now—now, when suffering has been stronger than all other teaching, and has taught me to understand what your heart used to be."

The understanding heart will be recognized, of course, as the great Dickensian virtue—a virtue which Dickens had himself to the utmost degree, and which he seems to have thought of as a panacea for humanity. No doubt such understanding is very admirable, and no doubt the world would be a better place if it were more common; however, true compassion is not idle and withdrawn, but looks for ways to remedy what is wrong. Dickens' heroes never *do* anything about the evils in society, the prisons, the government, and so on. The closest approach to action is the effort of Arthur Clennam in *Little Dorrit* to wring a decision on Doyce's invention from the Circumlocution Office. Clennam fails, of course, since Dickens did not believe that public or social institutions could be affected by individual or even group action. "As to the suffrage," he wrote to Macready in 1855, "I have lost hope even in the ballot."[41] His repeated refusal to stand for Parliament is well known, and his view of the proper attitude toward all evil public institutions seems to be exemplified by John Jarndyce's attitude toward Chancery in *Bleak House*—that one should unwaveringly hold oneself aloof from the whole dirty business.*

For all the weakness of the ending, however, *Great Expectations* is on the whole a powerful book. Part of its power must certainly be attributed to the remarkable suitability, the fine adjustment, of the plot to the view of society Dickens wished to convey. The interaction of the hidden and apparent strands, and their coming together in a moment of discovery and reversal, provide a kind of dialectic of deception, which is the equivalent in structural terms of the Dickensian conception of society and its institutions as a vast framework of false appearances. Particularly in *Great Expectations* the structure is nicely adapted to this theme, for the use of the first person gives Pip a centrality not available to the heroes of the other novels; and seen through Pip's eyes, the pattern of apparent and hidden actions serves as a structural paradigm of his conflict and his self-deception with much greater dramatic force than is possible in the objectively narrated novels. The peculiarly Dickensian use of delayed discoveries emphasizes the hero's self-deception and his fear of self-recognition. Only in the happy endings does Dickens' thematic use of structure appear to fail him, and such failures occur not

---

*Dickens, in his magazines and in his public speeches, continued throughout his life to promote various programs for the national welfare and to agitate for reform—in sanitation, in factory regulation, in governmental procedure, and so on; but in his private letters and in the novels his despair of any really effective program or protest becomes increasingly evident, especially after 1850.

because the return to innocence has no formal counterpart (it is represented in the revisiting scene), but rather because the new innocence strikes one as not quite earned, as an escape from responsibility rather than a revaluation of the proper relations between society and the self.

Much of the foregoing discussion might very well have been undertaken without any reference to dreams or the dream manner, but there are aspects of Dickens' novels which cannot be understood by mere formal analysis of plot and theme, just as the ordinary methods of stylistic analysis will not explain everything about Dickens' dreamlike rhetoric. Furthermore, although most fiction may be "psychoanalyzed" along the same lines I have followed here, Dickens' novels— because of their dreamlike character—*must* be analyzed in this way if we are to comprehend fully the means by which they achieve their remarkable power. For Dickens occupies a peculiar position halfway between the allegorist and the ordinary novelist. The work of the latter may often be read on two levels, but a psychoanalytic interpretation is not necessarily called for, since the writer's method is usually self-conscious and unhallucinated: to whatever degree he may use his imagination, he does not ordinarily employ it as freely and spontaneously as any dreamer does in dreaming. The ordinary writer does not invite his reader into the ambiguous world of dreams, where order and meaning are directed by unconscious needs and purposes. But that is just what Dickens does. On the other hand the allegorist, who always needs to be read on two levels, is also unlike Dickens, and the dual meanings of allegory call for a sort of interpretation unlike that of dreams. The allegorist may be read for the literal or the allegorical meaning, or both; but there is always a distinct separation between the two. They do not interpenetrate in the way that the levels of meaning in dreams do. One can imagine reading an allegory merely for the sake of its allegorical meaning. But Dickens cannot be read that way. Pip standing before Newgate, waiting for Estella, stamping and shaking the prison taint off him, cannot be understood unless one is to some degree aware of both levels of meaning—his inexplicable guilt and fear, and his hidden connection through Magwitch, Estella's father, with crime, violence, and retribution. The two levels cannot really be separated at all, without losing the essential and fundamentally single meaning of the image. This is how it is in dreams, where the image and its hidden significance are a single amalgam. Pip has dust on his clothes; he feels tainted with guilt. Miss Havisham still wears her decaying bridal dress; she is herself decaying because of her betrayal by Compeyson. Orlick slouches along the road growling out the blacksmith's song "Beat it out, beat it out—Old Clem!" and he has just "beaten it out" of Mrs. Joe. After office hours Jaggers washes his hands of his clients with scented soap. How effective is any of these unless both its surface meaning and its deeper significance are apprehended?

Similarly the whole structure of the plot depends on the interplay of meanings at the level of dream. Pip's story from beginning to end is both a sequence of events that happen to him and a projection into actuality of his own desires and fears. The discovery of Magwitch is also a revelation of Pip's own character, and leads to Pip's struggle toward a partial solution of the meaning of his life, which is also the meaning of his own motives and intentions. Even the weak and evasive ending needs to be seen from the dreamer's stance, for it is not clear what is being avoided unless we understand the psychological parallel of Pip's illness with that of Magwitch, and the too cheaply purchased symbolic rebirth as a consequence of this parallel, which rids Pip both of his guilt and also of his embarrassing responsibility.

In suggesting this interpretation of the novel as a dream, I do not mean to imply that every reader must have worked out such an interpretation himself in order to appreciate the story, any more than a dreamer needs to analyze his dream in order to have "had" it. As I have just remarked, Dickens is not an allegorist, nor are his novels mere codes to be deciphered. One must simply read any of the novels as one might experience a dream, attending and responding to it fully, aware that what happens is to be absorbed in a somewhat different way from the events of an ordinary story, because things in Dickens reverberate with special overtones, and fall into patterns governed by emotional congruities that are never explicitly verbalized. But the reader of Dickens scarcely needs instructions of this sort; everyone who takes to him at all reads him properly, for he himself sets us on the way and guides our responses. That is why we read him.

## Bleak House

The prominent fact of *Bleak House* is the division of the novel into two parallel narratives, one told in the third person, present tense, by an unnamed and "uninvolved" narrator, the other in the first person, past tense, by the heroine Esther Summerson. This division is the extreme example of the splitting into two plots found in all Dickens' later novels except *Great Expectations* and the unfinished *Mystery of Edwin Drood*. These novels written after 1850 tend toward greater unity of structure and a more direct expression of the dream content, with therefore less need to hold the novels together by melodramatic coincidence or any heavy-handed insistence on thematic parallels, repetition, and similar devices of secondary elaboration. *Bleak House*, as the first* of the dark novels, combined the most deeply divided of the plots with the most elaborately constructed network of superficial interconnections designed to bridge the gap. The gap is such and the interconnections are so many that critics who want to complain of Dickens' "incurable love of labyrinthine mystification" are likely to single out *Bleak House* as a hideous example, even while arguing on the other hand that its plot goes "all to pieces."[42]

The most important effect of the split narrative and the devices of secondary elaboration which lace across its surface is their obscuring of the dream meaning of the stories of Esther Summerson and Richard Carstone, the heroine and hero. The double plot is Dickens' major means of camouflaging the basic emotional contents of these novels, for it allows him to present the elements of sex, class, and violence and at the same time to keep them safely isolated from each other. The doubling of the plot may be compared to the use, at another level, of hidden and apparent strands, a separation that also works against confrontation until the crucial scene of discovery. With the doubled plot, however, there is no equivalent to this scene of discovery, for the two narratives are not alternative accounts of the same set of circumstances; rather, two completely different sets of circumstances are connected on the surface by patterns of secondary elaboration, and beneath the surface by the emotional congruities which the division in plot tends formally to obscure.

In the following analysis of *Bleak House* I shall concentrate on the effects of the split narrative rather than on the concomitant devices of secondary elaboration; for although critics have shown how the various patterns of repetition

---

*Before *Bleak House* there are traces of the typical line of action and the doubled narrative, but nowhere are they developed to the extent that they constitute the formal structure.

and parallelism give the novel a superficial unity, no one has attempted to sort out the distortions and displacements imposed on Dickens' materials by the double plot. In the next section, once the divisive effect of the double plot has been investigated, I shall go on to examine, in the novels between *Bleak House* and *Great Expectations*, the further obscuring of the dream meaning by devices of secondary elaboration. The dual point of view keeps the two stories apart in an odd, "inverted" way, for Esther's story is largely told not in her own narrative, but in the present-tense narrative, while she in turn tells most of Richard's story. This is made possible by the use of a representative or stand-in heroine—a typically dreamlike displacement. Lady Dedlock, Esther's mother, is also a surrogate for her. The apparent and hidden strands of her action, her reversal and discovery, and so on, are the mirror in which we see reflected (from the present-tense narrative) Esther's own story. The discovery, for both mother and child, is just that familial relation between them, of which they are both unaware. It is the secret that Tulkinghorn ferrets out and threatens to reveal to Sir Leicester; it is the guilty knowledge withheld from Esther by her aunt Miss Barbary. For Lady Dedlock the moment of discovery is at the end of Chapter xxix, in the present-tense narrative:

"O my child, my child! Not dead in the first hours of her life, as my cruel sister told me; but sternly nurtured by her, after she had renounced me and my name! O my child, O my child!"

For Esther the discovery is withheld for several chapters and is finally revealed by Lady Dedlock herself in the scene between them at Chesney Wold:

I looked at her; but I could not see her, I could not hear her, I could not draw my breath. The beating of my heart was so violent and wild, that I felt as if my life were breaking from me. But when she caught me to her breast, kissed me, wept over me,

139

compassionated me, and called me back to myself; when she fell down on her knees and cried to me, "O my child, my child, I am your wicked and unhappy mother! O try to forgive me!"— when I saw her at my feet on the bare earth in her great agony of mind, I felt, through all my tumult of emotion, a burst of gratitude to the providence of God that I was so changed as that I never could disgrace her by any trace of likeness; as that nobody could ever now look at me, and look at her, and remotely think of any near tie between us. [xxxvi]

That Esther's first thought is of her recent illness and the scars it has left, a mask to hide her mother's disgrace, is perhaps not so surprising when we realize that that illness has represented Esther's reversal, often in Dickens a warning of discovery to come. Just before her first exposure to the disease, Esther has a typical dreamlike premonition of this reversal and discovery:

I had no thought, that night—none, I am quite sure—of what was soon to happen to me. But I have always remembered since, that when we had stopped at the garden-gate to look up at the sky, and when we went upon our way, I had for a moment an undefinable impression of myself as being something different from what I then was. I know it was then, and there, that I had it. I have ever since connected the feeling with that spot and time, and with everything associated with that spot and time. [xxxi]

The connection between Esther's scars and her mother's disgrace goes very deep; it is in fact the essence of the dis-covery, though the full recognition is delayed, as usual in Dickens, until the secondary discovery. The illness, contracted from Esther's maid Charley, who has contracted it from the sweep Jo, is a symbol of the secret and guilty connections between the high and low in society—that is, between Jo and Lady Dedlock, between Lady Dedlock and Esther, and finally and most disgracefully between Lady Dedlock and

Captain Hawdon, Esther's father, the wretched Nemo. The third-person narrator particularly dwells on these guilty relationships:

What connexion can there be, between the place in Lincolnshire, the house in town, the Mercury in powder, and the whereabout of Jo the outlaw with the broom, who had that distant ray of light upon him when he swept the churchyard-step? What connexion can there have been between many people in the innumerable histories of this world, who, from opposite sides of great gulfs, have, nevertheless, been very curiously brought together! [XVI]

Dickens was fascinated with this idea, that secret, devious, multitudinous threads of connection run between the high and low in society. *Bleak House* is full of such threads and knots, and he makes one strand into the veritable spinal cord of an entire plot. Esther's lineage is such a bundle of vital connections, and much of her share of the plot consists in its slow laying bare by a series of patient anatomists—Tulkinghorn, Guppy, the Smallweeds, Bucket, the third-person narrator, even Esther herself. The ultimate anatomist is Dickens, who regards his heroine's lineage as diseased to the core, and uses the metaphors of pestilence and contagion to convey a sense of the hidden channels of corruption which connect high and low, respectability and bestiality, Chesney Wold and Tom-all-Alone's. As we slowly come to see, the connection at which Dickens hints is not limited to the coincidental collision of Lady Dedlock and Jo, but involves many other characters as well. Everyone is infected; society is corrupt. Dickens does not specify the exact place where Jo picks up the smallpox which he passes on to Charley, and through her to Esther, but the gruesome cemetery to which Lady Dedlock pays her secret visit, guided by Jo, is described as a source of both moral and physical infection:

...A hemmed-in churchyard, pestiferous and obscene, whence malignant diseases are communicated to the bodies of our dear brothers and sisters who have not departed; while our dear brothers and sisters who hang about official backstairs—would to Heaven they *had* departed!—are very complacent and agreeable. Into a beastly scrap of ground which a Turk would reject as a savage abomination, and a Caffre would shudder at, they bring our dear brother here departed, to receive Christian burial.

With houses looking on, on every side, save where a reeking little tunnel of a court gives access to the iron gate—with every villainy of life in action close on death, and every poisonous element of death in action close on life—here, they lower our dear brother down a foot or two: here, sow him in corruption, to be raised in corruption: an avenging ghost at many a sick bedside: a shameful testimony to future ages, how civilisation and barbarism walked this boastful island together. [xi]

Tom-all-Alone's, itself in Chancery and perhaps named after "the original plaintiff or defendant in Jarndyce and Jarndyce" (xvi), is a similar festering in the landscape of London; it was Captain Hawdon's haunt while he lived as Nemo, and it is Jo's home, or the closest thing he has to a home. Again in the descriptions of this slum, Dickens dwells on the subtle and pervasive implication of a guilt that knows no boundaries of rank or privilege. The metaphor remains that of disease, and Tom-all-Alone, the area personified, is no less likely a candidate for the source of Esther's sickness, both literally and symbolically, than the graveyard where her father lies:

[Tom] has his revenge. Even the winds are his messengers, and they serve him in these hours of darkness. There is not a drop of Tom's corrupted blood but propagates infection and contagion somewhere. It shall pollute, this very night, the choice stream (in which chemists on analysis would find the genuine nobility) of a Norman house, and his Grace shall not be able to say Nay to the infamous alliance. There is not an atom of Tom's slime, not a cubic inch of any pestilential gas in which he lives, not one obscenity or degradation about him, not an ignorance, not a wickedness, not a brutality of his committing, but shall work its retribution, through every order of society, up to the proudest of the proud, and to the highest of the high. Verily, what with tainting, plundering, and spoiling, Tom has his revenge. [XLVI]

The imagery here, in addition to the already familiar corruption and plague, has also the touch of moral evil, and particularly of sexual transgression, which is also hinted at by the conclusion of the love affair between Esther's parents in the filthy cemetery. Tom-all-Alone's disease seems to be a "social" one, in both senses of that term: there is mixed blood here, an "infamous alliance," infection "propagated," all in a context of "obscenity," "degradation," and "brutality."

The notion of the poor taking revenge for their sufferings by spreading disease is a familiar one in Dickens. We find it in *Dombey and Son*, for instance:

Those who study the physical sciences, and bring them to bear upon the health of Man, tell us that if the noxious particles that rise from vitiated air were palpable to the sight, we should see them lowering in a dense black cloud above such haunts, and rolling slowly on to corrupt the better portions of a town. But if the moral pestilence that rises with them, and in the eternal laws of outraged Nature, is inseparable from them, could be made discernible too, how terrible the revelation! [XLVII]

But this idea stems from a larger and deeper conviction running throughout the novels, namely that any relation, especially a sexual one, between the high and the low in society is to be regarded as filthy and diseased, as somehow immoral and unclean. Thus the bond between Lady Dedlock and Esther is set in the context of illness; and even more strikingly, the illicit love of Lady Dedlock and Captain Hawdon is symbolized by the gruesome image of the burial ground where Lady Dedlock comes to view her lover's grave. That the marriage of high and low in the liaison of Lady Dedlock and Captain Hawdon is guilty and unclean—this is the real discovery toward which Esther is impelled. The flight of Lady Dedlock (and of Esther, who in pursuing her mother is also in a sense fleeing with her) is away from this recognition, away from London, away from the burial ground; but the flight ends, nevertheless, at that very place:

At last we stood under a dark and miserable covered way, where one lamp was burning over an iron gate, and where the morning faintly struggled in. The gate was closed. Beyond it, was a burial-ground—a dreadful spot in which the night was very slowly stirring; but where I could dimly see heaps of dishonoured graves and stones, hemmed in by filthy houses, with a few dull lights in their windows, and on whose walls a thick humidity broke out like a disease. On the step at the gate, drenched in the fearful wet of such a place, which oozed and splashed down everywhere, I saw, with a cry of pity and horror, a woman lying—Jenny, the mother of the dead child. [LIX]

But it is Lady Dedlock dressed in Jenny's clothes; it is the *dead mother of the child*:

I passed on to the gate, and stooped down. I lifted the heavy head, put the long dank hair aside, and turned the face. And it was my mother cold and dead.

This is Esther's secondary discovery, the climax of her story. What is left out is only the explicit recognition that the burial ground, with its contagion and corruption, is the symbol of her mother's relations with Hawdon, and also the symbol of the taint in Esther's own life.

Esther cannot entertain any lover herself because of this taint. When Guppy (a suitor too ludicrously "low" for her) proposes marriage, Esther rejects him not only because she does not love him, or because he is too common for her, but also because she is tainted. In one of the most affecting scenes in her narrative, she gives us a symbolic clue to this motive, by means of another graveyard image. In early life she had had a doll which was her only comfort. Her aunt, Miss Barbary, was accustomed to harangue the child Esther:

"Submission, self-denial, diligent work, are the preparations for a life begun with such a shadow on it. You are different from other children, Esther, because you were not born, like them, in common sinfulness and wrath. You are set apart." [III]

Esther describes her reaction:

I went up to my room, and crept to bed, and laid my doll's cheek against mine wet with tears; and holding that solitary friend upon my bosom, cried myself to sleep. Imperfect as my understanding of my sorrow was, I knew that I had brought no joy, at any time, to anybody's heart, and that I was to no one upon earth what Dolly was to me.

Dear, dear, to think how much time we passed alone together afterwards, and how often I repeated to the doll the story of my birthday, and confided to her that I would try, as hard as ever I could, to repair the fault I had been born with (of which I confessedly felt guilty and yet innocent), and would strive as I grew up to be industrious, contented, and kind-hearted, and to do some good to some one, and win some love to myself if I could.

When she finally left Miss Barbary's, after that lady's death, Esther had buried the old doll in the garden. Now, having rejected Guppy,

I sat there for another hour or more, finishing my books and payments, and getting through plenty of business. Then, I arranged my desk, and put everything away, and was so composed and cheerful that I thought I had quite dismissed this unexpected incident. But, when I went up-stairs to my own room, I surprised myself by beginning to laugh about it, and

145

then surprised myself still more by beginning to cry about it. In short, I was in a flutter for a little while; and felt as if an old chord had been more coarsely touched than it ever had been since the days of the dear old doll, long buried in the garden. [IX]

Again, Esther's other suitors, her guardian John Jarndyce and her true love Allan Woodcourt, also suffer from the perverse caprice of Esther's guilty morality. Woodcourt—to spell out Dickens' pun—would court Esther if he could; but several obstacles prevent him: his mother's snobbism (she thinks Allan's Welsh ancestors too good for Esther, and even tells her so, indirectly); and Esther's sense of guilt. Esther agrees that she is not good enough for Allan; after her illness she is grateful for an excuse to forget about him as a potential lover:

But how much better it was now, that this had never happened! What should I have suffered, if I had had to write to him, and tell him that the poor face he had known as mine was quite gone from me, and that I freely released him from his bondage to one whom he had never seen! [xxxv]

In this excuse (that she is scarred) we can read her real fear (that she is tainted). The connection comes out even more explicitly in her decision to accept Jarndyce's proposal:

But he did not hint to me, that when I had been better-looking, he had had this same proceeding in his thoughts, and had refrained from it. That when my old face was gone from me, and I had no attractions, he could love me just as well as in my fairer days. That the discovery of my birth gave him no shock. That his generosity rose above my disfigurement, and my inheritance of shame. [XLIV]

Her acceptance of Jarndyce is possible because it is not really a lovers' union he proposes:

It was not a love letter though it expressed so much love, but was written just as he would at any time have spoken to me. . . . It told me that I would gain nothing by such a marriage, and lose nothing by rejecting it; for no new relation could enhance the tenderness in which he held me, and whatever my decision was, he was certain it would be right.

Indeed, Esther's acceptance of Jarndyce is really a renunciation of love, since she thereby gives up Woodcourt. It is a kind of punishment for her mother's sin. She is finally allowed (by the benevolent Jarndyce) to have her lover, only because once Lady Dedlock is herself brought low in the burial-yard scene, the punishment is over and the guilt has been expiated; we hear no more of barriers of class or family between Esther and Woodcourt, and Mrs. Woodcourt is miraculously converted, to become a doting mother-in-law.

For the most part, the flaws and gaps in Esther's line of action—and they are many—may be explained in terms of the method of narration, the split point of view. Before going on to examine Richard Carstone's share of the plot and the effects of keeping his story separate from Esther's, it will be useful to note some of these weaknesses of Esther's story, considered in isolation.

Most obvious of the defects of Esther's story is the failure explicitly to identify her problem as one of sexual-social conflict. Indeed, were it not for the evidence afforded by the other novels of this group, we should be hard put to defend the interpretation that has just been given of her story. Not only is Lady Dedlock's violation of sexual morality and class boundaries lost sight of in the present-tense narrative, where, for the sake of suspense and mystification, the "objective" narrator is allowed no knowledge of past or future, but also Tulkinghorn's threat to disclose the secret is so overdone that the reader's attention is distracted from the moral problem to the battle of nerves between Lady Dedlock and her solicitor, and finally to the apparently irrelevant mystery of Tulkinghorn's murder. (I shall return later to the question of how this murder functions in the dream meaning.) Moreover, because all of this takes place in the present-tense narrative, without direct reference to Esther and her own troubles, we are left to discover for ourselves the bearing of Lady Dedlock's sin on Esther's illness and her difficulties with her suitors. The use of Lady Dedlock as a surrogate for her daughter puts a distance between Esther and her problem which is widened still further by the separation between the two narrative points of view. Regarded as a device to provide mysteries and ambiguities in a detective novel, the dual or multiple point of view is an obvious advantage, as Wilkie Collins proved. But in *Bleak House* the ambiguity and mystery that arise from Esther's not knowing what goes on in the other narrative rob the discovery that Lady Dedlock is her mother of its full significance; and because Esther never knows anything about her father, she cannot see the symbolic meaning of the secondary discovery—her mother's death at the gate of the grisly place where Hawdon is buried.

That the split point of view is one cause of these gaps becomes more evident as we approach this secondary discovery. In order to represent the effect on Esther of Lady Dedlock's flight and death, it is necessary for the two points of view to come together, to coincide briefly in their focusing of time and space. This joining of the narratives occurs at the end of Chapter LVI, when Inspector Bucket calls at the Jarndyce residence in London to tell Esther of Lady Dedlock's flight and to ask her to join in the chase. This chapter is told by the third-person narrator; the next chapter is Esther's, and takes up the thread where the other has left it: "I had gone to bed and fallen asleep, when my guardian knocked at the door of my room. . . . " Bucket, who has appeared in Esther's narrative only once, and then only briefly at Gridley's death, is now taken into her story completely, as he and Esther rush through the countryside in pursuit of Lady Dedlock. This chapter and the next but one, both told from Esther's point of view, bring us to the gates of the burial ground, which also figures in Esther's narrative now for the first time, and Lady Dedlock is thus brought into her daughter's story, and out of the present-tense narrative, for good and all. Meanwhile, one chapter from the third-person point of view is inserted, marking the turnabout in the pursuit from St. Albans back to London; this inserted chapter does not break in on the temporal continuity, but only shifts the setting to Sir Leicester's sickroom, where he anxiously awaits news of his wife. The whole sequence, in which *single* chapters from the two narratives alternate for the first time in the novel, is constructed as a joining of the points of view in order to bring Esther and her mother together.

The previous meeting of Esther and Lady Dedlock could occur in Esther's narrative alone, for the discovery in that scene is purely Esther's—that Lady Dedlock is her mother; Lady Dedlock makes her own discovery of Esther in a still earlier chapter, told, of course, in the third person. The secondary discovery which Lady Dedlock's death represents is a discovery for *both* heroines, though only Lady Dedlock seems to be aware of its full meaning, as her final message shows:

"Cold, wet, and fatigue, are sufficient causes for my being found dead; but I shall die of others, though I suffer from these. It was right that all that had sustained me should give way at once, and that I should die of terror and my conscience." [LIX]

To die, Lady Dedlock goes back to the place that symbolizes her guilt, and to this extent she recognizes the meaning of her transgression and expiates it. Esther does not know that her father is buried there, and so she cannot consciously participate in the discovery; but the scene has its purgative effect upon her notwithstanding: afterwards she is ill for a time (an infallible Dickensian signal that a recognition has occurred and that a return to innocence is at hand); moreover, Jarndyce immediately relents and begins to plan the union of Woodcourt and Esther, acceptable now because her hereditary taint has been removed by her mother's death.

Still another weakness of the split point of view is evident in Dickens' treatment of Esther's reactions to Woodcourt and Jarndyce as suitors. Critics have been quick to deplore Esther's "coyness" in withholding information regarding her attachment to Woodcourt, and no doubt this awkward reluctance, which seems so femininely arch, is one of the inconveniences of having heroine and narrator combined in the same person, just as Esther's repeated demur to the sticky-sweet praise from Jarndyce, Ada, and the rest, is another. But the split narration—rather than merely the fact of Esther's being a narrator—must finally be called to account for the delay in bringing Woodcourt into her story romantically. We have already seen that her uneasiness with regard to him stems from her fear that she is tainted and her consequent belief that marriage with him would be a violation of caste. Hence her reluctance to think of him as a lover, even in "retrospect," is understandable on purely moral grounds. This, however, is just what is not made clear to the reader, because the two halves of the analogy—Lady Dedlock and Captain Hawdon, Esther and Woodcourt—are separated by the split narrative into mutually exclusive worlds. To be sure, Woodcourt appears in the present-tense narrative, is even introduced there, and is first seen in attendance on none other than Captain Hawdon himself, alias Nemo, who has just died from an overdose of opium. However, there is no room in the scene for a comparison of Hawdon and Woodcourt, because as yet we have no idea of their respective relations to Lady Dedlock and Esther, nor do we even know that the two women are mother and daughter. Woodcourt's appearances in the present-tense narrative are mainly there to show his goodness and industry, and accordingly his chief function is as a foil to Richard, rather than as a romantic figure whose connections with Esther and, through her, with her mother and father, might be exploited.

The case of John Jarndyce is even more to the point. His appearances in the present-tense narrative are far less frequent than those of Woodcourt, but he at least is acquainted with Lady Dedlock from earlier times, knows the secret of Esther's birth, and consequently is the logical choice as an interpreter of Esther's moral problem. Even these advantages, however, are not enough to counteract the effect of the split narrative. Jarndyce seems completely unaware that there might be a connection between the Dedlock-Hawdon story of illicit love across class lines and the Summerson-Woodcourt story of frustrated romance. He is perfectly unconscious of the possibility that the "pure" love he offers Esther is acceptable to her precisely because it goes against desire, not only in its sexless "purity," but also in its entailing a renunciation of her own desire for Woodcourt. Under other conditions—if the implications of Lady Dedlock's story for Esther's case were not obscured by the split in structure and point of view—*Bleak House* might have been an outsized and weirdly distorted *Jude the Obscure*, with a painful class-consciousness taking the place of Sue Bridehead's religious fanaticism. As it turns out, at least in Esther's story (told, we must remember, largely through the third-person narrative), the novel would seem to be a cautious trying out of themes that are treated more explicitly in *Great Expectations.*

If Esther's story gives us a certain foretaste of Pip's difficulties with Estella, the history of Richard Carstone's miserable decline would appear to foreshadow Pip's difficulty in settling on some useful vocation. Richard's problem is usually taken too much at face value: that he had the simple and overwhelming misfortune to be "born in Chancery." In consequence, critics* pay little attention to Richard as a character, especially in his relations with his guardian, and turn their efforts instead to analysis of the topicality, the justice, and so on, of Dickens' attack on the Court of Chancery. If, however, we consider Richard's story in the light of what we know about the typical Dickensian dream plot, we shall be forced to see Richard as a hero in his own right, instead of as a straw figure set up for Chancery to knock down. The failure of critical sympathy and interest in Richard has occurred largely because his story is told from Esther Summerson's point of view. If we try to see Richard's character and action as they are without the coloring given them by Esther's interpretation, then we may be able to state more precisely the effect of the split narrative on Richard's story.

Like Richard, the heroes of the other novels all have "reasons" for being unable to settle themselves in some interesting and honorable line of work: Tom Gradgrind is placed in Bounderby's bank for lack of anything better to do; Charles Darnay, as an emigrant who has renounced the duties of his previous station, is obliged to teach French for a living; Pip, after leaving the Forge, is trained up to be a gentleman—

---

*An interesting exception is Mark Spilka, who is led by the similarities of K in *The Trial* to consider Richard more seriously than most commentators—see *Dickens and Kafka* (Bloomington, 1963), pp. 215–222.

that is, for no occupation; Eugene Wrayburn is forced into the law by his family, and hates it; only Arthur Clennam seems to have a job of any positive importance to him—the partnership with Doyce—but even he has been through the same occupational mill, and his confession early in *Little Dorrit* reads like a manifesto for all Dickensian heroes:

"I have no will. That is to say," he coloured a little, "next to none that I can put in action now. Trained by main force; broken, not bent; heavily ironed with an object on which I was never consulted and which was never mine; shipped away to the other end of the world before I was of age, and exiled there until my father's death there, a year ago; always grinding in a mill I always hated; what is to be expected from *me* in middle life? Will, purpose, hope? All those lights were extinguished before I could sound the words." [1, II]

Richard Carstone, with his fatal absorption in the Jarndyce and Jarndyce suit in Chancery, is paradoxically more interested in his "occupation" than any of these other heroes. He is the only one with any devouring (indeed self-devouring, as it turns out) interest in a kind of work. Rather than fix halfheartedly on some dishonest and parasitical pursuit like the law, he gives himself wholly to the idea that besets him—of forcing Jarndyce and Jarndyce through Chancery. Admittedly this is a hopeless purpose, but it is a purpose, and it has the same virtue as Gridley's stubborn refusal to knuckle under to an evil institution; their intractability in giving themselves to a cause is at least more laudable than John Jarndyce's practiced indifference. Esther truly says, in justification of her guardian, that "he has resolutely kept himself outside the circle" (XXXVII), but the facts can be interpreted in another way. What sort of pattern does Jarndyce offer to a young man like Richard, what sort of model on which to form himself? Not only does Jarndyce abstain from the Chancery suit—sensibly enough—but he also puts nothing in its place. He has no consuming interest of his own, no job, no goal. He spends his time answering letters from charitable organizations and flitting about town "doing Good," after a fashion not unlike Mrs. Pardiggle's, except that his financial generosity really can accomplish something. But this is not a profession or a settled purpose. How can he expect Richard to do any better than he himself has done?

The characters all profess to believe that Richard's downfall is due to the influence of Chancery, yet Richard himself, in his most important scene, says just the opposite:

"I have done no good this long time. I have not intended to do much harm, but I seem to have been capable of nothing else. It may be that I should have done better by keeping out of the net into which my destiny has worked me; but I think not, though I dare say you will soon hear, if you have not already heard, a very different opinion. To make short of a long story, I am afraid I have wanted an object; but I have an object now— or it has me—and it is too late to discuss it. Take me as I am, and make the best of me." [LI]

Is Richard so wrong in his estimate of the situation? More important, why cannot Esther and Jarndyce take him as he is? They take Skimpole easily enough, pay his bills and buy him out of hock. Is it because Richard, by believing in the system and taking it seriously, threatens more than anyone else actually to destroy it? Indeed, to some degree this is what happens, and the events leading to that destruction constitute precisely his action in the novel.

From one standpoint Richard does not have a plot of his own at all. Instead, Jarndyce and Jarndyce, which has absorbed his interest, proceeds to take over his story as well; or, to put it the other way, he immerses himself in the story of Jarndyce and Jarndyce. Either way, the progress of action is the same for both absorber and absorbed. For Richard and for Jarndyce and Jarndyce, the apparent strand of the action consists in the belief that there is some sense to the lawsuit, that, as Richard puts it, "There is truth and justice somewhere in the case" (xxxvii). But in fact there is no truth or justice in any connection with the Court of Chancery; that is the hidden strand. The institution into whose clutches Richard was "born" is painted with the murkiest of colors, as a blight on society, a deadly trap from which none can escape and which benefits only legal thieves like the "respectable" Mr. Vholes and the more high-toned scavenger Tulkinghorn. The explicit comparison between Chancery and Krook's Rag and Bottle Warehouse is perhaps the most telling indictment of the Court; Krook, fancying himself a Lord Chancellor of his own court, draws the analogy:

"You see I have so many things here," he resumed, holding up the lantern, "of so many kinds, and all, as the neighbours think (but *they* know nothing), wasting away and going to rack and ruin, that that's why they have given me and my place a christening. And I have so many old parchmentses and papers in my stock. And I have a liking for rust and must and cobwebs. And all's fish that comes to my net. And I can't abear to part with anything I once lay hold of (or so my neighbours think, but what do *they* know?) or to alter anything, or to have any sweeping, nor scouring, nor cleaning, nor repairing going on about me. That's the way I've got the ill name of Chancery. *I* don't mind. I go to see my noble and learned brother pretty well every day, when he sits in the Inn. He don't notice me, but I notice him. There's no great odds betwixt us. We both grub on in a muddle." [v]

The discovery of this hidden strand also occurs symbolically, in Chapter xxxii, immediately after the chapter in which Esther's line of action is brought to reversal with her illness.

The death of old Krook, by Spontaneous Combustion, constitutes this symbolic discovery, a warning unheard by Chancery,
unheard by Richard:

The Lord Chancellor of that Court, true to his title in his last
act, has died the death of all Lord Chancellors in all Courts,
and of all authorities in all places under all names soever, where
false pretences are made, and where injustice is done. Call the
death by any name Your Highness will, attribute it to whom you
will, or say it might have been prevented how you will, it is the
same death eternally—inborn, inbred, engendered in the corrupted humours of the vicious body itself, and that only—Spontaneous Combustion, and none other of all the deaths that can
be died. [XXXII]

The dreamlike implication for Richard's story is that Jarndyce and Jarndyce is similarly constituted—all air, all paper,
all empty hopes—and that it too is destined to consume
itself—in costs. From this point on Richard becomes the
human counterpart of that fate; he slowly wastes away, of no
ailment but his absorption in Jarndyce and Jarndyce. The
secondary discovery fulfills the ominous prediction of the
earlier symbolic one: the lawsuit dissolves in its own spontaneous combustion when the disputed estate is completely
absorbed in costs. Shortly Richard himself finds a similar
fate, when, wasted away like the Chancery case, he leaves
this world, as Dickens says, to begin another (his fatal return
to innocence). Esther's account of the death scene is a moving one, in spite of the sentimental posturing by Jarndyce
in his reconciliation with Richard. The final paragraph, with
its sudden switch in time and place, is quite touching:

When all was still, at a late hour, poor crazed Miss Flite
came weeping to me, and told me she had given her birds their
liberty. [LXVI]

For once, the return to innocence does not seem so contrived.
Richard's death is inevitable from the time he becomes

absorbed in the lawsuit, and there is no chance now for him to do anything more in his struggle with Chancery. He has done his part in taking it seriously, thereby forcing others to take it more seriously too. His is a kind of martyr's death. But there is a weakness in the ending, even so; for the significance of Richard's martyrdom does not seem to be recognized by the others, though they see clearly enough that Chancery has destroyed him.

Most of the difficulties in Richard's story, as in Esther's, are the result of the distance which the split point of view artificially sets up between the hero and his action. This gap is most strikingly seen in the use of Krook's death as a symbolic discovery in Richard's plot. Because Richard is tied so firmly to Esther's narrative, while most of the Chancery characters are restricted to the present-tense narrative, the relation between Krook's spontaneous combustion and Richard's fate cannot be made explicit. This lack of connection is what makes the crucial difference between Richard's story and Pip's, because it means that Richard can never become self-aware, cannot have a recognition scene of his own, until it is too late for him to mend his ways.

Richard's blindness is not the only effect of the split narration. The attack on society and its institutions is prosecuted chiefly in the third-person narrative, in the descriptions of Chancery, in the contrasts between the fashionable world of Chesney Wold and the hideous poverty of Tom-all-Alone's. In these worlds lies the proof that society is rotten, and the true explanation of Richard's inability to find a place in it for himself; but because Richard is so little brought into contact with the society itself, there can be no elucidation of the problem. Would Jarndyce have Richard be a gentleman like those that frequent Chesney Wold, or a degraded tramp like Hawdon and the inmates of Tom-all-Alone's?

Such questions cannot be asked in the context of Esther's narrative, but they might have been in the third-person narrative.

If not into the worlds of Chesney Wold or Tom-all-Alone's, Dickens does bring Richard into the world of Chancery at last, and an interesting formal change takes place, much like the joining of points of view during the pursuit of Lady Dedlock in Esther's narrative. Again there is the shifting of a character from one narrative to the other, and again it becomes evident that the split point of view has prevented the character from taking part in his own action. For Richard the shift occurs in Chapter xxxix, "Attorney and Client," in which Richard is shown, in the third-person narrative, during an interview with Vholes. We have previously been informed of Richard's deadly fascination with Jarndyce and Jarndyce; now we see him actually in the clutches of his ghoulish lawyer. In the characterization of Vholes, that "*most* respectable man," Dickens gives us a living example of the abuses of the law—and thus provides Richard with a justification for his lack of enthusiasm for any of the "proper" professions—especially when he says, at the beginning of the chapter, "The one great principle of the English law is, to make business for itself." Such an indictment could hardly have been uttered in Esther's narrative, and certainly it is not offered in Richard's defense when he becomes dissatisfied with his work at Kenge and Carboy. Again, here in this brief chapter we find the one explicit indication that Krook's death is related to Richard's fate, when Guppy and Jobling (alias Weevle) observe Richard's aimless wandering through Lincoln's Inn:

"William," says Mr. Weevle, adjusting his whiskers; "there's combustion going on there! It's not a case of Spontaneous, but it's smouldering combustion it is."

Like the remark on English law, this observation could not have been made in Esther's narrative, for neither Guppy, Jobling, nor Krook himself is really part of that narrative, though they all make occasional appearances in it. Esther's own point of view is, in fact, the worst possible from which to narrate Richard's story justly. She has little opportunity to see him at work, and no sense of the society in which he must make a place for himself. Significantly, when Dickens wants to examine Richard's feelings and motives most closely, and to compare them with those of his ideal (Woodcourt), he finds it necessary for the first and only time in the novel to have Esther recount an interview at which she was not present. This is the meeting between Woodcourt and Richard in the passage already quoted from Chapter li, where Richard says his problem is that he has "wanted an object." This scene is remarkable for the relatively favorable light in which it places Richard—frank, manly, even responsible—and when Esther finally resumes the narrative again with her own voice, we suddenly become aware of how much her condescension and moralizing temper have conditioned our reaction to Richard:

"You see," said Richard, with something pathetic in his manner of lingering on the point, though it was off-hand and unstudied, "to an upright fellow like you, bringing a friendly face like yours here, I cannot bear the thought of appearing selfish and mean. I want to see Ada righted, Woodcourt, as well as myself; I want to do my utmost to right her, as well as myself; I venture what I can scrape together to extricate her, as well as myself. Do, I beseech you, think of that!"

Afterwards, when Mr. Woodcourt came to reflect on what had passed, he was so very much impressed by the strength of Richard's anxiety on this point, that in telling me generally of his first visit to Symond's Inn, he particularly dwelt upon it. It revived a fear I had had before, that my dear girl's little property would be absorbed by Mr. Vholes, and that Richard's justification to himself would be sincerely this.

Esther is right, of course, but her sympathy for Richard still leaves something to be desired. And almost the whole of his story is presented from her point of view.

The chief weakness of the split point of view in *Bleak House*, however, is not merely in the difficulties it raises for either of the two narratives in itself, but rather in its effect on the overall unity—a weakness in no way peculiar to this novel. If the author refuses to "come into" his story, either in his own person or that of a particular hero with whose point of view he is mainly identified, then there must result a loss of standard or measure, and a consequent fragmentation of perspective. In *Bleak House* there seems to be no controlling narrative stance; Esther's consciousness is the closest approximation, but the unity here is flawed, as we have seen, by the presentation of her story in the other half of the narrative. The two lines of action are kept apart not merely by their having separate protagonists, but also by the lack of any single, overriding point of view from which both actions might be seen and judged. Taking the narratives in isolation, we find that the two narrators, Esther and the anonymous disembodied observer, do not control even the stories they tell; that is, neither of the two separate plots is really distinct, since fragments of one crop up in the other, seemingly by chance but actually because it has become necessary to bring the protagonists in touch with the "estranged" elements of their lines of action. Thus the two themes—Esther's sexual-social dilemma and Richard's vocational one—are never forced into meaningful contact with each other.

This fragmentation of narrative is still more apparent when we come to consider the function of Tulkinghorn in the novel and the way his murder seems to complicate and obscure the major lines of action. Even in *Great Expectations*, where the single narrative voice helps to hold the elements together, and where the plot is not split into two stories, there are certain materials which Dickens seems unable to integrate into the action, especially the materials of violence represented by Orlick's attack on Pip at the old sluice-house. In *Bleak House* the same sort of violence is still more fragmented and encapsulated off from the main configurations of the plot.

Tulkinghorn's major function in the novel is to discover and threaten disclosure of Lady Dedlock's secret, and therefore he appears in the third-person narrative. However, as an attorney he also has a natural connection with Esther's narrative of Richard's fate in Chancery. No less than Vholes and Kenge, Tulkinghorn is also at work in Jarndyce and Jarndyce. In fact, he represents the interests of Sir Leicester and Lady Dedlock in that suit, and it is through a legal document connected with it that he first scents a connection between Lady Dedlock and the law-writer Nemo. The means of discovery is symbolically appropriate, since we are told that the Dedlock interest in the lawsuit was "the only property my Lady brought him" (II)—both ties go back to the period before Lady Dedlock's marriage. The appropriateness goes beyond this, for the struggle between Lady Dedlock and Tulkinghorn, although not firmly bound to the Jarndyce and Jarndyce case, is nevertheless very much a case at law, involving as it does illicit relations between Lady Dedlock and Captain Hawdon, an illegitimate child, judgment and exposure, guilt and punishment. The complex of crime and guilt is compounded further by the murder of Tulkinghorn and the hunt for his killer.

I have already mentioned the obscuring effect which the Tulkinghorn episodes have on Lady Dedlock and Esther's story, distracting the reader from the significance of Lady Dedlock's secret, first by focusing on the melodrama of its unearthing and then by raising false suspicions concerning her role in Tulkinghorn's murder. Viewed simply as part of the plot, these superficial complications seem disruptive and inessential. There is nothing in Tulkinghorn's character or history to justify his being the one to discover Lady Dedlock's secret, so long as we are reading the novel as ordinary realistic fiction. On the dream level, however, other more important relations may be discerned, which if directly expressed might have pulled together the whole fragmented novel. The key to these relations may be found in the very difficulty over the function of Tulkinghorn in Lady Dedlock's story. There is some question as to what his motives actually are, but if we remember that "the one great principle of the English law is, to make business for itself," Tulkinghorn's behavior is seen to be quite typical of all the attorneys in the book. Money, even, is not their object, though they live like parasites on "costs"; their purpose is to elaborate themselves, to glory in sterile arabesques like Jarndyce and Jarndyce, which they all consider a masterpiece of their practice. Lawsuits are like the pimples on Vholes' face, which he fingers "as if they were ornaments" (LX). Tulkinghorn's motives are as ingrown and self-decorating as those of his colleagues. He stands to gain nothing from the revelation of Lady Dedlock's guilty past, nor does it appear—his own statements to the contrary—that he has pried into her secrets for Sir Leicester's sake. Thus once he has proof of her guilt he warns her that he has it, but adds that he intends to keep his "own counsel" in the matter, perhaps indefinitely. The pun is marvelous, for it gives Tulkinghorn's legalistic character to a T: he is a man "severely and strictly self-repressed" (XLI), "the silent depository" (II) of family secrets, part of whose "policy and mastery" it is "to have no political opinions; indeed, *no* opinions" (xl), who in his intense scenes with Lady Dedlock carries on "in his business consideration of the matter, like a machine" (xli). His professed concern for Sir Leicester's honor is a blind, only—he himself makes clear—a "business precaution, in case it should be necessary to recall the fact in any communication with Sir Leicester." And when he reminds Lady Dedlock "that throughout our interview I have expressly stated my sole consideration to be Sir Leicester's feelings and honour, and the family reputation" (xli), the very ring of his prosing makes his hypocrisy evident. If his real purpose is known to himself, the novel is silent on the matter. In truth, he seems to have no purpose or motive in the ordinary sense; rather, it is *in his character and calling* to root out and gobble up such family secrets—not to divulge them. Lady Dedlock's estimate of him is correct: "He is indifferent to everything but his calling. His calling is the acquisition of secrets, and the holding of such power as they give him, with no sharer or opponent in it" (xxxvi). When he decides to reveal the secret, it is not for Sir Leicester's sake, but because of Lady Dedlock's "violation of our agreement" (xlviii), which is an intolerable affront to his legalistic way of life. He wants the feeling of power and stability that comes from being "in" on everything, having his fingers at every pulse, and holding the key to every lock. While Kenge, Vholes, Guppy, and the rest represent the tendency of the law to roll up endless precedents in a rigid edifice of useless order, Tulkinghorn represents its tendency to enclose, constrict, and imprison. It is in his nature to lock up, not to release or reveal. In his last meeting with Mademoiselle Hortense before his murder,

Mr. Tulkinghorn takes a small key from his pocket, unlocks a drawer in which there is another key, which unlocks a chest in which there is another key, and so comes to the cellar-key, with which he prepares to descend to the regions of old wine. [XLII]

Throughout the interview with her he rubs and taps the key on his head, his chin, his nose; finally he threatens her:

"Look, mistress, this is the key of my wine cellar. It is a large key, but the keys of prisons are larger. In this city, there are houses of correction (where the treadmills are for women) the gates of which are very strong and heavy, and no doubt the keys too. I am afraid a lady of your spirit and activity would find it an inconvenience to have one of those keys turned upon her for any length of time."

Later, on the night of Tulkinghorn's murder, the theme recurs: "Mr. Tulkinghorn, in repairing to his cellar, and in opening and shutting those resounding doors, has to cross a little prison-yard" (XLVIII). This association of law and prison is echoed in a hundred different passages in *Bleak House*, from Vholes' tight-fitting gloves to Kenge's characteristic gesture, "moving his right hand as if it were a silver trowel, with which to spread the cement of his words on the structure of the system, and consolidate it for a thousand ages" (LXII). More than anyone else in the novel, Tulkinghorn is the warder of the law, a disagreeable predecessor of Jaggers in *Great Expectations*.

Tulkinghorn's particular victim is Lady Dedlock. Not only is he the immediate agent of her destruction, but also it is his repressive, legalistic attitude which is seen in Lady Dedlock's own character to be her undoing. Tulkinghorn himself admires her constraint and composure, the self-control which is self-imprisoning to her and which breaks down only after his death. On the surface she is the iciest of women. Her manner of speech, especially with Tulkinghorn, is a remarkable instance of the barriers she throws up between herself and the world. Their dialogues are many of them reported in *erlebte Rede*, the represented speech that signals the excessive formality of Chesney Wold society—

Mr. Tulkinghorn with his usual leisurely ease advances, renders his passing homage to my Lady, shakes Sir Leicester's hand, and subsides into the chair proper to him when he has anything to communicate, on the opposite side of the Baronet's little newspaper-table. Sir Leicester is apprehensive that my Lady, not being very well, will take cold at that open window. My Lady is obliged to him, but would rather sit there, for the air. Sir Leicester rises, adjusts her scarf about her, and returns to his seat. Mr. Tulkinghorn in the meanwhile takes a pinch of snuff [XL]

—so ritualized that it does not need the particularity and concreteness conferred by quotation marks. It is as if all their confrontations took place, as the one at the beginning of Chapter XLI actually does, through glass doors.

The function of Lady Dedlock's self-control is to conceal her passionate nature. She is a woman who has broken the laws of her society in a wild love affair; she gives way to fits of rage and grief in the privacy of her boudoir. Only a strict constraint—imitative of the very laws she has broken— allows her to keep up the front of gentility she shows the world. Just as society and its laws by suppressing natural impulse and desire until they explode in unnatural violence, produce the spontaneous combustion that is the symbolic climax of the Chancery half of the novel, so in Lady Dedlock herself the pressure exerted by Tulkinghorn combined with her own characteristic restraint finally results in a murderous explosion of violence. For, in a reading of the novel as dream, Lady Dedlock herself must be regarded as the murderess.

We have already seen how Lady Dedlock is a surrogate for Esther in the third-person narrative; similarly, Mademoiselle

Hortense becomes the surrogate of Lady Dedlock in killing Tulkinghorn. Lady Dedlock has often wished him dead, and she is naturally suspected of the murder: "If she really were the murderess, [her horror and fear] could hardly be, for the moment, more intense" (LV). Typical dream devices connect her desire with Mademoiselle Hortense's act. They are lady and maid; each disguises herself in order to be mistaken for the other; each acts out of excessive pride, yet each finds herself a suppliant to Esther at some point in the novel (XXIII, XXXVI). Both hate Tulkinghorn, both visit his chambers on the fatal night, and so on. In the chief difference between the two lies a clue to the true meaning of the doubling: the violence Lady Dedlock has suppressed is fully embodied in Mademoiselle Hortense's character and action. Like Lady Dedlock, she also combines constraint and violence, as in her barefoot walk through the wet grass (XVIII); but the balance of passion is much higher in the complexion of the maid. Dickens' favorite image for her is that of a savage animal—she is called a "vixen" and a "tiger." It is she who acts out Lady Dedlock's deadly wishes, with the result that the deadlock of impulse and constraint suggested by her name is finally shattered:

What was his death but the key-stone of a gloomy arch removed, and now the arch begins to fall in a thousand fragments, each crushing and mangling piecemeal! ... The complication of her shame, her dread, remorse, and misery, overwhelms her at its height; and even her strength of self-reliance is overturned and whirled away, like a leaf before a mighty wind. [LV]

This final "key" image releases Lady Dedlock from the prison of her life of pretense. Tulkinghorn has represented the repressive and secretive aspects of her character, Mademoiselle Hortense the violence; the conflict between them results in the destruction of the restraint, and frees Lady

Dedlock for her punishment and the expiation of her guilt. This is expressed by the plot, in Lady Dedlock's flight and death. It is also suggested by Mademoiselle Hortense's final speeches in justification of her own act:

"Can you make a honourable lady of Her? . . . Or a haughty gentleman of *Him*? . . . You cannot do these things? Then you can do as you please with me." [LIV]

Mademoiselle Hortense's motives seem to have shifted now that the murder is done. Whereas it appeared to be directed against Tulkinghorn (who had threatened her) it now seems to have been a means of punishing Lady Dedlock. This inference corresponds almost exactly with what would have been Lady Dedlock's motives for killing Tulkinghorn, *had* she done it herself:

For as her murderous perspective, before the doing of the deed, however subtle the precautions for its commission, would have been closed up by a gigantic dilatation of the hateful figure, preventing her from seeing any consequences beyond it; and as those consequences would have rushed in, in an unimagined flood, the moment the figure was laid low—which always happens when a murder is done; so now she sees that when he used to be on the watch before her, and she used to think, "if some mortal stroke would but fall on this old man and take him from my way!" *it was but wishing that all he held against her in his hand might be flung to the winds, and chance-sown in many places.* [LV; my italics]

Like Carton and Darnay in *A Tale of Two Cities* or Wrayburn and Headstone in *Our Mutual Friend*, Lady Dedlock and Mademoiselle Hortense are symbolic twins, projections onto separate characters of the conflicting impulses of the dreamer. Through them Dickens conveys the ambivalence and complexity of his dream meaning without expressly stating it. The mystery of Tulkinghorn's murder thus has the following place in the total configuration of sex, class, and violence: Society, whose systematizing, delimiting, law-making aspects are represented by Tulkinghorn and the legal profession, enchains and represses human nature, which nevertheless expresses itself in violations of these laws (the crossing of class boundaries, the breaking of sexual mores); the result is illegitimacy, guilt, and the need for deception and hypocrisy; finally the deception must be uncovered, the illegitimacy punished, the guilt expiated; and all this is accomplished when the repression—originally a cause of the crime, now a part of the guilt and the attempt to hide it—becomes so constrictive that the system itself splits open in an explosion of violence, representing both a return to nature and impulse and also a punishment and atonement for the sin. This pattern of repression and explosion may be seen again and again in the novel—in the symbolic connections between Chancery and Krook's spontaneous combustion, and in the stories of Tom Jarndyce and Gridley, as well as in the main plot involving Lady Dedlock. Minor exemplars of the same motif crop up everywhere: in the bars of the gate to the burial ground where Nemo lies, in the numerous threats and warnings, arrests and imprisonments, in the explosions of guns, the images of lightning flashing, floodgates opening, arches tumbling. In the symbolic weave of the hidden dream meaning, all these fragments repeat the larger pattern.

Again, these connections may be traced back to the black-ing-warehouse experience and the jailing of Dickens' father for debt. No doubt it was during that time that the image of prison first grew large for Dickens as a sign of the forbidding and constraining forces of society, opposed to his own nature and freedom. But his novels do not merely reflect his own past, or even his judgment of the society of his day and its problems; their hidden content also provides a close analogue of the dream manner in his writing. The forces of order and repression in the stories are equivalent to the censorship and secondary elaboration which obscure and layer over the true meanings of his dreams, the impulses of fear and desire which, thus repressed, erupt throughout the novel in apparently unrelated scenes of violence like Krook's spontaneous combustion or Tulkinghorn's murder. Split narratives, doublings of characters, displacements of emotion and life from the characters into their surroundings—these all are comparable to the devices of dreamwork, at once concealing and revealing the meaning, just as the legalistic mores of society have cramped and distorted human beings into grotesques like Miss Flite and Krook, Phil Squod and Volumnia Dedlock, Mr. Turveydrop and Grandfather Smallweed, or like Tulkinghorn himself, who "dwelling among mankind but not consorting with them, aged without experience of genial youth, and so long used to make his cramped nest in holes and corners of human nature...has forgotten its broader and better range..." (XLII).

In dealing with actual dreams it is usual to regard the distortions and concealments of the dreamwork as hindering analysis. But at the same time it must be recognized that these very impediments are the means of expression and the clues to understanding the dream, without which there could be no dream at all, no coming to the surface of what has been repressed. In Dickens' novels, one may complain that the dream manner obscures the deeper significance of the story, but again these devices of concealment are also devices of revelation, and further, in the dream novel, the aura and texture of dream is itself a characteristic value (as perhaps it is not in actual dreams, though this would bear argument). It is thus hardly fair to accuse Dickens of failure when a novel like *Bleak House* does not express his dream meaning so clearly or directly as, for example, *Great Expectations.* There are obscure elements, and these are often essential to the central action and meaning, but one might go so far as to say that the techniques of displacement, condensation, and other dream mechanisms used to reveal by means of distortion are not only more characteristically Dickensian but also ultimately more satisfying than direct expression and straightforward plotting. For many readers (myself included) *Bleak House,* for all its murky complexities, is a greater novel than the paradigmatic *Great Expectations* with its formally neater and better integrated structure. As a step in Dickens' development as a novelist, however, *Bleak House* must be regarded as preliminary and tentative, not the full expression of his view of society or the full realization of his talent; for in the nature of the dream manner is embedded the necessity of repeated attempts to clarify meaning and to render it with greater insight and self-awareness.

### *Hard Times, Little Dorrit,* and *A Tale of Two Cities*

Between *Bleak House* and *Great Expectations* Dickens experimented with various methods of unifying his sprawling and fragmented novels. His concern with greater unity and integrity was partly an expression of his need to come to terms with the emotional substance of his fiction, to bring the elements of his dream novels to more direct awareness and control (*Great Expectations* shows his success); but the unifying devices he used had another, even contradictory purpose—that of hiding from himself the true significance of the content by layering it over with tissues of superficial order and unity, patterns of secondary elaboration which concealed as much as they revealed about the deeper meanings of the novels. These two kinds of unity are not always immediately distinguishable, but for the most part it was the larger structural design that was modified in the direction of underlying integrity, while on the level of individual incident he continued to use techniques of repetition, parallelism and doubling, mystery and foreshadowing, to plaster smooth the surface of meaning.

One might suppose that the very decision to work in less space, with novels of the length of *Hard Times* and *A Tale of Two Cities*, was a step in the direction of overall simplicity and unity. But even in *Hard Times*, the shortest of his later books, where he found himself "crush[ed] by the lack of elbow room,"[43] Dickens did not abandon the double plot, the main structural hindrance to direct presentation of the dream content. Had he done so, *Great Expectations* would not have been the innovation it was, and the action in the novels preceding it would have been less complicated and roundabout. Yet, if Dickens continued to use the double plot, he also changed it so that its divisive effects were less and less at odds with his theme.

The two plots of *Hard Times* center around Mr. Gradgrind and Stephen Blackpool. Although Mr. Gradgrind is the protagonist of his part of the novel, most of the action is not his own but that of his children, who stand to him as Lady Dedlock does to Esther in *Bleak House*. Tom and Louisa are products of the Gradgrindian system, raised in Stone Lodge, taught in the school of hard facts, model grindings off the parent stone. When Louisa flees from her disastrous marriage and the temptation of adultery, her reversal and discovery bring on a like crisis for her father: the destruction of his system, his apparent strand; the discovery of the one great factor left out of his calculations—the passions—his hidden strand. Similarly Tom's catastrophe is also his father's, the major secondary discovery which completes Mr. Gradgrind's humiliating recognition of his failure.

Although the Blackpool plot had to be pared to the bone for weekly serialization, it has the full sequence of hidden and apparent strands, discovery and reversal, and so on. Stephen is suspected of being a thief (his apparent strand) but is actually an upright man; he disappears, is thought to be fleeing from the law but has actually gone in search of work; his discovery, reversal, suffering, death, and return to innocence are all given in the single scene at the old mine pit, where every mystery is solved before he dies.

As in *Bleak House*, the double plot keeps the sexual and the social problems from intermingling, and the guilt and punishment are again displaced and not clearly related to their psychological sources. Louisa's loveless marriage to Banker Bounderby and her adulterous attraction to Harthouse are paralleled by Blackpool's unfortunate marriage and his love for Rachael; and the class question is raised briefly by the partiality of the law, dissolving Bounderby's marriage while ignoring Blackpool's more "legitimate" claim to annulment. But this irony is no more than a minor theme of the novel, and the inflammable materials are so dispersed throughout that there is no major confrontation of the classes on the sexual question or really, for that matter, on any other. The two protagonists, Gradgrind and Blackpool, meet but once, and their contact has no consequences issuing from their characters or conditions. For Stephen, the meeting only means a chance to clear his name, and its effect on Mr. Gradgrind can be measured by his next dialogue with Tom, when he charges his son with the betrayal of family and honor, but says not a word of Stephen, the victim of Tom's perfidy. The impact of one world upon another is not felt, and there can be no final integration without it. What should occur in the meeting between them is impossible to say, but nothing can happen unless there are some probabilities given in the novel for their confrontation and its results; the split narrative, by enforcing the social stratification, does its share in preventing any such probabilities from developing.

In spite of these weaknesses, *Hard Times* is a slight advance over *Bleak House* in respect to plotting, though its flaws are nonetheless more serious and more apparent. Dickens attempted to pull his two stories together by various means, but most of these—for example, the connections between Gradgrind and Blackpool, which are tenuously threaded through Mrs. Pegler and Bounderby—are merely devices of secondary elaboration, irrelevant lines in the pattern. Some headway is made, however, in joining the plots concerning Blackpool and young Tom Gradgrind, his father's representative. This is managed by allowing two separate hidden strands to coincide: Blackpool is not the thief, Tom is the thief. Although this unification has no bearing on the sexual questions of the novel, it does help to bring the relations of class structure, vocation, crime, guilt, and punishment into focus. Even here the reader must look beneath the surface for the meaning of events, but at least the structure is supportive rather than disruptive.

Since Tom and Stephen have the same hidden strand, we may regard them as another doubling, and consider their two situations as if they were one. Both work for Bounderby— Tom at the bank, Stephen at the factory—and both have difficulty in their jobs. The cause of their vocational problems is the hard-facts philosophy of Gradgrind and Bounderby, which leaves human nature and feelings out of account in the calculation of *what is*:

Fact, fact, fact, everywhere in the material aspect of the town; fact, fact, fact, everywhere in the immaterial. The M'Choakum-child school was all fact, and the school of design was all fact, and the relations between master and man were all fact, and

everything was fact between the lying-in hospital and the cemetery, and what you couldn't state in figures, or show to be purchaseable in the cheapest market and saleable in the dearest, was
not, and never should be, world without end, Amen. [1, v]

This system of orderly relations between men has the same
characteristics as the legal system of *Bleak House*, the same
constriction and imprisonment (the descriptions of the *factor*-
ies make them seem very like prisons), and the same suppressed violence. If it is true that Stephen did not commit
the crime of which he is accused, and that Tom did, it is
also true that both had good enough reason for wanting to
break the law that confines and suffocates them.

In presenting Stephen as a pastoral figure like Joe Gargery,
Dickens displaces the bad side of the proletarian image to
Tom's character, as he did with Magwitch and Orlick in
*Great Expectations*. Here, however, it is not the violence
and passion so much as the sordid meanness and degradation
that are transferred to Tom, the supposedly respectable son
of Coketown's cornerstone of middle-class sobriety. The final
transformation occurs in the circus scenes late in the novel,
where Tom appears in blackface, as a clown:

In a preposterous coat, like a beadle's, with cuffs and flaps
exaggerated to an unspeakable extent; in an immense waistcoat,
knee-breeches, buckled shoes, and a mad cocked hat; with nothing fitting him, and everything of coarse material, moth-eaten and
full of holes; with seams in his black face, where fear and heat
had started through the greasy composition daubed all over it;
anything so grimly, detestably, ridiculously shameful as the whelp
in his comic livery, Mr. Gradgrind never could by any other
means have believed in, weighable and measurable fact though
it was. And one of his model children had come to this. [3, vii]

The oddness of this passage—the intensity of disgust so much
in excess of anything the situation would appear to warrant—

may be accounted for, as in the Orlick scenes of *Great Expectations*, by the repression and displacement of revulsion which would naturally be attached to the proletarian figure, Stephen. Between them, Tom and Stephen express Dickens' inner conflict—his moral revulsion from a society whose laws are a prison, and his equally strong counter-revulsion (a rebellion compounded with guilt) against those who break its laws. It is Tom who actively responds to the oppression and constriction imposed on Stephen, while it is Stephen who undergoes the punishment deserved by Tom. And this series of dreamlike displacements is economically handled by the identification of their hidden strands, so that every act of the one is felt as critical in the fortunes of the other. This is particularly interesting as a sign of Dickens' development, since the two characters belong to different plots, and their joining is therefore a partial amalgamation of the split narrative, accomplished not by the patchwork of secondary elaboration, but by an integration of structure at its deeper levels.

*Hard Times* may thus be regarded as an advance in Dickens' gradual bringing together of his double plots, even though in most respects it is a rather tinny version of the dream materials that reverberate through *Bleak House*. Dickens' next novel, *Little Dorrit*, represents a return to the denser atmosphere of the long monthly serials, and though not so inventive and energetic a book as *Bleak House*, it has most of that novel's virtues as well as a new attempt to get round the difficulties of the double plot.

The two plots of *Little Dorrit*, Arthur's and Amy's, differ from the earlier split narratives in that Arthur's story contains more elements of sexual and social transgression and guilt and punishment than any of its predecessors, while Little Dorrit's story is peculiarly empty.

We may begin by analyzing Arthur's hidden strand, a complicated series of mysteries the clues to which form his rather confusing and fragmented apparent strand. These mysteries are: the mystery of Merdle, the mystery of Clennam's love for Little Dorrit, the mystery of Affery's dreams, the mystery of the watch, and the mystery of the noises in the house.* The solutions to these mysteries constitute Arthur's discoveries, the revelation of his hidden strand.

The first discovery brings with it Arthur's reversal; it is a typically distorted dream event, for at first glance there seems to be no good reason why Arthur's fortunes should hinge on Merdle's financial speculations. Merdle and Clennam have never met, have never been linked in any way except by Clennam's ill-advised venture of his firm's money in Merdle's swindle. Yet Arthur regards his offense as a "crime" almost equivalent to Merdle's forgery and fraud, and of course he is jailed in the Marshalsea for debt, just as Dickens' father had been in the blacking-warehouse days. Arthur's guilt is explained—insofar as it is explained at all— as part of the general guilt of society, which, here as in *Bleak House*, is expressed in images of contagion and disease:

Bred at first, as many physical diseases are, in the wickedness of men, and then disseminated in their ignorance, these epidemics, after a period, get communicated to many sufferers who are neither ignorant nor wicked. [2, xiii]

Just as Richard Carstone is infected by his contact with Chancery's institutional deceit, so Arthur, though not nearly so much involved as Richard, is implicated in Merdle's

*Compare the list given by Viktor Shklovsky in his *O Teorii Prozy* (Moscow, 1929), p. 152: "the mystery of the watch, the mystery of the dreams, the mystery of Pancks (inheritance), the mystery of Merdle, the mystery of the noises in the house, the mysteries of the loves of [Little] Dorrit and Clennam."

betrayal of public trust. The dream logic of this involvement goes something like this: Chancery, the Circumlocution Office, Merdle—all are examples of the humbug which young Ferdinand Barnacle extols as the proper function of civil servants: "We must have humbug, we all like humbug, we couldn't get on without humbug. A little humbug, and a groove, and everything goes on admirably, if you leave it alone." The parallel with Chancery is obvious; Ferdinand himself points out the parallel with Merdle: "One cannot help admiring the fellow. Must have been such a master of humbug" (2, xxviii). The law in *Bleak House*, capitalism and utilitarianism in *Hard Times*, high finance and the civil service in *Little Dorrit*, are all aspects of the same rigid system, which fills the scene and squeezes out human nature.

It is perfectly appropriate, on a symbolic level, that Arthur's reversal should coincide with Merdle's downfall and suicide. Not that Arthur is a humbug; on the contrary, his earnestness is harped on. But his earnestness is peculiarly sterile, because of his heritage and situation in life. He succumbs to the general contagion because—in spite of his earnestness—he lacks will, purpose, and hope, which he says have been ground out of him by his rigorous upbringing (1, ii). Mrs. Clennam justifies her harsh treatment of him by saying that "there was an angry mark upon him at his birth," the sin of his illegitimacy, which called for stern therapy "that the child might work out his release in bondage and hardship" (2, xxxi). Arthur's sin combines Esther Summerson's illegitimacy and Richard Carstone's ambiguous struggle/embrace with the System. His guilt is at once inherent and socially caused; he is simultaneously guilty and innocent, both victim of and accessory to the crime.

Paradoxical as it is, Mrs. Clennam's insistence that Arthur's release must come from "bondage" proves prophetic. Only after his imprisonment does the burden of guilt begin to lift and free him for love and work. It is in the Marshalsea that he discovers Little Dorrit's love for him, and his for her; thus is halted his timid withdrawal from the life of the affections and his premature drifting into moody middle age. Moreover, it is during his imprisonment that the mysteries of Affery's dreams, of the watch, and of the noises in the house are all solved, bringing to light as well the secret of Arthur's illegitimacy and providing a sacrificial victim—Rigaud—to atone for his guilt. As happens frequently in Dickens (Darnay's imprisonment is an exact parallel), the confinement of the hero produces an eruption of violence elsewhere in the novel. Also typically, the exposures and explosions do not touch the hero; Arthur himself never learns the truth about his parentage or the solution to any of these mysteries. The closest he comes to discovering the meaning of his own past is in reading Miss Wade's autobiography, "The History of a Self Tormentor" (again strikingly like the revelation in *A Tale of Two Cities*, which is presented by means of Doctor Manette's first-person manuscript).

Miss Wade's history has little direct connection with any other character in the story except Henry Gowan (who turns out to be her former lover). Dickens was aware that this intense little set piece made an odd contrast to the rest of his novel, but he was determined to work it in, and, as he wrote to Forster, he hoped "to make the blood of the book circulate through both."[44] Whatever its success, the episode is a dreamlike displacement and condensation of all the elements of Arthur's story suppressed and scattered cryptically throughout the novel. Lionel Trilling has ingeniously suggested that Miss Wade's story "becomes the more interesting if we think of her as the exact inversion of Esther Summerson of *Bleak House*," but the more striking and instructive comparison is with Arthur himself. Miss Wade's "bitterness," as Trilling shows, is "the perversion of the desire for love," and her self-torture "is the classic manoeuvre of the child who is unloved, or believes herself to be unloved—she refuses to be loveable, she elects to be hateful."[45] It is the painful knowledge of her illegitimacy—in her own words, the feeling "that I was not like other people"—that provokes Miss Wade's sense of being "unloved," and her convulsive withdrawal:

I learned that I had no grandmother [she has been reared by a woman who charitably assumed that title] and no recognised relation. I carried the light of that information both into my past and into my future. It showed me many new occasions on which people triumphed over me, when they made a pretence of treating me with consideration, or doing me a service. [2, xxi]

Although in every respect more violent and perverted than Arthur's, Miss Wade's revulsion from human warmth and love is akin to his self-willed malaise. Her touchy awareness of class distinctions corresponds to Arthur's feeling, after Little Dorrit's rise in station, "that she was far divided from him by more than distance" (2, viii). Similarly, Miss Wade's belief that she cannot be loved for herself, but only pitied, matches Clennam's refusal to admit that Little Dorrit loves him:

Had he ever whispered to himself that he must not think of such a thing as her loving him, that he must not take advantage of her gratitude? [2, xxvii]

The difference between Miss Wade's rejection of *pitying* love and Arthur's rejection of *grateful* love marks the difference in their characters. Miss Wade's early misfortunes have left her sullen, mistrustful, and self-pitying, while Arthur's rigorous upbringing has made him reticent and shy of his feelings, even morose, but not mean or bitter. Perhaps the difference is in Miss Wade's awareness of her illegitimacy as opposed to Arthur's ignorance of his. But for both the illegitimacy seems to be the inner sore, known or unknown, which rankles and sensitizes the whole being. Here we have the explanation of the relation between the central secret, Arthur's illegitimacy, and his specific character failing, his self-willed retirement from the life of the affections. According to Mrs. Clennam's stern moral logic, since Arthur is the fruit of sin, he must work out his penance "in bondage and hardship," and the result of his forty years' penance is his inability to commit himself to any personal action—an inability represented not only in his avowed lack of "will, purpose, hope," but also in his withdrawal from love, his habit of thinking himself too old and jaded for such emotions. In short, his illegitimacy is to blame for his upbringing, and his upbringing is to blame for the weakness in his character. Part of this logical chain is given in Arthur's own reflections on his upbringing, his prospects, his various afflictions; part is given in Mrs. Clennam's admissions and justifications. However, the whole argument is finally brought together and summarized, not as an explicit interpretation of Arthur's case, but indirectly, in the parallel case of Miss Wade.

From this displacement of Arthur's problems into Miss Wade's character and history, it will be seen that Dickens still keeps his dream materials at one remove from his hero, but that nevertheless there has been a growth in unity from the confusion of heroes in *Hard Times*. When we come to examine the second plot of *Little Dorrit*, Amy's own story, we find that Dickens has shifted all the interest to Arthur at some cost.

In the first place, although Little Dorrit is nominally the

heroine of the whole novel, she is not even at the center of her own half of the plot. Her father, William Dorrit, fills that place: his apparent strand is his self-deceiving pretension to gentility, both in his capacity as "Father of the Marshalsea" and later, when he supposes that he "can emerge before the world a—ha—gentleman unspoiled, unspotted" (2, v); his hidden strand is the fact that the "prison shadow," the "prison taint," is so strong on him, even after his release, that he can never escape its influence; his reversal and discovery are provided by the sudden change in his condition wrought by Pancks' discovery of his great inheritance; his secondary discovery is his breakdown at Mrs. Merdle's party, when, in his senile fancy, he shocks the dinner guests by imagining himself back in the Marshalsea (in his soul he has never got free of it) and addressing them as his "fellow Collegians"; his expiation is the ten days' sickness that follows; his return to innocence comes with his death, as the lines of age and suffering vanish from his face:

The reflected marks of the prison bars and of the zig-zag iron on the wall-top, faded away. Quietly, quietly, the face subsided into a fair younger likeness of [Little Dorrit's own face] than she had ever seen under the grey hair, and sank to rest. [2, xix]

Little Dorrit, of course, is deeply involved in her father's story, but as the quotation suggests, her function in the action is not so much structural as it is "attitudinal"—she provides a point of view, a perspective; her reactions to her father's discoveries and sufferings furnish us with a guide to what our reactions should be. Except in her influence over the narrative perspective, Little Dorrit is not like Esther Summerson, who occupies the center of her story even though it is her mother who undergoes the suffering and expiation in her place. William Dorrit is not a surrogate for his daughter, as Lady Dedlock is for hers. Indeed, the device of the surrogate will not work here, and Little Dorrit cannot have an action of her own, not even at one remove—because she is *too good*. The Dickensian plot requires, for its sequence of hidden and apparent strands leading to discovery, a hero or heroine who has some secret flaw or sin which can be disclosed. Esther Summerson, good as she is, has the secret of her guilty birth to learn; but Little Dorrit already knows the worst that she can know about herself and her condition. For her there can be no reversal or discovery. While her father and his other children glory in their new riches, Little Dorrit sees all along that they remain under "the well-known shadow of the Marshalsea wall" (2, v).

If, because of her goodness and her immunity to deception, Little Dorrit cannot be the principal of her action, there are still two plots, and the novel suffers, as most of Dickens' later books do, by the split in its structure. This time the split is less damaging to the overall unity than in *Bleak House* or *Hard Times*, because the attraction between the hero and heroine of *Little Dorrit* brings their stories together in a more natural way than is possible, for instance, with the stories of Gradgrind and Blackpool. Yet there remains a gulf between the stories of Little Dorrit and Clennam, one which becomes especially apparent at the end of the first half of the novel, when Arthur is literally shoved out of the Dorrit family's acquaintance:

The attendant, getting between Clennam and the carriage-door, with a sharp "By your leave, sir!" bundled up the steps, and they drove away.

The second book is almost finished before Little Dorrit and Clennam meet again, and by that time Little Dorrit's story (or rather, her father's) has already unfolded, leaving her free to act a part in Clennam's story. Until her surprise appearance in his room at the Marshalsea, Little Dorrit has almost no contact with Arthur's plot in this second book. The fact is that the two plots—although both are stories of men imprisoned by the past, who are slowly approaching the discovery of what that imprisonment means—nevertheless have very little to do with each other. Dickens apparently understood this, and utilized every stray stick of circumstance in his effort to bridge the structural gap—by the multiplication of thematic parallels between the plots, by the melodramatic use of accidental meetings and coincidental relations among the secondary characters, by the intimation (never borne out in fact) that the mysteries of one plot are somehow connected with those of the other. Letters from Little Dorrit to Clennam are inserted into both narratives so as to draw them closer together; Clennam is the subject of conversations in the bosom of the Dorrit family, and Little Dorrit is often in Clennam's thoughts. But no amount of such contrivance can bind up the two actions into one. The most promising attempt to knit them is the hint, extensively developed through much of the book, that the secret wrong of which Arthur suspects his father and stepmother is some injury done to Little Dorrit or her family. If it had been true that the Clennams had somehow caused the Dorrits' imprisonment, that *might* have brought the stories together. As it happens, the charge has a certain symbolic justice, for the Mrs. Clennams of the world, being themselves imprisoned by choice, are anxious to impose their narrowing and confining morality on others. But in fact the solution of the mystery of the watch does not correspond to Arthur's fears: Mrs. Clennam is only guilty of suppressing a small legacy left Little Dorrit by old Gilbert Clennam, Arthur's great-uncle. This disclosure is an unpleasant surprise to the reader, first because it is not what has been expected, but mainly because the main thread joining Little Dorrit's story to Arthur's is thus severed for good and all. The love of hero and heroine—even their marriage—cannot repair this damage; for although Arthur "carries his story with him," so to speak, being its enactor and its product, Little Dorrit brings no such dowry with her—she is not the principal in her own half of the plot and consequently cannot bear the weight of its actions. The marriage creates a superficial unity at the end of the novel, but the story of the Dorrits is never really integrated with that of the Clennams.

In spite of this unclosed gap, *Little Dorrit* is a more unified book than *Bleak House* or *Hard Times*, both because Arthur brings together in his own story more of the basic dream materials scattered and fragmented in the preceding novels, and also because *Little Dorrit*, as one of Dickens' full-length books, is provided with an amplitude of symbolic resonators tucked away in the background and corners of the plot, causing the main events of Arthur's action to echo convincingly, no matter how displaced and distorted they may seem on a merely schematic view. To see the mechanics of this reverberation of the background (an effect largely missing from the much shorter *Hard Times*) we may return to the final mystery of Arthur's plot—the mystery of the noises in the house—and note how its solution is related to Arthur's guilt and expiation.

The climactic scene, which solves the mystery of the noises, takes place before the eyes of Little Dorrit and Mrs. Clennam as they return to Mrs. Clennam's house after their meeting at the Marshalsea:

In one swift instant, the old house was before them, with the man [Rigaud] lying smoking in the window; another thundering sound, and it heaved, surged outward, opened asunder in fifty places, collapsed, and fell. Deafened by the noise, stifled, choked, and blinded by the dust, they hid their faces and stood rooted to the spot. The dust storm, driving between them and the placid sky, parted for a moment and showed them the stars. As they looked up, wildly crying for help, the great pile of chimneys which was then alone left standing, like a tower in a whirlwind, rocked, broke, and hailed itself down upon the heap of ruin, as if every tumbling fragment were intent on burying the crushed wretch deeper. [2, xxxi]

As a consequence of this traumatic scene, Mrs. Clennam is struck immobile and speechless as a statue, and "the rigid silence she had so long held was evermore enforced upon her," a fitting punishment for her sins. But the chief victim of the retribution from the skies is the villain Rigaud, whose body is discovered after two days' digging in the ruins, his head "shivered to atoms, like so much glass." Ironically, the retribution comes to him as he sits "upon the window-seat of the open window, in the old Marseilles-Jail attitude," that is, in the identical posture he had fallen into while, in the first chapter of the novel, he awaited trial for the murder of his wife. That judgment he escaped; this one he cannot lie his way out of, for it is a judgment from Heaven.

Rigaud is particularly well suited to expiate Arthur's guilt. If Miss Wade's rejection of society seems an extreme version of Arthur's withdrawal, Rigaud's more energetic contempt for mankind, his eagerness to "turn the tables on society" (1, xxx), represents the ultimate in this sort of alienation. Like Miss Wade, and like Arthur to some extent, Rigaud has been mistreated by society, though with far greater provocation and less injustice: "'I am a man,' said Monsieur Lagnier [Rigaud's alias], 'whom society has deeply wronged. ...But society shall pay for it'" (1, xi). Rigaud himself compares his antisocial campaign with Clennam's unwitting betrayal of Doyce's trust ("Have you sold no friend?"), and there is a kind of caricature of the hero's illegitimacy in Rigaud's insistence that he has no family or heritage, that he owes allegiance to no country, but is "a citizen of the world" (l, i).

The manner of Rigaud's death, in the collapse of the Clennam house, is also appropriate. In the very first description of the old house the catastrophe is already being prepared:

Many years ago, it had had it in its mind to slide down sideways; it had been propped up, however, and was leaning on some half-dozen gigantic crutches: which gymnasium for the neighbouring cats, weather-stained, smoke-blackened, and overgrown with weeds, appeared in these latter days to be no very sure reliance. [l, iii]

The noises Affrey hears in the house—"whisperings," rustlings "like the falling of dry leaves"—are signs that the house is settling, that the props are giving way. At first they seem to hint at some other mystery, some secret prisoner in the house, but as the climax approaches, the signs grow more explicit and unmistakable. When Affrey proposes her theory that Arthur's true mother is locked up somewhere in the place, Mrs. Clennam rebukes her:

"Kept here? She has been dead a score of years or more. Ask Flintwinch—ask *him* [Rigaud]. They can both tell you that she died when Arthur went abroad."

"So much the worse," said Affery, with a shiver, "for she haunts the house, then. Who else rustles about it, making signals by dropping dust so softly? Who else comes and goes, and marks the walls with long crooked touches, when we are all a-bed? Who else holds the door sometimes?" [2, xxx]

Affrey's fears are ignored; no one worries over sagging doorframes or cracks in the plaster, and in the next chapter the house tumbles down, burying Rigaud in its ruin.

The motif of the rotting or collapsing house may be seen in *Bleak House* too, but in *Little Dorrit* it is more clearly and directly related to the larger motif of the "prison-house." The central image here is the Clennam house itself, which is likened again and again to a prison. Thus Arthur's return to his childhood home, after twenty years' absence, calls up memories of restriction and punishment:

There was the old cellaret with nothing in it, lined with lead, like a sort of coffin in compartments; there was the old dark closet, also with nothing in it, of which he had been many a time the sole contents, in days of punishment. [1, iii]

Mrs. Clennam's long invalidism is referred to as "her cell of years" (2, xxxi), and she regards her room as a kind of prison:

"Look at me, in prison, and in bonds here. I endure without murmuring, because it is appointed that I shall so make reparation for my sins. Reparation! Is there none in this room? Has there been none here this fifteen years?" [1, v]

"Look round this room. If it is any compensation for my long confinement within these narrow limits—not that I complain of being afflicted; you know I never complain of that—if it is any compensation to me for my long confinement to this room, that while I am shut up from all pleasant change, I am also shut up from the knowledge of some things that I may prefer to avoid knowing, why should you [that is, Flintwinch], of all men, grudge me that relief?" [1, xv]

Mrs. Clennam's compensation is exactly that which is cherished by the prisoners of the Marshalsea; in Dr. Haggage's words,

"Elsewhere, people are restless, worried, hurried about, anxious respecting one thing, anxious respecting another. Nothing of the kind here, sir. We have done all that—we know the worst of it; we have got to the bottom, we can't fall, and what have we found? Peace. That's the word for it. Peace." [1, vi]

Both Mrs. Clennam's "compensation" and Dr. Haggage's "peace" are types of the rejection of society which is Arthur's sin and indeed the chief sin of the novel; they are varieties of Arthur's desire to be like the river, "to compound for its insensibility to happiness with its insensibility to pain" (1, XVI).

Throughout the novel people are represented as *choosing* to live in prison-houses, walling up their own humanity in narrow and narrowing confines:

Mews Street, Grosvenor Square, was not absolutely Grosvenor Square itself, but it was very near it. It was a hideous little street of dead wall, stables, and dung-hills, with lofts over coach-houses inhabited by coachmen's families, who had a passion for drying clothes, and decorating their window-sills with miniature turn-pike-gates.... Yet there were two or three small airless houses at the entrance end of Mews Street, which went at enormous rents on account of their being abject hangers-on to a fashionable situation; and whenever one of these fearful little coops was to be let (which seldom happened, for they were in great request), the house agent advertised it as a gentlemanly residence in the most aristocratic part of town, inhabited solely by the élite of the beau monde. [1, x]

The dowager Mrs. Gowan's house, also chosen for its shabby-genteel neighborhood, is described by her son as a "dreary red-brick dungeon"; like the Marshalsea, it has, in its mere physical properties, a morally deteriorating effect upon its inhabitants:

The venerable inhabitants of that venerable pile seemed, in those times, to be encamped there like a sort of civilised gipsies. There was a temporary air about their establishments, as if they were going away the moment they could get anything better; there was also a dissatisfied air about themselves, as if they took it very ill that they had not already got something much

better. Genteel blinds and makeshifts were more or less observable as soon as their doors were opened; screens not half high
enough, which made dining-rooms out of arched passages, and
warded off obscure corners where footboys slept at night with
their heads among the knives and forks; curtains which called
upon you to believe that they didn't hide anything; panes of
glass which requested you not to see them; many objects of
various forms, feigning to have no connection with their guilty
secret, a bed; disguised traps in walls, which were clearly coal-
cellars; affectations of no thoroughfares, which were evidently
doors to little kitchens. Mental reservations and artful mysteries
grew out of these things. Callers looking steadily into the eyes
of their receivers, pretended not to smell cooking three feet off;
people, confronting closets accidentally left open, pretended
not to see bottles; visitors, with their heads against a partition
of thin canvas and a page and a young female at high words
on the other side, made believe to be sitting in a primeval silence.
There was no end to the small social accommodation-bills of this
nature which the gipsies of gentility were constantly drawing
upon, and accepting for, one another. [1, xxvi]

The Merdle neighborhood exerts a slightly different influence, in keeping with its more exclusive gentility:

Upon that establishment of state, the Merdle establishment in
Harley Street, Cavendish Square, there was the shadow of no
more common wall than the fronts of other establishments of
state on the opposite side of the street. Like unexceptionable
Society, the opposing rows of houses in Harley Street were very
grim with one another. Indeed, the mansions and their inhabitants were so much alike in that respect, that the people were
often to be found drawn up on opposite sides of dinner-tables, in
the shade of their own loftiness, staring at the other side of the
way with the dulness of the houses. [1, xxi]

In the world of *Little Dorrit* houses are never mere shelters;
they are the prisons of civilization, engaged in a subtle inter-

action with their prisoners, whereby a house cramps and twists its inhabitants into some inhuman shape (Flintwinch's "head was awry, and he had a one-sided, crab-like way with him, as if his foundations had yielded at about the same time as those of the house, and he ought to have been propped up in a similar manner"—l, III), while in turn the architecture of the dweller's soul seems to influence the structure of his dwelling. This mutual influence is observable in the living arrangements of both "bad" and "good" characters. Miss Wade's house, for instance, was

A dead sort of house, with a dead wall over the way and a dead gateway at the side, where a pendant bell-handle produced two dead tinkles, and a knocker produced a dead, flat, surface-tapping, that seemed not to have depth enough in it to penetrate even the cracked door. However, the door jarred open on a dead sort of spring; and he closed it behind him as he entered a dull yard, soon brought to a close at the back by another dead wall, where an attempt had been made to train some creeping shrubs, which were dead; and to make a little fountain in a grotto, which was dry; and to decorate that with a little statue, which was gone. [2, xx]

Miss Wade's enemies, the Meagles, live in a house which contrasts with hers just as their cheerful "practicality" contrasts with her deadly reserve:

It was a charming place (none the worse for being a little eccentric), on the road by the river, and just what the residence of the Meagles family ought to be. It stood in a garden, no doubt as fresh and beautiful in the May of the Year, as Pet now was in the May of her life; and it was defended by a goodly show of handsome trees and spreading evergreens, as Pet was by Mr. and Mrs. Meagles. It was made out of an old brick house, of which a part had been altogether pulled down, and another part had been changed into the present cottage; so there was a hale elderly portion, to represent Mr. and Mrs. Meagles, and a young picturesque, very pretty portion to represent Pet. There was even the later addition of a conservatory sheltering itself against it, uncertain of hue in its deep-stained glass, and in its more transparent portions flashing to the sun's rays, now like fire and now like harmless water drops; which might have stood for Tattycoram. [1, xvi]

For once a house seems not to be a prison; the Meagles do not will themselves into jail. Moreover, it is not the house itself so much as the garden, the river, the countryside environment, that make it a "charming place." This fits in with the contrast, developed throughout the novel, between the walled-in gloom of the city and the peace of the open countryside. On Sunday afternoons in her childhood Little Dorrit had sometimes been taken far from the iron gates of the Marshalsea, to "meadows or grass lanes" where "she picked grass and flowers to bring home" (1, vii). In the chapter called "The Child of the Marshalsea" Little Dorrit herself is depicted as a sort of human flower, blooming in the unlikely surroundings of the debtors' prison; she brings the benign influence of nature even into the Marshalsea, just as her brother "appeared to take the prison walls with him" into the outside world.

This thematic contrast between the prison-house and the freedom of nature plays a part in the symbolic atonement scene at the end of the novel. In the very moment of collapse of the old Clennam prison-house with the one-time inmate of the Marseilles jail inside it, Dickens inserts a symbolic commentary on the event—a sudden parting of the dust cloud, which shows us the "placid sky" and the stars. Nature has reasserted itself. Earlier, when the sun's rays fell aslant the city, they had been perceived as "bars of the prison of this lower world" (2, xxx), but now they appear in "great shoots of light...like signs of the blessed later covenant of

peace and hope that changed the crown of thorns into a glory"
(2, xxxi).

The triumph of Nature and its representative, Little
Dorrit, over the prison-house and its prisoner, Rigaud, soon
results in amnesty for one more prisoner—Arthur Clennam.
The last chapter of the novel begins with a symbolic rendering of a rural autumn landscape, full of peace and joy; then
we are taken into the Marshalsea again, where Clennam sits
listening while Little Dorrit reads to him:

> Changeless and barren, looking ignorantly at all the seasons with
> its fixed, pinched face of poverty and care, the prison had not a
> touch of any of these beauties on it. Blossom what would, its
> bricks and bars bore uniformly the same dead crop. Yet Clennam,
> listening to the voice as it read to him, heard in it all that great
> Nature was doing, heard in it all the soothing songs she sings
> to man. At no Mother's knee but hers, had he ever dwelt in
> his youth on hopeful promises, on playful fancies, on the har-
> vests of tenderness and humility that lie hidden in the early-
> fostered seeds of the imagination; on the oaks of retreat from
> blighting winds, that have the germs of their strong roots in
> nursery acorns. But, in the tones of the voice that read to him,
> there were memories of an old feeling of such things, and echoes of
> every merciful and loving whisper that had ever stolen to him
> in his life. [2, xxxiv]

This passage clearly shows the effect of the symbolic atonement, the purging of Clennam's guilt, his return to innocence.
He remains a "natural" child, but no longer in the guilty
sense; now purified, he can ask Little Dorrit to marry him.
Other obstacles fall away in the face of his new innocence:
Little Dorrit discloses that her fortune, like his, had been lost
in the Merdle collapse; Doyce appears—a sort of poor man's
Jarndyce—to forgive Arthur, to pay his debts, and to an-
nounce that the great invention has at last been accepted

by a foreign government and that the money will soon be rolling in.

Still, the new innocence does not extend beyond the charmed circle of the "good" characters. The final scene of the novel makes this clear. Married at last,

Little Dorrit and her husband walked out of the church alone. They paused for a moment on the steps of the portico, looking at the fresh perspective of the street in the autumn morning sun's bright rays, and then went down.

Went down into a modest life of usefulness and happiness. Went down to give a mother's care, in the fulness of time, to Fanny's neglected children no less than to their own, and to leave that lady going into Society for ever and a day. Went down to give a tender nurse and friend to Tip for some few years, who was never vexed by the great exactions he made of her, in return for the riches he might have given her if he had ever had them, and who lovingly closed his eyes upon the Marshalsea and all its blighted fruits. They went quietly down into the roaring streets, inseparable and blessed; and as they passed along in sunshine and shade, the noisy and the eager, and the arrogant and the froward and the vain, fretted, and chafed, and made their usual uproar.

Society has not changed. There will be other Merdles and Rigauds; there will always be a Circumlocution Office. But from the final symbolic discovery in Clennam's story we are meant to carry one more lesson away: if human beings so far abdicate their humanity as to legislate against Nature, to bind themselves over in custody to stultifying institutions and a lock-and-key morality, Nature itself will revolt, with destructive violence. As in the spontaneous combustion in *Bleak House*, the "crash" of Merdle's vast fraud, or the collapse of the Clennam prison-house, some day the pressures from without and the decay from within will be too much, and the whole unnatural edifice will fall in upon itself:

...Look to the rats young and old, all ye Barnacles, for before God they are eating away our foundations, and will bring the roofs on our heads! [1, xiv]

Dickens' is a stern optimism.

The importance of a full background in Dickens' dream novels should be evident if one compares the symbolic overtones of Rigaud's death with the much less resonant expiation scene of Stephen Blackpool in *Hard Times* (where all the complications of the double plot simply left no room for the dense texture of "unnecessary" detail which provides the medium of dream meaning). Stephen's fall into Old Hell Shaft has a certain appropriateness, for the abandoned mining pit stands for the whole Coketown system of industrial oppression: "When it were in work, it killed wi'out need; when 'tis let alone, it kills wi'out need. See how we die an' no need, one way an' another—in a muddle—every day!" (3, vi). But the echo is weak and fades quickly. There is no mass of circumstance to be pulled together by the image of the pit. In *Little Dorrit* the collapse of the Clennam prison-house is perhaps even more fortuitous and implausible, but the dreamlike texture makes the coincidence seem "right" because it attaches to so much else in the novel. The magical connections of houses and their inhabitants, the identification of houses and prisons, the mysterious noises in the house, Rigaud's history as a prisoner, and so on, all combine to make the collapse of the house upon Rigaud seem inevitable; and likewise the associations with Arthur's story make it a fitting atonement for his guilt, so that we are not surprised or annoyed when his release from prison follows upon it. The dream logic is perfect, even though the literal facts might otherwise seem scarcely able to bear the weight put on them. Just as such seeming disproportions are the rule in dreams, so they are in Dickens' dream novels; but in order to stand up, such deeper meanings must have an emotional basis in the atmosphere and texture of detail. *Little Dorrit* provides this, whereas *Hard Times* does not.

Dickens' next novel, *A Tale of Two Cities*, was written for weekly serialization, and thus is not much longer than *Hard Times*. But like *Great Expectations*, which followed it, the *Tale* is less handicapped by the enforced compression. *Great Expectations* was actually begun as a longer novel, intended for monthly serialization; yet even when Dickens had to change his plans (to meet an emergency in his weekly magazine) there was less cramping in it than in *Hard Times*, because for the first time Dickens had chosen to use only a single plot. The *Tale*, on the other hand, finds space for textural complexity because it has a single hero—even though there is the usual divided plot, as the very title suggests.

Through most of the *Tale* the two stories are separated geographically as well as structurally, one centering in London, the other in Paris. In the Paris story the usual formula of hidden and apparent strands can be traced in the opening paragraph: "It was the best of times, it was the worst of times...." On the surface, "things in general [seemed]... settled for ever"; but behind these appearances the Woodman Fate and the Farmer Death are at work, preparing their guillotine and their tumbrils. Although the cruelties of Monseigneur seem to be merely devices of the ruling class to maintain order and power, these very repressions—the secret prisoners, the trampled child, the tortured father—are also the making and storing of lightning, or the preparing of an earthquake, as Madame Defarge puts it, which must lead to the catastrophe when the people *discover* themselves, when Saint Antoine marches on the Bastille, and the Jacquerie (the multiple hero of the Paris tale) wrest from the hands of Monseigneur the bloody prerogatives of power. Expiation and return to innocence are also represented, although not dramatically, in Carton's final prophecy:

"I see a beautiful city and a brilliant people rising from this abyss, and, in their struggles to be truly free, in their triumphs and defeats, through long long years to come, I see the evil of this time and of the previous time of which this is the natural birth, gradually making expiation for itself and wearing out."

This is the familiar vision of happiness which symbolizes a return to innocence.

If Carton, through his prophetic vision, is the means of presenting the expiation in the Paris story, he is even more useful in the London tale, as a scapegoat to bear the burden of suffering for Darnay, the real hero, and even as a scape-grace to deserve it for him—a device we have just seen in *Little Dorrit* with Rigaud. Darnay is the real hero, for all the crucial actions except for Carton's sacrifice are his. Beginning with his first appearance in the novel, Darnay's multiple trials and reprieves form the backbone of the London narrative. In the treason trial at the Old Bailey the apparent and hidden strands of his action are introduced: Lucie Manette and her father seem to be connected with his story only by chance, but their lives are already secretly entangled with his, through Doctor Manette's old imprisonment by the family St. Evrémonde. With Darnay's final arraignment before the Paris tribunal, this hidden connection emerges, in the chapter appropriately titled "The Substance of the Shadow." This scene represents the secondary discovery—the revelation of Darnay's true relation with his father-in-law, and the guilty family history behind it.

Like Arthur Clennam, Darnay combines in his story most of the dream material which the earlier novels doled out to separate characters and incidents. But also like Clennam,

Darnay is therefore kept at one remove from these forbidden contents, by their stipulation as part of his inheritance, so that his guilt is indirect and obscure. What little there is of personal guilt in Darnay is presented, again as with Clennam, in terms of renunciation and withdrawal. At the end of the second book the hidden strand of the Paris narrative has pushed its way into the presented action, reaching even to London by means of the crowds of aristocratic emigrants who flock each day to Tellson's Bank for news of the Revolution and for mutual commiseration. Dickens shows Darnay, himself an emigrant, in the midst of these monseigneurs, feeling rather uncomfortable with his secret. A messenger arrives with a letter addressed to the Marquis St. Evrémonde (that is, to Darnay himself) and when no one claims it, all the refugees join in the recriminations against the missing addressee:

"Nephew, I believe—but in any case degenerate successor—of the polished Marquis who was murdered," said one. "Happy to say, I never knew him."

"A craven who abandoned his post," said another. . . .

"Infected with the new doctrines," said a third, eyeing the direction through his glass in passing; "set himself in opposition to the last Marquis, abandoned the estates when he inherited them, and left them to the ruffian herd. They will recompense him now, I hope, as he deserves." [2, xxiv]

Darnay is disturbed by the remarks—but not merely because of their disagreeable tone. In an important sense, every charge against him is true. A "latent uneasiness in Darnay's mind" is explained to us as a sense of hereditary guilt for the past sins of his family, a feeling that "his renunciation of his social place...had been hurried and incomplete."

Here we have the familiar class problem in Dickens, now put in a new light. The hero has renounced his upper-class status in order to escape the guilt of being rich while peasants are starving; and he has been rewarded with the lower-class heroine. This seems ideal. The bother is that Darnay *has* "given up"; his renunciation *was* an abandonment. In Dickens no crossing of class lines goes unpunished. The problem follows him—no matter if he changes his name—and now he finds he must return to France to justify his position and save Gabelle (whose letter of appeal it was) from the guillotine.

Doctor Manette has enjoined Darnay never to reveal his true name, but has not told his son-in-law why he asks this. The reason is not simply that the public admission would be painful to the Doctor, but that it would reveal the whole story of Darnay's family shame. It was Doctor Manette's fatal knowledge of that shame—the rape of Madame Defarge's sister and the murder of her brother by the evil Marquis, Darnay's uncle—that sent the Doctor to the Bastille. This double sin, first a brutal violation and then an unjust imposition of the law, is behind the hereditary guilt which Darnay instinctively feels. But the meaning of all this is not made clear by Dickens until much later. As usual in his dream novels, he is left with a hero who must atone, but whose personal guilt does not seem to warrant the punishment that is required, namely death. Except for the single hint that he has neglected his responsibilities, all Darnay's guilt appears to be hereditary. So in the dream structure Darnay's double, Sydney Carton, must provide both sins and expiation. The atonement here has a more distinctly Christian overtone than is usual in Dickens, for in spite of Carton's dissipated ways, it is quite rightly emphasized that his sacrifice is of an *innocent* life—though his is a clearer case of the abandonment and renunciation of responsibility than Darnay's. The Christian theme of redemption and resurrection pervades the book, not only in the use of words like "recalled," "restored," "revived," and so on, but also in events such as Manette's rescue from prison and madness, Darnay's several reprieves, and even Cly's reappearance from the "dead." All this prepares for Carton's rebirth, framed by several references to children in the final chapters, and crystallized in his last words: "I am the Resurrection and the Life...." In his innocent atonement for and redemption of Evrémonde (whose sin is hereditary), in his "sublime and prophetic" look on the scaffold, and in his assured resurrection and new life (not only spiritually, but *in fact*, through the child who is to bear his name and make it "illustrious")—in all this, Carton may be regarded as a Christ figure.*

This use of the Christian story is calculated to provide thematic unity, to foreshadow and so lend probability to the conclusion, and to strengthen and deepen its meaning. In all but the last of these purposes, Dickens is successful, but at the expense, I think, of other more characteristic Dickensian virtues. The "recalled to life" theme usurps too much from the hidden strand of the London narrative. The weight of emphasis, particularly in the third book of the novel, is shifted away from Darnay and his guilt in favor of Carton and his resurrection motif. This weakens everything in the novel that depends on Darnay—including even Carton's sacrifice, for if Darnay does not capture the reader's sympathy, the sacrifice is pointless and annoying. Dickens' heroes are sometimes weak, but not usually in this way. They may often be vague figures without color or distinctive outline, as compared with the brilliantly rendered minor characters; but they need not be meticulously drawn, for the action is theirs. The hero is the focus of the line of action, and

*K. J. Fielding lists still other Christian patterns in *A Tale of Two Cities;* see *Charles Dickens: A Critical Introduction* (London and New York, 1958), p. 165.

gathers his interest from its structure and movement, which, although "outside" him, reflects and represents him. But much of the total effect depends, as I have suggested, on the texture of dreamlike images, the interweaving of symbols with the action. If these center about Carton and his death, Darnay must suffer a consequent loss of interest, unless he is somehow enmeshed in them as well. And he is not.

The Paris tale is also a peculiar one, because it has for its hero not a man but a whole class, variously represented by the Jacquerie—Jacques One, Jacques Two, and so on— and by the personification of Saint Antoine. In Dickens even the inanimate world takes an active part in the story: houses collapse, raining destruction upon their inhabitants; lightning flashes ominously; holes open in the earth to swallow the unsuspecting wayfarer; the very air is foul with pestilence. Thus it is entirely fitting that in the Revolution scenes of the *Tale* Saint Antoine should come alive, shout, dance, kill, and sleep—all in his own person; the actions of the characters in the Paris tale are the actions of Saint Antoine, and the setting takes over. Even in Soho, where the Manettes live, "backs and ends of houses peeped at them as they talked, and the plane-tree whispered to them in its own way above their heads."

These two locales, framing, and even initiating action, are presented alternately through the first two books of *A Tale of Two Cities*. With the approach of the catastrophe the tempo quickens, not merely in the increasing violence of the action presented, but also in the parallel montage. The two story lines introduced in the first book are brought closer and closer together in the second: *four* weekly numbers set in London, *two* set in Paris and the château; then *three* in London, *two* in Paris; then *two* in London, *two* in Paris; and finally *one* in London. The London tale slowly narrows (four, three, two, one) up to Darnay's reversal (the London equivalent to the Revolution), while the Paris narrative looms correspondingly large. It is as if Saint Antoine in person were hammering at the door of the house in Soho, louder and louder, with the echoes in the street. In the second book the Paris narrative does in fact break in on the London tale when Chapter XXI, begun in Soho, suddenly switches from "the little circle...in the dark London window" to "the foot-steps raging in Saint Antoine afar off." After a few Revolutionary scenes we are brought back to London again for Darnay's crucial decision to go to France. The two tales are violently juxtaposed, equated, and finally even joined, at least in setting. During the whole alternating montage of the Paris and London tales, clusters of symbols not only differentiate the two parts (Paris: ragged people, dirty streets, gloomy skies; London: the quiet corner, the plane tree in the garden), but also equate them and thus prepare for their joining at the end of the second book (Paris: footsteps, tempest, lightning; London: footsteps, tempest, lightning). Everything is in readiness for the merging of the two tales.

The third book, however, is again disappointing; the two tales do not become one, though they now share a single locale. Were it not for their enforced confinement, Lucy and Charles might as well be safe at home in Soho, for all they learn from their experience. The violent confrontation we expect between the Defarges and the Evrémondes never comes off. Instead, the flat and uninteresting character of Miss Pross is elevated to improbable heroism as she defends Lucie from the vengeful Madame Defarge; and Sydney Carton, who is completely uninvolved in the Paris plot, is allowed to die for Charles. The closest thing to a genuine showdown is the reading of Doctor Manette's long-hidden denunciation of the evil Marquis and his family; but this is unduly formalized in the trial scene, by the device of the interpolated story, and the most inflammable content—the rape of Madame Defarge's sister—is discreetly muffled. The exciting scenes in this book are the set pieces: the grindstone passage, the Carmagnole. These have nothing directly to do with the Darnays, who are merely observers. Although Charles is supposedly threatened by all this, he is not *in* the scenes, and what we feel is not fear for him but horror at the violence and butchery before us.

In these isolated set pieces we have the usual Dickensian displacement of violence and punishment, which, once over, allows the hero to return to freedom and innocence. Their failure here to provide the sense of expiation and purgation that similar scenes accomplish in other novels may be attributed to Dickens' attempt, also a failure, to join the two plots. In *Bleak House*, for instance, the murder of Tulkinghorn and the death of Lady Dedlock will serve as violence and atonement in Esther's plot, but not in Richard's, who must die his own death. In the *Tale* Dickens tries to get extra mileage out of the scenes of violence in the Paris streets, but they simply will not work for both plots. Darnay is too detached and protected, too uninvolved in the whole Paris side of the novel. The symbolic violence in *Little Dorrit* also takes place while the hero is in prison, but there the prison-house motif serves to make the connection. The bloody outrages committed by the mob in the *Tale* have no relation to Darnay's guilt or imprisonment, beyond the bare fact that the Revolutionaries are responsible for imprisoning him. Ironically, then, it is Dickens' very attempt to draw his two plots together that weakens them most in the final episodes.

This irony should not surprise us too much. As I suggested at the beginning of this chapter, Dickens' gradual integration of his dream materials was accompanied by a growing need to hide their significance by means of devices which give a superficial and misleading unity to the novels. Often the same structural elements might both reveal and conceal the dream meaning. As he comes closer to the breakthrough of *Great Expectations,* where so many of these motifs are brought into the open, Dickens seems more and more reluctant to let the hero act out his own story, and even the surrogate figures and symbolic events in which the action is allowed to go forward are more and more detached and remote from the hero's apparent problems and fate. The result is in some ways more and more dreamlike—certainly in the major scenes involving displacement, the Carmagnole or the Grindstone, in fact all the Revolutionary scenes, where there is no hero—but less and less so in the scenes with the hero himself, who is robbed of his vitality as it were to protect him from his own guilty desires. The hero becomes the center of the secondary elaboration, the attempt to make "realistic" sense of what is not realistic at all, but hallucinatory and nightmarish. In *Great Expectations* Dickens finally found a means—very much dependent on his use of the first person there—to bring his forbidden contents into relatively direct relation with his hero. The double plot disappeared, and the usual dream displacements and distortions became part of the hero's story—by necessity, since it was he who experienced and reported them. Toward this integration and clarification of the dream content all the novels from *Bleak House* had been tending, with the results we have seen. After *Great Expectations* Dickens returned to the double plot, but with quite different effects.

## Our Mutual Friend

Halfway through the writing of *Our Mutual Friend,* Dickens paused to take stock of his story. He has left us a record of this inventory, as it was set down in the number plans which he prepared as the narrative progressed, and which are now bound up with the manuscript itself at the Pierpont Morgan Library. That record reads as follows:

Position of affairs at the end of the Second Book (No. X)

Lizzie has disappeared, by the aid of the good Jew: leaving as to that part of the story:
> Eugene
> The Doll's Dress Maker
> Mr bad child
> Bradley Headstone (and Charley?)
> Miss Peecher

John Harmon is known to the reader, and involves on to that part of the story:
> Bella
> Mr and Mrs Boffin

With the Bower are concerned:
> The Dustmounds
> The friendly move between Silas Wegg and Venus
> Check-mate on the part of Harmon and Sloppy

With the chorus, rest:
> Humbug, Social and Parliamentary
> Twemlow's promise as to Georgiana
> Mrs Lammle's development
> Fledgeby's use of power?

There remain, besides, for implements and otherwise:
> The Wilfers (notably Rumty)
> George Sampson
> Riah
> Betty Higden
> Lightwood
> Riderhood and his daughter
> The Six Jolly Fellowships.—Miss Abbey Potterson
> Job Potterson
> Jacob Kibble[46]

A glance tells us that we have here the familiar division of the novel into two main story lines, as revealed by Dickens' classification of his characters under five heads: Lizzie, Harmon, the Bower, the chorus, and implements. Leaving the last group out of the count, we can lump Harmon and the Bower, Lizzie and the chorus, as the two major configurations, easily demonstrated by the large number of connections between the characters under these heads. The title of the novel, which refers to John Harmon, alias Julius Hanford, alias John Rokesmith (see page 111 of the Oxford edition), confirms the impression given by Dickens' notes that Harmon was the intended hero of the novel. In the superficial working out of the story, too, Harmon's supposed drowning in the first chapter makes his role central, for the action of both plots seems to stem from it: Eugene's interest in Lizzie as well as the comic Boffin intrigue—even the dinner conversation at the Veneerings' table.

On the other hand, neither Harmon nor Lizzie undergoes the sequence of actions we have learned to expect of a Dickens hero. Instead of being confused and deceived, by self, by other characters, or by society, they themselves represent enigmas, to be solved by the real hero and heroine of the two plots, Eugene and Bella. This should be clear to any reader of the novel: Eugene and Bella are the two characters whose fortunes matter to us, whose stories command our interest, whose natures are explored in their actions. Like Pip in *Great Expectations*, or the Gradgrinds in *Hard Times*, they are the problem children, whose destinies are uncertain and therefore matter to us. John Harmon and Lizzie Hexam are too much in control of themselves to make us at all tender of their fates.

If we turn to the "Memoranda" book to trace the development of the drowning-disguise idea on which Harmon's story is based, we find it relatively well formed before Dickens started writing. On page [8] appears the following note:

Found Drowned. The descriptive bill upon the wall, by the waterside.

Later on the same page Dickens writes,

A "'long shore" man—woman—child—or family

—and he wonders whether he might not "connect the Found Drowned Bill with this?" On page [19] he hits upon the central idea of the new book:

LEADING INCIDENT FOR A STORY. A man—young and eccentric?—feigns to be dead, and *is* dead to all intents and purposes external to himself, and for years retains that singular view of life and character.

By the next page Dickens has the title as well—"Our Mutual Friend."

There is no doubt that the combination of these ideas gave Dickens the beginning of the novel, and the "leading incident" is clearly defined—no vague, wandering notion. Still, had we not the "Memoranda" book notation—"Done Rokesmith"—who would recognize this as the "leading incident" of *Our Mutual Friend?* In the novel itself, the whole cluster—title, hero, incident—loses power and is handled perfunctorily. Another story usurps its place.

In *Our Mutual Friend* the split narrative does not quarantine or conceal the sexual and social problems or the scenes of violence that are the contents of the dream; Dickens puts them all into the Wrayburn half (just as he does in the single plot line of *Great Expectations*), and the Wilfer-Harmon story is chiefly a frame to allow the real subject to take shape. Consequently, the Wilfer-Harmon half lacks interest and gives rise to such comments as that of Henry James that the novel "is wanting in inspiration."[47] But the Wrayburn plot is very interesting, as Pip's story is, so much so that some modern critics take issue with James, and even praise the book as Dickens' finest. As I have suggested earlier, both are right, for the novel is very good or very bad, depending on which plot you are talking about.

Bella's part of the novel follows the usual formula with undeviating fidelity. She describes herself as "the most mercenary little wretch that ever lived in the world" (2, VIII), and this, in combination with Harmon's assumed identity as John Rokesmith, constitutes her apparent strand. Bella does everything she can to convince herself and her society that she is looking out for a rich husband. She rejects Rokesmith's proposal on these grounds (she thinks she hates Rokesmith, while in fact she loves Harmon), and she is well on the road to a bad end when the Boffins step in with their benevolent conspiracy, Mr. Boffin acting the role of a miser to show Bella the awful consequences of greed. The result is that Bella, in a discovery-and-reversal scene with Mr. Boffin and Rokesmith, renounces her patron and her mercenary hopes, and flees—not homeward, for the redoubtable Ma Wilfer awaits her there, but to her father; her lover follows; she accepts his renewed offer, and is shortly whisked off to Greenwich to become Mrs. John Rokesmith. Good and sweet as Dickens paints her in her new role, according to the formula Bella must yet prove that she is purged of her sins. This she accomplishes by remaining faithful and trusting, in the face of her husband's suspicious evasiveness with Lawyer Lightwood, and in the face of an even greater trial, expressly designed by Rokesmith in a veritable paroxysm of pride in his wife's virtue:

"She shall see me under suspicion of having murdered myself, and *you* [the Boffins] shall see how trusting and how true she'll be." [4, XIII]

Trusting and true she is, of course, and with folktale justice her patience is rewarded with all those riches she has renounced, complete with innocent Boffins, and even their house, gotten up like a childish palace (in lieu of a return to innocence).

It is hard to be serious about the Boffins and Bella and John Harmon, much harder than to accept Little Nell or Paul Dombey or even the cloying Esther Summerson. At least they have the distinction of being grotesques, "monster[s] of virtue" as Eugene Goodheart has put it.[48] The unconventionality (cuteness) of the Boffins is bad enough; but Dickens' doting approval of the suddenly reformed Bella and her gallant suitor is quite beyond pardon. One can only smile grimly in agreement with Mr. Boffin's pretended reaction to Rokesmith's stiff declaration of love:

"Win her affections," retorted Mr. Boffin, with ineffable contempt, "and possess her heart! Mew says the cat, Quack-quack says the duck, Bow-wow-wow says the dog! Win her affections and possess her heart! Mew, Quack-quack, Bow-wow!" [3, xv]

We hope that Dickens' heart was in the ridicule more than he knew.

Eugene, like Bella, is a favorite type with Dickens, but still more deeply meaningful for him. Richard Carstone, Pip, Arthur Clennam, Sydney Carton, even Harthouse in *Hard Times*—all represent the bright young man who is made miserable or whose talents are wasted by a lack of purpose. Eugene's chronic inability to be serious, his lack of purpose or interest in anything, are the traits of the "misplaced" man, that is, the man who for some reason avoids placing himself. Eugene explains his condition to his friend Mortimer:

"You know that when I became enough of a man to find myself an embodied conundrum, I bored myself to the last degree by trying to find out what I meant. You know that at length I gave

it up, and declined to guess any more. Then how can I possibly
give you the answer that I have not discovered? The old
nursery form runs, 'Riddle-me-riddle-me-ree, p'raps you can't
tell me what this may be?' My reply runs, 'No. Upon my life,
I can't.'" [2, vi]

Even more clearly than the long line of heroes before him,
Eugene is an emptied character, totally detached and dis-
interested, his energy and ambition drained by the system
and society which in all these novels is represented by his
profession, the law. The main difference is that there is more
of Harthouse and Gowan in his character than we have seen
before in Dickens' protagonists. He is, in other words, closer
to being the villain as well as the hero of his story.

"If there is a word in the dictionary under any letter from
A to Z that I abominate," Eugene says in Chapter iii of the
first book, "it is energy. It is such a conventional superstition,
such parrot gabble!" When we see him next, in Chapter viii,
he is parrying Mr. Boffin's small talk—"But there's nothing
like work. Look at the bees"—with a diatribe against odious
entomological comparisons:

"Ye-es," returned Eugene, disparagingly, "they work; but don't
you think they overdo it? They work so much more than they
need—they make so much more than they can eat—they are
so incessantly boring and buzzing at their one idea till Death
comes upon them—that don't you think they overdo it?"

Again, in Chapter xii, the same theme is taken up: "In suscep-
tibility to boredom...I assure you I am the most consistent
of mankind." Not until his last appearance in the first book
(Chapter xiv) does Eugene act outside the expectations set
up by this characterization, and even when he does finally
contract an interest in something—Lizzie Hexam—he keeps
the matter to himself. We later learn that it was he who
broke the news to Lizzie of her father's death, and who saw

to it that she had friends to comfort and care for her then; but his first explanation to Mortimer of his mysterious disappearance offers no hint of this:

"My dear fellow," said Eugene, sitting on his bed, "I felt that we had bored one another so long, that an unbroken continuance of those relations must inevitably terminate in our flying to opposite points of the earth. I also felt that I had committed every crime in the Newgate Calendar. So, for mingled considerations of friendship and felony, I took a walk." [1, XIV]

Again Eugene's boredom presents a smooth, impenetrable surface. What is behind his mask of ennui? As in the other novels, so in *Our Mutual Friend*: in order to understand the hero's nature and problem, we must study the structure of his plot, and especially his scenes of discovery.

Eugene's initial discovery comes to him at the Veneerings', when Mr. Dolls brings him the address of Lizzie's hiding place. But we do not see its effect; the chapter ends with Eugene muttering,

"A stroll and a cigar, and I can think this over. Think this over." Thus, with a thoughtful face, he finds his hat and cloak, unseen of the Analytical, and goes his way.

This is the briefest and least marked of all discovery scenes in Dickens; we only know that it is the discovery because (1) it comes at the end of the third book, the usual position in the long four-book novels; (2) it is literally a discovery— of Lizzie's whereabouts; and (3) the next time we see Eugene, he is changed.

This last—Eugene's change—argues most heavily, of course, for identifying the end of the third book as the discovery scene. Something must have caused the changes that are dwelt on in his next interview with Lizzie. Moreover, these changes themselves breed changes; the discovery leads to secondary discoveries. When Eugene reveals himself to Lizzie—

"Lizzie! I never thought before, that there was a woman in the world who could affect me so much by saying so little. But don't be hard in your construction of me. You don't know what my state of mind towards you is. You don't know how you haunt me and bewilder me. You don't know how the cursed carelessness that is over-officious in helping me at every other turning of my life, won't help me here. You have struck it dead, I think, and I sometimes almost wish you had struck me dead along with it" [4, vi]

—he is also discovering himself. This secondary discovery is much more revealing and more powerful than the initial one. The first is a simple objectification of feelings and motives which had previously been only loosely structured in him. He has already told us,

"I am bent on finding Lizzie, and I mean to find her, and I will take any means of finding her that offer themselves. Fair means or foul means are all alike to me."

But he has also said,

"I ask you [Mortimer]—for information—what does that mean? When I have found her I may ask you—also for information— what do I mean now? But it would be premature in this stage, and it's not the character of my mind." [3, x]

When he discovers Lizzie's hiding place, he also discovers (partly) what he wants to do: he wants to go to her; and, what is the same thing, he wants to leave Society—the dinner party at the Veneerings'. Eugene's characteristic way of solving (or *not*-solving) a problem is to "hang around" it in his careless, accidental manner, without really confronting it, hoping something will happen. Since Lizzie now seems to be his problem, he goes to where she is, in order to hang around.

This is only typical behavior for Eugene, and hardly seems to be an important discovery or change; but the fact that he *goes to her* instead of waiting for her to come to him (which she will never do) constitutes a major innovation in his behavior. It is an outgoing act, even though its purpose (merely to hang around) is not outgoing.

Eugene's second discovery builds on his first. His initial reaching out to Lizzie, timid and guarded as it is, makes a second advance easier. In his conversation with her at the Paper Mill he wavers on the brink of a real avowal:

"Are you so determined, Lizzie—forgive the word I am going to use, for its literal truth—to fly from a lover?" [4, VI]

To say the word is hard for him, as his embarrassed levity indicates, and he has not yet accepted the implications of his love; but he does say it, and the excitement of the scene comes from just this tension between his inhibitions and his desires, between what he has been and what he is about to become. It is this scene, therefore, that I want to concentrate on, because in it the conflict in his character is closer to the surface than at any other point.

The scene occurs in Chapter VI of the fourth book. It begins with an idyllic rendering of the countryside near the Paper Mill where Lizzie has taken refuge (the idealization prepares us to accept the same locale as the haven necessary for a later return to innocence). Then suddenly and significantly Dickens wanders from the scene itself to a satirical description of a "little Fair" going on in the village. Two things make this digression curious: first, it *is* a digression, and seems to have no function in the plot; second, the tone, although intense, is strangely ambiguous.

Fearful to relate, there was even a sort of little Fair in the village. Some despairing gingerbread that had been vainly trying to dispose of itself all over the country, and had cast a quantity of dust upon its head in its mortification, again appealed to the public from an infirm booth. So did a heap of nuts, long, long, exiled from Barcelona, and yet speaking English so indifferently as to call fourteen of themselves a pint. A Peep-show which had originally started with the Battle of Waterloo, and had since made it every other battle of later date by altering the Duke of Wellington's nose, tempted the student of illustrated history. A Fat Lady, perhaps in part sustained upon postponed pork, her professional associate being a Learned Pig, displayed her life-size picture in a low dress, as she appeared when presented at Court, several yards round. All this was a vicious spectacle, as any poor idea of amusement on the part of the rougher hewers of wood and drawers of water in this land of England ever is and shall be. They *must not* vary the rheumatism with amusement. They may vary it with fever and ague, or with as many rheumatic variations as they have joints; but positively not with entertainment after their own manner.

We can guess from similar passages in *Hard Times* and other books (for instance, see the chapter in *American Notes* on the factory girls at Lowell) that Dickens means to be praising village amusements and condemning puritanical suppression of them. But why bring it up here? With whom is he arguing?

Dickens *himself* disapproves of the want of taste, the lowness and vulgarity of the scene. As F. R. Leavis has pointed out concerning the amusements praised in *Hard Times*, Dickens deliberately avoids any reference to the "squalor, grossness and vulgarity" which he must have known was part of a traveling circus.[49] What is further apparent is that although Dickens refuses to admit it, his own revulsion comes through regardless, when he pictures the degradation of young Tom Gradgrind dressed and painted up like a clown, and similarly in the passage just quoted from *Our Mutual Friend*, where obvious distaste frowns behind the phrase "entertainment after their own manner," not to mention the condescending tone of the whole description.

The apparently out-of-place and certainly ambivalent sketch of lower-class amusements is a prelude to the treatment of the sexual-social problem that faces Eugene and Lizzie. Dickens' ambivalence about these lower-class amusements corresponds to Eugene's conflict over Lizzie. Eugene himself states the dilemma: "Out of the question to marry her,...and out of the question to leave her. The crisis!" The alternative, as Dickens hints, is to seduce her, and we are supposed to take Headstone's vicious attack on Eugene as providential punishment for this "wickedness." This is made obvious by the juxtaposition of Eugene's decision and Headstone's assault, which follows immediately. "Was he struck by lightning?" Dickens asks, implying that the gods are angry.

The "decision" for which Eugene is punished, however, has as little of the "decisive" about it as we should expect from him. He merely "decides" to "try her again." The wavering and uncertainty in Eugene's conduct toward Lizzie is the result of his noncommittal attitude toward life in general. Eugene himself has no confidence that Lizzie can make a better, more earnest man of him. His lack of earnestness or commitment is too ingrained. Its extreme expression occurs at the Veneering dinner parties, where Eugene is always discovered gloomily contemplating his goblet, "buried alive in the back of his chair," refusing to "come out" (l, ii). This defense is perfectly adequate to the Veneering dinner parties, but the mechanism is unhappily characteristic of all his behavior. His refusal to act or take part *is* his character, and all his behavior is colored by this abstention.

His going to Lizzie is therefore almost daring, his putting

his arm around her and kissing her even more so; observe how hedged with reservations these acts are:

"Will you walk beside me, Mr. Wrayburn, and not touch me?" For his arm was already stealing round her waist.

. . . . .

"Will you walk beside me, and not touch me," for his arm was coming about her again.

. . . . .

He held her, almost as if she were sanctified to him by death, and kissed her once, almost as he might have kissed the dead.

Eugene stands back as far as possible from the emotions which his body is expressing. *His arm* makes the move, but not *he*. He kisses her as if she were dead (that is, as if *he* were dead). Finally, after she has gone, he is forced to admit that he is moved: "...there were tears upon his hand, as he stood covering his eyes." Again the emotion is divorced from the man (why not say "He was weeping"?), but the tears are real and cannot be overlooked:

"A most ridiculous position this, to be found out in!" was his next thought. And his next struck its root in *a little rising resentment against the cause of the tears.*

"Yet I have gained a wonderful power over her, too, *let her be as much in earnest as she will!*" [my italics]

His resentment is twofold: (1) resentment of her earnestness, which he lacks; and (2) resentment of her ability to call up earnestness in himself, which he fears. A sorry case, perhaps, but at least he does get angry, and this is one way of getting in contact with the situation. Curiously enough, Eugene's anger provides the necessary feeling to solve the problem. There are three possibilities: (1) to leave (this would be flight); (2) to marry her (this is impossible, for it would require that he give himself, exactly what he is not willing or able to do); (3) "to try her again" (this means merely to hang around, to see what comes up). The third possibility is his "reckless" choice—a wicked one, according to Dickens—and Eugene makes it in anger and the sense "of his power" with Lizzie. Given the circumstances, it is the right choice, for if he hangs around something *will* come up, as has already been proved by his tears. What does come up is Headstone's attack, and the schoolmaster's murderous passion seems to be just what is needed (equivalent to Eugene's resentment) in order for Dickens to allow Eugene and Lizzie to marry. Once the violence has been expressed, the love can take over.

Eugene's anger is primarily self-directed. What he ought to hate is the society that frustrates and emasculates him, but he cannot admit that society is really evil, nor can he be actively aggressive. Orwell points out how rarely a fist fight occurs in Dickens, and puts it down to the fact that "he belongs to a cautious urban class which does not deal in socks on the jaw, even in theory."[50] Of course it is more than this; there are no passionate love scenes either, and we can account for both absences only by positing a general inhibition of strong feeling expressed in bodily contact. Headstone and Eugene are not allowed to clash face to face; the schoolmaster must strike from behind so that Eugene can remain passive. Often the violence must wait until the hero is literally in prison. In *Great Expectations* Pip is shown in anger only when Orlick has him tied up; compare Eugene's powerlessness:

Eugene was light, active, and expert; but his arms were broken, or he was paralysed, and could do no more than hang on to the man, with his head swung back, so that he could see nothing but the heaving sky.

He is not even allowed to look at his attacker, though it can make no difference later, since he is convinced on his recovery that it must have been Headstone.

Because Eugene cannot act out his feelings, all his anger is turned inward. More than once he voices his wish for death (punishment), and he certainly courts disaster in baiting the violent Headstone. When the attack finally comes, it is almost a relief. First, it satisfies Eugene's need for punishment and seems to give him new confidence—at least enough to defy Society and his father, by marrying Lizzie. His guilt is atoned for in much the same way as Pip's, and he is freed to pursue his real desires, as far as he understands them. Lizzie's class background is no longer a disadvantage because she turns it to good: her waterfront experience enables her to save Eugene from drowning, and he in turn can then be grateful to her and offer his love. She proves, *in spite of her background*, to be a game girl: "she was rowing down the stream as never other woman rowed on English water." In other words, the class question is avoided by making her an exceptional case.

This means that the ending must be false. Eugene cannot hope to be happy unless he faces the class question. He asks Lizzie, "If I had not been *what you call* removed from you and cut off from you, would you have made this appeal to me to leave you?"—"Let me know how you would have dealt with me *if you had regarded me* as being *what you would have considered* on equal terms with you" [my italics]. The style marvelously conveys his refusal to commit himself, his inability to ask himself the same question. However, after Lizzie has gone, he does pose it to himself, as if from his father: "You [Eugene] wouldn't marry for some money and some station, because you were frightfully likely to become bored. Are you less frightfully likely to become bored, marrying for no money and no station?" The question is immediately brushed off then as "levity," but surely it is the real problem. Can love make all the difference? Dickens says yes; Eugene wonders; the novel itself seems to say no, or at any rate everything that happens in the novel seems to preclude Eugene's happiness. We are not shown any convincing picture of Eugene *being* happy, though we are urged to believe he will do his best to make Lizzie so. His father turns out to approve of Lizzie (that is, like Eugene, he really doesn't care, one way or the other); but what will Eugene do about a job and a social life? When Dickens says, at the end, that Mortimer and Eugene "discoursed of the future, until Lizzie came back," we cannot really imagine what they would have to discuss. They speak of "turning to at last" and "in earnest," as if everything could be changed because of Lizzie, as if *she* were "something really worth being energetic about." But Eugene's sickbed confession to his new wife has the more convincing ring to it:

"...Well. If I live, you'll find me out."

"I shall find out that my husband has a mine of purpose and energy, and will turn it to the best account?"

"I hope so, dearest Lizzie," said Eugene wistfully, and yet somewhat whimsically. "I hope so. But I can't summon the vanity to think so. How can I think so, looking back on such a trifling, wasted youth as mine! I humbly hope it; but I daren't believe it. There is a sharp misgiving in my conscience that if I were to live, I should disappoint your good opinion and my own—and that I ought to die, my dear!" [4, xi]

We may perhaps attach even more weight to Eugene's pessimistic declaration, knowing that the "Memoranda" book contains a still gloomier version of it, one which shows the peculiar ambiguity of Eugene's newfound earnestness in a colder light:

As to the question whether I, Eugene, lying ill and sick even unto death, may be consoled by the representation that, coming through this illness, I shall begin a new life, and have energy and purpose and all I have yet wanted: *"I hope* I should, but *I know* I shouldn't. Let me die, my dear."

Very few passages in the "Memoranda" book found their way into the novels, and most of those only as ideas for events and characters and not as actual dialogue. The presence there of this speech suggests that Dickens must have regarded Eugene's story as demanding a pessimistic conclusion, soften it as he might in the final pages, and that he therefore recognized and accepted Eugene's conflict as unresolved, even unresolvable.

From the foregoing analysis one thing ought to be particularly noticeable: for the first time in our study of these novels, it has been possible to state much of the meaning of the plot without appeal to the dream logic, the underground connections between superficially unrelated events and acts. Eugene even more than Pip is openly and directly involved in the problems of sex and class from which the earlier novels tend to insulate the hero. Eugene's guilt is not hereditary, nor is it expressed by some surrogate; he is the one who wishes to break down the social and sexual barriers between himself and Lizzie. Since he is a lawyer, of course, his acts go precisely against his nominal commitment to society, and in this too his dilemma is more immediately represented than that of the earlier Dickensian hero, whose legal antagonist was likely to exist objectively in his world as a Tulkinghorn or Barnacle or Jaggers. As the terms of the hero's problem are concentrated more and more in his own character and action, there is correspondingly less displacement of these same materials into the surrounding plot and scene. The proportion is much lower in *Our Mutual Friend* than in its predecessors, just as the integration of its subject matter around Eugene Wrayburn is much more complete. One consequence of this rise to the surface of the dream content is that the novel may be discussed much more straightforwardly, without constant reference to dream devices and the like. The psychological analysis previously focused on the whole novel may here be narrowed to the hero himself, who contains in his own character the elements previously scattered throughout his plot.

This integration and concentration of the dream content in the hero is not complete in *Our Mutual Friend,* and it is interesting to see which elements of the forbidden problems are most resistant to direct expression. In general, it may be said that Eugene is a withdrawn and detached hero, thoroughly unwilling to admit his own feelings and desires; but this is not surprising, given the heroes of earlier novels, who were not allowed to embody such feelings at all. The main area in which Eugene is still deprived of his own nature, so that it must be expressed by means of displacement, is the area of violence and crime. Although some of his antisocial passion gets expressed in his pursuit of Lizzie, a much stronger and more violent version is seen in the two figures who act as surrogates for him in this area, Bradley Headstone and Rogue Riderhood. Since these two characters function as the major displacements in the novel, it is worth paying them some special attention.

Appropriately enough, given Eugene's malaise of boredom and lack of earnestness, it is his alter ego, Schoolmaster Headstone, who provides the only example of genuine earnestness in the novel. He cares for his job, and has been promoted in it. His ill-repaid kindness to Charley Hexam shows that he takes a real interest in his pupils. He cares passionately for Lizzie and would probably make a good husband for her, though perhaps one prone to jealous rages. He cares about social injustice, and is not too timid to tax Eugene with taking advantage of Lizzie; he hates Eugene cordially for his upper-class arrogance, as well he may:

"You reproach me with my origin," said Bradley Headstone; "you cast insinuations at my bringing-up. But I tell you, sir, I have worked my way onward, out of both and in spite of both, and have a right to be considered a better man than you, with better reasons for being proud." [2, vɪ]

Eugene in turn hates Headstone for both his lower-class origins and his seriousness of purpose, which puts Eugene's frivolity to shame. Eugene sneers at the schoolmaster's coarseness in coming round to warn him away from Lizzie; but it is not the coarseness that troubles Eugene so much as it is that Headstone *cares* about anything enough to *do* something about it:

"I suppose you," said Eugene, "judging from what I see as I look at you, to be rather too passionate for a good schoolmaster." [2, vɪ]

The passion irritates Eugene, because he himself is so lukewarm. In fact, much as Eugene denies it, the schoolmaster is extremely interesting to him, and he spends a good deal of time and goes a good bit out of his way just to humiliate Headstone:

"Then soberly and plainly, Mortimer, I goad the schoolmaster to madness. I make the schoolmaster so ridiculous, and so aware of being made ridiculous, that I see him chafe and fret at every pore when we cross one another. The amiable occupation has been the solace of my life, since I was baulked in the manner unnecessary to recall. I have derived inexpressible comfort from it." [3, x]

Eugene's behavior arises partly out of simple hatred for the man who has what he lacks—intensity of purpose; but even more than that, Eugene hangs around him as he does around Lizzie, in order that something may happen. It is plain that Headstone is violent and dangerous, and that if Eugene persists he may be attacked by his rival. This is what Eugene wants, for it will put feeling into his life and satisfy his need

221

for punishment. The physical confrontation of the assault scene produces the final change in Eugene's character and allows him to marry Lizzie, though with the misgivings we have seen. But Dickens' failure to resolve the class theme leaves Headstone without a function in the plot after the rescue. Once Eugene's "good side" has emerged, the contrast is no longer wanted, and the schoolmaster is relegated to a watery grave with the wharf-rat Riderhood, outside the charmed circle of hero and heroine.

Headstone's fate is especially interesting, though, because it makes still clearer his function as a foil and surrogate for Eugene. There is much evidence to show that just as Headstone is a kind of double for Eugene, so Riderhood is for Headstone. When he attacks Eugene, Headstone dresses in clothes identical to Riderhood's, hoping thus to place the blame for the murder on him. Symbolically, it is as if he *had* done it, and it would not be out of character for him, though he has less motive. Riderhood is already associated with drowned men, and may possibly have had a hand in some of the drownings. In their final scene, he and Headstone die together, Headstone declaring that he will drown himself in order to drown Riderhood, almost as though he regarded himself and Riderhood as one. Obviously a violent criminal type, Riderhood represents one extreme on a continuum of passion and restraint, crime and law-abiding order, which runs from him through Headstone to Eugene. (This may be compared to the continuum in *Great Expectations*—Joe, Pip, and Magwitch—which has the hero in the center. Riderhood, as Pleasant's father and a "business" associate of Gaffer Hexam, is thus in another way similar to Magwitch, who is Estella's father.) The three characters represent the ambivalence in Dickens' feelings about law and order, crime and punishment. To borrow (and modify slightly) Riderhood's own version of their relations to each other, they stand for the "one, t'other, and t'otherest" aspects of the same conflict between legality and crime. It is a curious development of the relations between the actual doubles, Darnay and Carton, in *A Tale of Two Cities*. In *Our Mutual Friend*, although the meaning of the split characterization is more openly displayed, so that there is less need to express it indirectly in other elements of the story, it is nevertheless the same story once again: society and its laws forbid the crossing of sexual and social boundaries; this proscription is a kind of imprisonment and is enforced by the threat of violent punishment; the impulses against which the laws are applied break out regardless, with a degree of energy proportionate to the repression exerted by society; thus the criminal act condenses both guilt and punishment in a single explosion of violence. Eugene represents the law, Riderhood the criminal, Headstone the alternately repressed and violent victim of the conflict; but actually all three must be taken together, to see the full range of Dickens' ambivalence. Convention and nature struggle indecisively, and the outcome is hedged, in spite of the mutual destruction of the two more violent types, by Eugene's sickbed pessimism—a pessimism partly necessary because the energy and purpose of which he feels the lack are precisely those qualities which Headstone and Riderhood have usurped to his cost.

In all this, the familiar mechanisms of Dickens' dream manner may be seen. But, as I have suggested, *Our Mutual Friend* is in some ways less a dream novel than any that preceded it—less Dickensian, if you will. There are fewer displacements, and those that do occur are presented less deviously, their meanings less concealed and distorted. I do not believe that we should account for this change by saying Dickens has abandoned the dream manner, but rather that, while continuing to write his dream novels with their characteristic manner and matter, he has come now to accept the dreaming as his own (the first-person narrative of *Great Expectations* suggests this), and to feel more at his ease in the midst of ambivalence and conflict, readier to admit his fears and desires to full and direct expression. The effect is a change from magic to myth, from the vibrations of nightmare to the elegiac quality of wish-fulfillment. The atmosphere is pastoral; it depends on a kind of direct symbolism rare in Dickens, save in the still purer example of *Drood*. I do not of course mean that there are no mysteries in Eugene's story, any more than I would suggest that there are none in *The Mystery of Edwin Drood*. But the mysteries in both are deeper, less "cooked," than in the other novels. They are mysteries of character and emotion rather than of circumstance or contrivance. The resultant change in atmosphere is quite striking. One feels it most in the river scenes in *Our Mutual Friend*: the setting is no longer quite so weirdly alive as it is, say, in *A Tale of Two Cities*, and yet it continues to affect the characters and the reader symbolically, rather as in a dream, where things look to be their ordinary selves and yet are deeply suffused with emotion. Does it sound odd to say that these last two of Dickens' novels strike us as the work of an old man, no longer struggling with his materials, but letting the feelings speak as they will?

In any case *Drood* so far as we have it seems to confirm some such analysis of the changes and the reasons for them in the Wrayburn half of *Our Mutual Friend*. Like *Great Expectations*, it has a single plot, and as in *Our Mutual Friend*, the atmosphere is calmer, the scenes less fantastic, the plot more integrated around one protagonist. In *Drood* there has been still further development of all these qualities, and perhaps most striking is the condensation of the double-figures (Carton and Darnay; Joe, Pip, and Magwitch; Eugene, Headstone, and Riderhood) into a single character—Jasper, who is apparently a double in himself, a split personality. This further concentration of the dream materials into a single hero-villain must account for the dreamy peacefulness so often praised in the scene: the elements of violence are no longer displaced into the landscape, and it is clear that Jasper himself is the murderer in this novel; one guesses that he was ultimately to be his own victim as well—Eugene and Headstone combined.

I do not intend any full-scale analysis of *Drood* here, but it is perhaps appropriate to close this section on the novel as dream with a conjecture that could not be made without taking Dickens' final work into consideration. The conjecture is this: in order to explain the relaxation of Dickens' dream manner, its shift into a calmer and less desperate mood, I have suggested that he had at last accepted the dream materials which had come to the fore in *Great Expectations* and *Our Mutual Friend*. We may go further, and suppose even that he had seen into his own artistic method, had finally understood not only the dream, but also that it was a dream and that he had used a dream manner to tell it. At least we have the evidence of *Drood*, that much of the book was apparently to be cast quite straightforwardly *as* dream, and that everything in the outcome seemed arranged to hinge on that fact.

# 5

# The Meaning of the Dream

IN this chapter we shall turn again from practical to theoretical concerns. The intention is to summarize the results of our analysis of Dickens' dream novels, and to venture some general account of these results, as well as some broad speculations regarding Dickens' reasons for writing such novels. Although I have argued in the preceding chapter for a particular view of Dickens' development as a dream novelist, in this chapter, for the sake of clarity and simplicity, I shall largely ignore the growth and changes in his art, and the discussion will center mainly on the dream materials and manner of the middle novels, before *Great Expectations*.

What appears first of all is that these novels have in common a characteristically Dickensian plot. The hero is presented a surface of event and circumstance which seems to constitute reality, a world of which he has a ready understanding, and which corresponds to his view of his own nature and place in the scheme of things. This is the *apparent strand* of action. But regularly intruding into the plot are a series of mysterious occurrences which do not make sense in this ordered sequence of event and interpretation. These mysteries constitute the *hidden strand*, and at this stage are hardly more than loose threads not yet worked into the tightly spun apparent strand. They intrude more and more insistently into the time and space of the plot, with a greater and greater sense of menace and foreboding accompanying them. Finally their force can be resisted no longer. This is the *discovery*. From underneath the surface of appearances emerges the hidden truth: all the supposed facts of the plot are false, or have been falsely interpreted by the hero; and the consequence of this discovery is the *reversal* of his fortune.

Throughout the early unfolding of the plot, while the apparent strand still holds the attention in the hero's world, the isolated forewarnings of the hidden strand are connected, as they arise, with some vaguely felt guilt which infects the hero. With the full emergence of the hidden strand, the nature of this guilt begins to appear: in some way the hero's very being is tainted, and he has further aggravated his sin of existence by avoiding all recognition of its nature, by clinging to a false view of reality and his place in it. All along he has deserved to be punished, and now as the discovery of the hidden strand presses this truth upon him, it also initiates an *atonement* by bringing about the reversal.

But the hero does not come easily to the recognition of his guilt. The major discovery that leads to reversal does not immediately make his inherited sin clear to him. He must face a series of *secondary discoveries*, which explain all the mysteries that have arisen in his earlier life, and show the connections between these mysteries and those remaining fragments of his former view of himself and his life. In terms of the plot, this series of secondary discoveries serves to account for all the loose ends of the apparent strand, explaining or redintegrating them into the emergent hidden strand. In terms of the characterization, these discoveries amount to the hero's slowly developing *recognition* of his own complicity in both strands and, through this, of his true nature and the true nature of his world. In this resolution, guilt is simultaneously recognized and expiated, for the hero's involvement is such that he cannot see the truth without changing his own nature at its deepest levels. This is equivalent to *rebirth*, with its trauma as well as its new innocence. The hero's suffering is generally marked by an illness, followed by a symbolic return to some earlier scene in the novel, already associated with childhood and innocence, where he may begin a new life.

Because the materials dealt with are so loaded with repressed feeling, for both Dickens and his heroes, much of this typical line of action—especially in the earlier novels—is displaced and distorted, so that parts of the hero's story hardly seem relevant to him at all, or affect him drastically without apparent reason. In particular, the extent of the reversal often seems out of proportion to his actual guilt, and the final violent retribution often falls not on him but on some surrogate. A symbolic reading of the novels, as if they were dreams, makes the best sense of these various twists and turns of action and character.

The typical Dickensian plot is further complicated, in all the later novels except *Great Expectations* (and the unfinished *Edwin Drood*), by the doubling of the complete sequence— apparent and hidden strands, discovery and reversal, secondary discovery, recognition, atonement, and rebirth—so that there are two heroes, each with a full line of action according to the formula. The two plots are interrelated, with elements from the strands of one plot also functioning in those of the other, with innumerable parallels of character, action, and setting; nevertheless they remain two fundamentally separate stories, and the lines of action, although sometimes crossing and often running parallel for short stretches, never merge in a single structure. As Sergei Eisenstein put it in an essay on "Dickens, Griffith, and The Film Today," the alternating montage technique which Dickens utilized (and which Griffith seems to have borrowed) contains no dialectic, goes "no deeper than the image of an intricate race between two parallel lines" which could meet only in "some hypothetical 'reconciliation' where...the parallel lines would cross, that is, in...infinity."[51] The dialectic of hidden and apparent strands, which meet in discovery and reversal, has no counterpart at this higher level of structure.

Such is the paradigm that emerges from a comparative examination of Dickens' later novels, each of which appears to follow the formula more or less closely. In it several characteristic features of Dickens' dream technique may be seen at work. Perhaps most obvious is the treatment of the hero's experience as though it were his dream. The events of both the apparent and the hidden strand are not mere outward circumstance; they also represent the character of the hero himself, his hopes and fears, his self-deception, his guilt; and thus we see his complicity in the creation of his own world. This is clearest where the hero is a figure with whom Dickens has reason to identify—especially so with Pip, whose story is told in the first person. Dickens' usual identification with all the characters, even with the setting and events, may be seen operating here in an interesting way. To speak for a moment as if *Great Expectations* actually were a dream, we may say that by putting himself (as Pip) into his own dream, Dickens has accepted the dream meaning more fully here than elsewhere, so that for once the events that occur may be allowed to *be* their own meanings rather than merely symbolic of them. One need only compare Pip's discovery of

Estella's parentage with the discovery of Miss Wade's story in *Little Dorrit*, or with the discovery of Doctor Manette's manuscript in *A Tale of Two Cities*, to see the difference between a hero whose dreams are at once symbolically and literally functional in his life, and one whose dreams need critical interpretation before the connections between the literal and the symbolic become clear.

Related to this simultaneity of the literal and the symbolic in *Great Expectations* is the absence of the double plot, for when Dickens steps into his dream as Pip, he is forced to tell the dream from "inside" it, and thus there can be no second hero, no parallel action as in the other novels. Nor need there be, for the primary function of the double plot was to ensure the very disjunction between the literal and the symbolic, between events and their meanings, which in *Great Expectations* is no longer quite so necessary. There less than in any previous novel is there a need to rely on parallels and juxtapositions to give the connection between action and feeling, for the choice of Pip as narrator automatically introduces a new tension between background and foreground, a new Gestalt in which, because events are focused by a single, involved consciousness, they no longer appear as isolated, random elements in a pattern which is *all* background. To develop such a Gestalt is the natural function of discovery in the plot line of these novels, but the double plot continually worked against this function by allowing the discovery to come symbolically, without being integrated in the hero's actuality—as Mr. Merdle's downfall functions symbolically for Arthur Clennam, both as discovery and reversal, whereas viewed literally as part of Arthur's career it has at most only an accidental and tangential connection with his secret guilt. Within the framework of the double plot, events from one world can thus "randomly" affect those of another;

but with a first-person narrator telling his own story, everything tends to cohere merely by virtue of being noticed and
reported by the same involved consciousness. There can no
longer be any pretense that the narrator is detached or absent. The dream must be taken as reality; responsibility for
it is fixed.

We may take it then as a general rule in Dickens that the
paradigm line of action works toward revelation of the
dream content of the novels, while the doubling of the plot
works to conceal and confuse these meanings, to hide them
under a superficial network of connections and parallels,
the secondary elaboration of dream theory. Thus although
the intricate pattern of correspondences across the two plots
provides a certain unity of tone and texture, in the final
analysis it operates to hold elements in solution, while the
formula of discovery and reversal, and so on, works as a
precipitant of these elements and organizes them according
to their deepest meanings and relations, as a significant action
rather than a static set of possibilities and alternative views.
It is the function of the secondary discoveries, for instance, to
clarify all the major displacements and condensations of the
dreamwork (the metonymies, personifications, metaphors, and
image-clusters of the style), which on the superficial level of
correspondence and parallel are all means of concealing the
truth, but at another, deeper level of structure become the
means of revealing it. So in *Bleak House* the murder of
Tulkinghorn, the flight of Lady Dedlock, and the pursuit by
Esther and Bucket, are all part of the melodramatic structure
of secondary elaboration, while on a deeper level of the novel
we see that Tulkinghorn's murder represents the violent
destruction of the prison of forms in which Lady Dedlock
lives, that Lady Dedlock's flight to the grave of her lover is
the symbolic revelation of Esther's true nature as a child of

sin (the explanation of her smallpox), and that Lady Dedlock's death is a symbolic atonement for that sin, and a freeing
of Esther from hereditary guilt. The sequence of events has
two organizations, the one designed to camouflage the other,
which is structurally deeper and on which depends the whole
meaning of Esther's self-discovery and acceptance of her own
nature.

With the example of Esther before us we may note still
another way in which the elements of the novels are differently organized, according to the level of structure on which
they are considered. On one level, Lady Dedlock's secret
connection with Esther is that she is Esther's mother, and
Esther's discovery of the fact constitutes a crucial juncture in
the melodrama. Viewed more deeply, Esther's discovery is
her self-recognition, the discovery symbolically conveyed
by the death scene at the entrance to the graveyard that she
is tainted by the sin of her mother—just as all society is infected by the guilty relations between high and low represented by the graveyard, the pestilential Tom-all-Alone's,
Jo's smallpox, and even Richard's grim disease, "smouldering
combustion." The numerous parallels of imagery seen here
are the fretwork of secondary elaboration. Obviously, they
add to the novel's effectiveness: we see how general Dickens'
indictment is, and how consistently it is maintained. But we
lose something by this device too, for the multiplication of
guilty parties dilutes the strength of the central action.
Dickens splits his heroine as he splits his plots, and separates
the good heroine from her guilty surrogate, Esther from
Lady Dedlock. The notorious result is Esther's thin and uninteresting character, robbed of its vitality at the same time
that it is whitewashed of its sin. Like Little Dorrit and Charles
Darnay, Esther is deprived of her very *raison d'être* in the

novel. This is the price we pay for the double plot and its thematic reverberations.

Another variety of displacement seen in the novels is the use of the composite hero, the Jacquerie in *A Tale of Two Cities* and—even more curious a "hero"—the Jarndyce and Jarndyce case in *Bleak House*. In the *Tale* Saint Antoine is the hero of the Paris plot, and this personification results in an extraordinary intensification of violence in that part of the novel. The use of a personified class to enact the characteristic drama of the hero seems to enable Dickens to bring together elements that he ordinarily kept apart. The degradation and brutality of the revolutionaries is a far cry from the restraint and gentility of Pip, the self-effacement of Clennam—who refers to himself and is referred to by the narrator as "Nobody"—or the inhibitions of Wrayburn, whose lovemaking is so painfully embarrassed and strangely disavowed. One gathers that it was not simply Dickens' horror of mobs or his respect for law and order that produced this violence in the Revolutionary scenes of the *Tale*, though that certainly had something to do with it; equally important must have been the freeing of his imagination from a restricting conception of what a hero ought to be. With Saint Antoine there was no need to protect his respectability or preserve his goodness-at-heart.

The major displacement involved in making Saint Antoine the hero of the Paris tale relieved Dickens of the need for the innumerable minor displacements ordinarily required to keep his heroes untouched by the very sins that gave them their right to be in the novels at all. Consequently the set pieces of the *Tale*, "The Carmagnole" and "The Grindstone," are not purely symbolic displacements like Miss Wade's "History of a Self Tormentor" or the sluice-house scene with Orlick in *Great Expectations*. But at the same time that the

composite hero of the Paris tale is thus freed of certain re-
strictions, he is limited by others. The most important development in the typical Dickensian line of action, namely
the series of secondary discoveries with their attendant suffering and atonement eventuating in rebirth, must necessarily
be omitted from the Paris tale. *A Tale of Two Cities* is not
*War and Peace*, and there is no room in it for the elaboration
of plot that would have been necessary with a whole class as
hero. The ultimate regeneration of the French people is
therefore only predicted, by Carton in his final vision on the
scaffold.

The same difficulty is seen in *Bleak House* with the use of
the Jarndyce and Jarndyce case as a "complementary hero."
There, the merging of Richard's character and fate with the
legal struggle results in an abridgment not only of the plot
line concerning the case itself, but of that concerning Richard
as well. Obviously, a legal case cannot suffer or atone for its
sins; it can only end. Accordingly Richard is allowed only a
brief final moment of enlightenment before he expires along
with the case, used up in its costs. The identification of
Richard's fate with that of the legal case is in some ways very
effective, just as the device of the composite hero is in the
*Tale*, but only—again as in the *Tale*—at the expense of the
symbolic force of the usual Dickensian plot.

The composite hero, like the surrogate, is a displacement
which tends to obscure the line of action, but which is ultimately bound to it just as much as the other formal elements
we have been examining in this chapter. The typical functions and interrelations of all these elements appear to be
organized according to principles very like those found in
dreams. Therefore, if we now wish to push the inquiry
further, to ask why it is that so many of these elements seem
to work at cross purposes, obscuring the basic line of action

as much as they promote it, we must look for an answer in the *content* of Dickens' dream novels, the symbolic meanings conveyed by the formal structures. As in dreams, such meanings in Dickens are suffused with emotion, and a large part of the effort involved in rendering them goes into disguise and distortion—to relieve anxiety, to avoid taboo subjects, and to make the emotional content both literally and figuratively more presentable.

I have already suggested that the kernel from which the action of all these novels grows is a preoccupation with sex, class, and sin, which seems to originate in Dickens' childhood experience at the blacking warehouse, and which he typically represents as the love or seduction or rape of a heroine from one class by a hero from another. In the earlier novels embodying this theme the seminal event is buried in the past, underneath an elaborate structure of more recent incidents and concerns, so that its full significance is kept from the reader. In later books it is brought nearer the foreground, both as part of the temporal sequence actually presented and as avowed subject matter. Eugene Wrayburn's pursuit of Lizzie in *Our Mutual Friend*, and Pip's infatuation with Estella in *Great Expectations*, are much more in the center of attention than Lady Dedlock's affair with Captain Hawdon, or Mr. Clennam's liaison with the dancing-girl, or the Marquis' rape of Madame Defarge's sister. This gradual coming to the surface of the hidden content is accompanied by an increasingly intelligible, even formulistic plot, so that as the content becomes more available, the structure becomes more capable of expressing it. (This, of course, is quite the same as with recurrent dreams; as under analysis the repressed content is brought to consciousness, the dreamwork becomes more and more directly expressive.) But once expressed, what precisely is the significance of the central story that Dickens keeps telling? To understand this, we must separate the elements of the story.

The problems of a young man in the Victorian age were, as they still are, to find a job, a mate, a place to live, a position in a community, a goal in life. These are interrelated problems—the job is in order to support the mate and maintain the place, the goal is in order to justify the position in the community, the mate is in order to continue the community, and so on—but for exposition's sake we may treat them as only three distinct problems: finding a job, finding a community, and finding a mate.

(1) *Finding a job.* Consider the situation of Richard Carstone in *Bleak House*. Born in Chancery, as Dickens puts it, Richard has from his earliest years been under the influence of that emblematic institution. His one ambition is to overcome his past, by bringing the case of Jarndyce and Jarndyce to a profitable close. But in order to win, he must play the game according to Chancery's rules; and so he compromises himself at the very beginning, by placing his faith in the justice of an unjust system. Moreover, because he is so inextricably caught up in it, he cannot place himself as an individual. All his attempts at finding a profession must fail, because he is only marking time, role-playing, while he waits for the disclosure of his secret fate. He is nothing more than another helpless cog in the great Chancery machine, and all his actions have a fatal necessity about them. He does not choose his own life. Everything in Richard's world is ultimately linked to the system; all the professions he tries are shown to be infected by the same humbug and time-serving hypocrisy; and one of them, the law, is at the very center of corruption. The only men who manage to remain uncontaminated are John Jarndyce, who has so completely cut himself off from society that he holds no job at all, and

Allan Woodcourt, a physician who—because he refuses to be a part of the general evil—has no paying patients (only Nemo, Miss Flite, Jo, Gridley, Jenny, and Richard himself, none of them able to contribute a farthing to the doctor's subsistence). It is significant that the only sort of job shown favorably in *Bleak House* is one in which the worker subverts the system by working for next to nothing and in which he cannot expect to succeed except by relying on some benevolent *deus ex machina* like John Jarndyce.

Nor is Richard the only Dickens hero who cannot find a place in society. Compare Eugene Wrayburn in *Our Mutual Friend*—

"I hate," said Eugene, putting his legs up on the opposite seat, "I hate my profession" [1, III]

—or Arthur Clennam, whose complaint in *Little Dorrit* has already been cited as typical of Dickensian heroes—

"I have no will. That is to say," he coloured a little, "next to none that I can put in action now. Trained by main force; broken, not bent; heavily ironed with an object on which I was never consulted and which was never mine; shipped away to the other end of the world before I was of age, and exiled there until my father's death there, a year ago; always grinding in a mill I always hated; what is to be expected from *me* in middle life? Will, purpose, hope? All those lights were extinguished before I could sound the words." [1, II]

The problem of vocation is an important one in Dickens, for it reveals a great deal about his attitude toward society. George Orwell, for example, is puzzled by "an enormous deficiency in Dickens, something that makes the nineteenth century seem remote from us—that he has no ideal of work":

The feeling, "This is what I came into the world to do. Everything else is uninteresting. I will do this even if it means starvation," which turns men of differing temperaments into scien-

tists, inventors, artists, priests, explorers and revolutionaries—
this motif is almost entirely absent from Dickens's books.[52]

Humphry House in *The Dickens World* makes a curiously
opposite observation concerning Dickens' attitude toward
work—"Nearly everybody in Dickens has a job: there is a
passionate interest in what people do for a living and how
they make do."[53] It is not that House and Orwell have
contradictory perceptions, but that they are noticing different
things. House points out the *interest in jobs*, while Orwell
points out the lack of *interesting jobs*. House notes that, for
Dickens, "the typical restless, baffled person is one who, like
Richard Carstone, cannot settle to a profession and make
good," but we remember that Richard is enthusiastic about
almost any job—until he has tried it. Dickens' interest in
jobs resembles Richard's; it is the interest of a man who is
occupationally bored, who cannot see the value of any job
in the system. Notice the vocations represented, for instance,
in *Our Mutual Friend*: Wrayburn and Lightwood are dis-
contented lawyers, Boffin is a retired scavenger, Wegg a ballad-
monger, Venus a taxidermist (one of the more satisfactory
jobs in the novel), Fledgeby a usurer; Riderhood and Hexam are body-robbers, Rumty Wilfer is a nondescript clerk,
and Mr. Dolls a jobless drunk. John Harmon acts as Boffin's
secretary for nonvocational reasons. The most respectable
positions are held by the villains: Veneering and Podsnap are
businessmen, Headstone is a teacher. There are plenty of
jobs in Dickens' world, but there is little manly work. And,
as Arthur Clennam learns in *Little Dorrit*, if a man has something really important to contribute to his society (as Daniel
Doyce is made out to have), society, in the person of the
Circumlocution Office or some other institution, refuses to
be interested and in fact actively hinders the contributor.
It is the Court of Chancery all over again.

(2) *Finding a community.* The difficulty the Dickens hero has in finding useful work is in large part not his fault at all. It is "Nobody's Fault," as the discarded ironic title of *Little Dorrit* was to suggest—that is to say, it is everybody's fault, it is the community's fault, and most of all, it is the fault of social institutions like the Circumlocution Office, the Court of Chancery, the Marshalsea Prison, the *Fact*ory System, Monseigneur, and Society. These institutions encourage young men to become gentlemen, to hang around (Eugene), to look about (Herbert Pocket), in short to do nothing, as a kind of training for taking their position in the community where "How Not To Do It" is the one indispensable skill. Relations between men—and what else *is* community?—are conceived legalistically, bureaucratically, autocratically, but not humanly. There is no community beyond the formal patterns for relations between men, who are litigants, masters, servants, prisoners, officials; who are Bar, Bench, Physician, Bishop, Chief Butler; who are Boodle, Coodle, Doodle, Foodle, Goodle, Hoodle, and so on through the alphabet.

In such a noncommunity, a man will perhaps settle for a role instead of a job. He will become a flat caricature of his vocation, known by his post-office mouth (Wemmick in *Great Expectations*) or by his hook nose, bright eyes, and ruffled head (which "bore a certain likeness to a roused bird of prey" in the physiognomy of the body-robber Gaffer Hexam in *Our Mutual Friend*—1, 1). Further, he will perhaps settle for a setting instead of a place in the community, and the scene of his activities will take on the life that has been squeezed out of his relations with his fellow human beings. What in a humanly constituted world would be a dramatic event becomes, in this world of roles and institutions, a vibration of the scene itself, for the people have all receded into the places and objects which are the formal signs of their role-existence. This is the displacement of nightmare, come true.

That anyone living in such a world might have a goal in life is out of the question, as Clennam typically complains. And indeed, so far is any goal from being conceivable in Dickens' world that it is hard to imagine what could constitute a meaningful goal for one of his characters. His best types, men like Jarndyce, have no purpose beyond the vague intention of doing good, and the more energetic sort, like Woodcourt or Doyce, are so intent on the practical moment that they seem not to have any long-range plans. How could they, when even their short-term accomplishments always depend on the benevolence of a Jarndyce or the luck of finding some vague foreign power to back their efforts?

(3) *Finding a mate.* When men are baffled in their desire for meaningful work, for a genuine community, and for a goal in life, they may turn to the hearth and home for substitutes or consolation. So in *Our Mutual Friend*, Eugene's boredom is relieved by his interest in Lizzie. But the change supposed to have been worked upon Eugene by his marriage is not convincing. A wife like Lizzie might make life tolerable, but how could she make "a good opportunity" (1, iii) for her husband's professional and public needs and responsibilities? One imagines for him at best the solace Ada provides Richard, at worst the domestic felicity which is so offensive in the Harmon household, complete with "inexhaustible baby" and a Boffin for godfather.

The women in Dickens' world are of two main kinds, good and bad. Whatever possibilities there might otherwise be for a man who has neither worth-while job nor sense of community to find bliss by the fireside, it is very difficult to imagine normal flesh-and-blood satisfaction with any of Dickens' grotesque child-wives. These sexless Victorian clichés have been drained of all human vitality by their opposites, the bad women who represent the other side of the melodramatic split, and who in addition to laying claim to all the guilt and shame of the feminine spectrum have a corner on sexuality as well.

But no one needs to be reminded of the Victorian heroine's deficiencies. What may perhaps be worth pointing out is how Dickens' female characters seem to correspond in type to the various women who were most prominent in his own life: his wife Kate, a clumsy and ineffectual woman whose character in the early years of their marriage must have provided the raw materials for David Copperfield's simpering child-bride Dora; Georgina Hogarth, Kate's sister and the equivalent of Esther Summerson in the Dickens household, who knew how to entertain the children and kept the keys to the cupboard; Mary Hogarth, another sister who lived with the newlyweds until her sudden death at seventeen (Dickens adored her and dreamed of her nightly for months afterward); Maria Beadnell, Dickens' first romantic interest, whose family kept them apart; and Ellen Ternan, who became Dickens' mistress in the late 1850's, when she was scarcely older than Mary Hogarth had been at her death. In the last three of these women—Mary, Maria, and Ellen—may be found the elements which make up Dickens' idealized virgins and his sentimentalized fallen women, the two feminine figures which, with the child-bride and the competent housewife, fill out the sexual range of Dickens' imagination. Other figures which appear are variations on these types, not counting of course the asexual caricatures which abound in the novels. One exception may be Helena Landless in *Drood*, though one cannot be sure how she would have turned out.

What is striking in all this range of feminine figures is the absence of any real objects of sexual desire. Virgins,

child-brides, competent housekeepers—even the fallen woman is a helpless victim rather than an attractive object. One
is drawn to the conclusion that, strong as the motif would
seem to be in the kernel situations of the novels, erotic desire
is not at the heart of these plots after all. If anything, the
woman represents security, acceptance, purity, innocence, a
place and a role—all things somehow forbidden the hero,
just as the other goods of life, jobs and community, are closed
to him. Such sexuality as may be found in the novels seems
to be there less as an enticement in itself than as a pretext
for forbidding the hero access to home and family. And
perhaps just this is the clue to the content of Dickens' novel-
dreams.

Dickens' heroes are waifs, orphans, unfortunates whose
lineage is somehow defective. Even Eugene Wrayburn is in
some sense an orphan, for whom the initials "M. R. F." (My
Respected Father) must serve in lieu of a parent. In a number of cases, the hero is illegitimate, born out of wedlock.
In others he himself is seeking to transgress the boundaries
of society in some sexual liaison (including marriage above or
below one's station), regarded as another sort of illegitimacy.
These heroes are engaged in a struggle to gain entrance to
the social world. Generally they do not understand why they
are outcasts, since they do not know they are illegitimate,
much less who their parents were. Still they intuit their
unworthiness, and society makes them smart for it. Denied
family, vocation, and community, the heroes regard themselves as somehow flawed and undeserving of the social goods.
What they do not understand is that their personal dissatisfaction is everywhere matched in the social world. It is not
merely for them that there are no worth-while jobs, no
human bonds, no community. The problem is omnipresent.
But for them, it seems a thoroughly just rejection by society;

their ways of coping with it are to pass as gentlemen (Pip, William Dorrit), or to seduce a woman (Eugene, Harthouse), or to change their identities (Darnay, Harmon), or to force the world into giving up its goods (Richard), or rob it of them (Tom Gradgrind). But these methods are also illegitimate. And indeed the legalistic and bureaucratic world the hero wishes to enter is such that he can hardly avoid some impropriety or other. It is the world of rules and roles that has proclaimed him illegitimate, unwanted, unfit for the available slots.

Actually, what the hero wants is not to get into or out of society, but to break down the bars which mark the boundary line. His task is to escape from the prison society makes for him and yet, at the same time, achieve admission to that society. This dilemma (the society that is there is the only society there is) cannot be solved by the hero. Consequently the most intense scenes of the novels contain some explosion of violence—the collapse of a house, a fall into a pit, a spontaneous combustion—which represents neither escape nor successful entry, but simply the uncontrollable assertion of a nature too long repressed and confined. Moreover, these are the last elements to be integrated into the hero's own life and action (not until *Drood*), because they do not express merely his own anger and frustration nor merely the punishment that society reserves for its enemies, but both at once—and because, even more, they represent the simple impossibility of any solution at all, given the terms of the impasse—so that the violence really does seem to belong neither to the hero nor to the society, but hovers menacingly between them.

Ultimately, the deceit which the world has practiced upon the hero forms part of his discovery. He sees at last that society will crush whomever it can, as it has crushed Magwitch and William Dorrit and Richard and Carton. But the hero's most important discovery is not about the world he lives in but about himself. He finally discovers his true parentage, and with it the fact of his illegitimacy, the terms of his rejection by society. And yet this amounts to the same discovery he has already made about society, for in recognizing his own illegitimacy, he must see that society condemns him, that there is no place for him in the legitimate system. The primary emphasis on the personal recognition, on his own illegitimacy rather than on the discovery that society has made him so, produces the characteristic outcome of the novels. The rebirth and return to innocence, which is a wiping clean of the slate, a purging of the taint of illegitimacy, must take place in some haven beyond society itself, for it is not imagined that anything can be done to change the social order. Laws must be obeyed, and thus the only way for the hero to avoid breaking them by his very existence is to remove himself to some nonsocial realm. Dickens cannot imagine the world as other than it is. For all his dissatisfaction with the way things are, he cannot write utopian fiction; he must contrive an ending in which social evils are simply not faced. His dream is a dream of some secret hideaway where the evil in the world cannot touch him; but in order to imagine such a refuge, he must continue to believe in the evil from which it will be a refuge. Furthermore, the refuge must necessarily become still another prison-house, of one's own making. *There is no refuge.* The Dickens hero is being punished for his guilty nature, as he conceives it. Therefore he needs the society that imprisons him; he needs the prison in order to expiate his sins. The vision of a secret place is another symptom of Dickens' compulsion for order, his insistence that things be in their places, that the universe be moral. But in order to believe that there is certainly a good place somewhere, one must believe that there is an inevitably bad place here. And thus he finds no place for himself, no satisfaction however great his achievements.

Dickens' dissatisfaction with his own life seems to date from *David Copperfield*, in which he told enough of his early history to call forth just such self-assessment. In January 1855, five years after *Copperfield*, he wrote to Forster:

Why is it, that as with poor David, a sense comes always crushing on me now, when I fall into low spirits, as of one happiness I have missed in life, and one friend and companion I have never made.[54]

This "one happiness" or "one friend" cannot refer obliquely to Ellen Ternan, who did not appear on the scene until the late summer of 1857. Thus it is not fair to interpret his complaints as mere self-justification, though later on there may have been something of that in them too. That the sense of waste is somehow related to his unhappy marriage is shown by another letter to Forster, about a year later:

However strange it is to be never at rest, and never satisfied and ever trying after something that is never reached, and to be always laden with plot and plan and care and worry, how clear it is that it must be, and that one is driven by an irresistible might until the journey is worked out! It is much better to go on and fret, than to stop and fret. As to repose—for some men there's no such thing in this life. The foregoing has the appearance of a small sermon; but it is so often in my head in these days that it cannot help coming out. The old days—the old days! Shall I ever, I wonder, get the frame of mind back as it used to be then? Something of it perhaps—but never quite as it used to be. I find that the skeleton in my domestic closet is becoming a pretty big one.[55]

Probably about the same date (certainly before the completion of *Little Dorrit*) Dickens jotted the following idea for a story in his "Memoranda" book:

A misplaced and mismarried man. Always, as it were, playing hide and seek with the world and never finding what Fortune seems to have hidden when he was born.

Although the sense of sexual unfulfillment ("misplaced and mismarried") is strong in all three complaints, it is not the essential difficulty, which seems rather to be a general discontent with life, expressed as a feeling that Fortune has somehow passed him by. The blame is more and more laid on his wife, but in *no* area does he feel that he has or is what he really wants or values. Compare another entry in the "Memoranda" book:

The man who is incapable of his own happiness. Or who is always in pursuit of happiness. Result. Where is happiness to be found then. Surely not Everywhere? Can that be so, after all? Is *this* my experience?

It is something of a shock to discover how exactly Dickens' understanding of the particulars of his own life parallels his conception of life in the novels. What is striking is not so much the use of his own predicament as story material, but rather the application of his artistic principles to real situations: if it sounds rather self-dramatizing for him to speak of his own condition as "always laden with plot and plan and care and worry,...driven by an irresistible might until the journey is worked out," one could not ask for a more accurate formulation of the world of the typical Dickens novel. His fatalistic view of life, the feeling that Fortune has not dealt fairly with him, corresponds precisely with the impression of his stories, that they merely happen instead of being told by him. His notion is that life offers itself to the individual, rather than the other way round. Thus he feels "misplaced" and "passed by," whereas in reality he refuses to place himself. This refusal is at the heart of his dreamer's total immersion not only in his characters, but in places, events, and

images as well; he is constantly searching for further life
to fill out his own. Yet the attempt always fails, for he never
really places himself, never finds what it is he is "missing";
or to put it the other way, he never accepts his lot as it is, he
cannot believe it is his lot, and never allows himself whole-
heartedly to be Charles Dickens.* Instead, he plays roles—as
writer, actor, and public performer of his own works (like
Macready and Kean, he was a brilliant "method actor"). Yet
in spite of his huge popular success, this life was never ultimately satisfying to him; after the exhilaration of losing himself in the part, there was always the letdown of coming
back to his own character. "I want to escape from myself,"
he wrote Wilkie Collins after the final performances of *The
Frozen Deep.* "For when I *do* start up and stare myself
seedily in the face, as happens to be my case at present, my
blankness is inconceivable—indescribable—my misery, amaz-
ing."[58] No role, on stage or off, could provide the vague
something—the "one happiness"—which "Fortune seems to

---

*In some ways, of course, he was terribly aware of himself; his
egotism could be monstrous, as in his playful references to himself
in his letters as "the Inimitable." He thought of naming his magazine
(*Household Words*) after himself—"Charles Dickens: A Weekly journal
designed for the instruction and entertainment of all classes of readers:
Conducted by Himself."[56] But these too are obvious examples of a kind
of role-playing; his notion of his public self was a complex fabrication,
sometimes downright repulsive in its resemblance to the patronizing
benevolence of John Jarndyce, but more often made pathetic by the
sense of mission ("the instruction and entertainment of all classes
of readers") which is noble in spite of its condescension. He cut a
rather pompous figure in the public role he felt a duty to maintain;
doubtless he would have been more comfortable in the fanciful persona
he envisioned (until Forster talked him out of it) for the animus of his
weekly miscellany: "a certain SHADOW, which may go into any place, . . .
and be supposed to be cognizant of everything. . . ."[57] The anonymity,
the mystery, the omnipresence of such a schoolboy conception appealed
to him hugely. The consequence for the novels is the peculiarly Dickensian narrator, omnipresent yet nowhere to be seen.

have hidden," because there was no such thing. It is said that children reach maturity when they discover that *there is no secret* which the adults are keeping from them. Dickens seems to have learned this lesson late (much of what critics call his childlike imagination consists in exactly this continuing search for some key that will unlock all the doors); only in *Drood* does he seem to have abandoned the fruitless attempt.

Writers of the sort Dickens is do not regard themselves as "historians" or even "imitators" of life. They often undertake research for the background materials of their novels—Dickens himself went north to explore an industrial town before he wrote *Hard Times,* and he read through two cartloads of books which Carlyle had provided him before beginning *A Tale of Two Cities*—but for this sort of novelist the act of writing is not a report or a re-creation. It is an imaginative act, an undergoing of experience rather than a recounting of it. After finishing Paul Dombey's death scene Dickens was too distraught to sleep, and walked the streets till dawn. He "half began," he said, "to think it the only reality in life, and to mistake all the realities for shortlived shadows."[59] A reading of the letters seems to bear out this intensity of involvement with his characters, and of course a reading of the novels themselves gives the strongest sort of proof, for we feel there just how powerfully those characters can take hold of the imagination and become—if for a reader, then all the more so for the writer—the focal points of reality, the test and measure of *what is*. The mimetic act for such a writer is quite unlike that of most authors. Imitation becomes participation.

Novelists ordinarily find themselves involved in their works, but in different ways. For instance, there is a kind of novelist who writes in order to experience vicariously what she writes about. I use the feminine pronoun, because the writer of this category is so often female—the sex of its first great representative, Richardson, notwithstanding. This is the epistolary tradition, the vein of Fanny Burney and Jane Austen and innumerable novel-writing English ladies. The tone of such novelists is the gossipy one of a private letter, and the subject matter tends likewise to be the same combination of trivia and rumor that once flourished in middle-class parlors and now enlivens suburban kitchens. In this sort of fiction mundane matters provide the solid ground on which more exciting conjecture may be based. The heroine is just like the authoress, except that her life is complicated by experiences which only occur to her creator as possibilities, and never actually happen to her. For the writer and her readers alike, boredom is relieved by endowing present circumstances with a set of more exciting alternatives that are always in the offing, though perhaps never to be chosen. It is precisely here, in the sense of such experience as only possible, that we see the difference between fiction as vicarious life and fiction as imagined life, between Jane Austen and Dickens. For the sort of author who writes stories in order to experience events vicariously is ordinarily quite comfortable in real life, at worst chronically bored but not really interested in doing what her heroines do. The identification with the protagonist tends to be rather superficial—for pleasure only, as it were—and not a matter of intense commitment (one thinks of the difference between Emma Woodhouse and Catherine Earnshaw). That is to say, there is a great difference between vicarious experience and imaginative experience. It is the difference between shivers-up-and-down-the-spine and fear, between a-lump-in-the-throat and love.

Other novelists write a kind of fictionalized autobiography. They gather up fragments of their own lives into a coherent pattern and render them as a story. This sort of fiction is akin to allegory, for the invented elements of the story must be continually tested against a set of facts or truths which already exist complete. The outcome is predetermined, not by the givens of the story, but by the actuality of the past, or of the way things are now. It is a repeating to himself of what the author already knows, and its psychological function is to reassure him that his world exists. Again, this is very different from Dickens' fictive manner; he does not report things as they are or have been, but invents them. Life for him is the tenseless present moment of his imaginative world, rather than the hypothetical future perfect of the gossip novelist or the still-reverberating past of the autobiographical writer. Dickens prefaces his stories with neither "I wish" nor "I believe," but somehow manages to say both at once, as the dreamer does in his dream.

In Dickens' kind of mimesis, the imitation creates the imitated object. Fiction becomes reality. Life is a plot, and the plots of novels are life. This is not like vicarious experience or fantasy, for Dickens is neither identifying his own life with someone else's nor simply avoiding reality. He presents an imagined world which is essentially his own world, with precisely its problems; only in the imagined version all the ordinary beliefs, desires, possibilities, and alternatives blossom into a new sort of existence. Every wish and fear is embodied in setting and character and incident. In ordinary life the mind searches out the circumstances which will answer to its thoughts. It fixes on images from the past, or hunts a perspective in the present, that will permit it to see what it wants. But past and present do not invariably rise to the occasion. Much of a man's vision of reality fades when tested against the hard facts. One loses faith. The world of dreams is different because there one finds an object ready to every thought or feeling. Reality caters to one's vision of it where the mind invents whatever it needs. Faith is automatic. And these two worlds are what Dickens managed to combine in his fiction. Feeling dissatisfied and misplaced in his own life, and driven to try to understand why, in the manner of a dreamer he created a world where feelings could represent themselves in action, and where he might test them against the possibilities he could imagine. The language of dreams gave him a way of simultaneously saying and doing, as though he were acting out his desires instead of just talking about them. And he did precisely that, for as he continued to press his imaginative inquiry he discovered more and more exactly what he felt, and came steadily closer to the truth about himself and his life. Like his heroes, he had put himself into a situation where he could not avoid the recognition—the very plot forced it upon him.

But the greatness of Dickens is neither in his analysis of society nor in his understanding of himself; rather, it is simply his imagination that one marvels at, the dream manner that creates a world where anything might happen, where the possibilities of life seem infinite and man's imagination, after all, more than adequate to them. Finally one comes back to the incomparable scenes in Dickens, where fantasy and realism are so immortally blended that there is nothing for the critic to do but gasp—Pip wheeling Miss Havisham about her decayed apartments, Bitzer defining "horse," the Jacquerie bloodier and bloodier as they sharpen their knives on the grindstone under Lucie's window; Gaffer Hexam pulling bodies out of the Thames, the dialogues in *erlebte Rede* between Tulkinghorn and the Dedlocks, Mrs. Merdle's parrot gazing at her "as if he took her for another splendid parrot of a larger species." It is not that such things never happen in ordinary life, nor that they often happen, for we are in another realm altogether, where they *are* happening.

# 6

# Faith in Dreams:

# Some Notes on the Victorians

FOR the most part, men who act as if they were living in a dream (including, of course, some of our greatest prophets) end up in hospitals, asylums, and jails. Dickens was not a dreamer of this sort. Artists may be allowed to live out their dreams in their work, so long as their visions seem sufficiently dissociated from reality to leave the status quo undisturbed. Unlike some writers—Blake and Yeats for example—Dickens does not fit into the category of pure visionaries, for his dreaming is more grounded in a point-by-point specification of the way the world actually seems to be; nor does he offer, in the manner of the Victorian sage, any final recommendations for a better world—any utopian or mythic image of the past or future. His only advice is to live better in this one. And yet Dickens does not quite accept the world around him, but assumes the distorting dreamer's stance in dealing with it. He cannot accept his world, yet equally he cannot reject it or imagine a better one.

However much Dickens' dream world may appear to stem from his personal inability to find or place himself, in the final analysis his difficulty is not merely private: it is the dilemma of the age—an age of greatness also unable to define itself—and his appeal to his contemporaries is largely owing to the typicality of the plight in which his heroes find themselves. What sort of age was it that could foster and nourish a genius like Dickens', and hunger after the dream world of his novels with such unexampled voracity?

It is not really very important what name we give to the literary manner in which Dickens works; I have suggested "super-naturalism" as appropriate, but other names would do as well. Nor is the dream analogy itself the only possible means of delineating this literary manner, even though it is extremely useful, as I hope by now to have demonstrated. The essential characteristics of the manner remain in any case. In moving now to a discussion of Dickens' place in literary and cultural history, I shall continue to rely on the analogy to dream, as a means of connecting Dickens' manner with the problems of his age, his stance with that of other artists and thinkers, his style with his enormous popular success among Victorian readers. Such relations could be shown without reference to dreams, but since the questions to be raised now are of broader cultural and historical import, the analogy has more significance in its own right, *what-is-like-dream* being, from a social historian's point of view, a convenient category for the study of activities in which men engage. In examining these broader questions of culture and society, I shall limit my attention to such aspects of the Victorian period as seem particularly relevant to Dickens' style and manner. In so brief a compass I could not present anything like a fair or balanced picture of the age. But I do hope to offer a way of looking at a number of curious Victorian phenomena so that they may become more comprehensible, more of a piece, than they ordinarily appear to be.

Not only do these phenomena shed light on Dickens' means and purposes as an artist—his work being a reflection of his age, with its problems and its possibilities—but also, by the same token, the quality and texture of Victorian life may also be illuminated when seen in relation to his special appeal to his contemporaries.

### Representationalism and Escapism: Fact and Fancy

Confronted with the Victorian world, Dickens neither made an intellectual peace with it, as George Eliot seems to have done, nor retreated from it into the lyricism of a Tennyson or the historicism of a Browning. He accepted enough of it to be able to name its parts, even taking great pains to specify them with a literalism of imagination verging on the naturalistic; yet he was also alienated from his world, and so refused to perform the ultimate artistic act of integrating the parts, of evaluating and passing judgment on reality. Of course I do not mean that he took no stands in his novels; he was always taking stands—for charity and justice and good will, against the delays of the law, or the worship of money and power, or the excesses of tyranny and rebellion. Yet, at the heart of his style, as he named off the components of everyday reality—the furnishings of a room, the habits of a man, the mechanics of an institution—he did not distinguish the important from the unimportant, the necessary from the inconsequential. Everything is potentially crucial in his world; since the slightest detail may turn out to be the key to a mystery, nothing is really judged or evaluated as essential or trivial. Dickens knew what he loved or hated well enough, but he seems, on the evidence of his whole literary technique, to have been unwilling either to embrace or to discard a single bit of concrete reality. For him, the world is in pieces, and he can find no trustworthy organizing principle to help him decide which pieces are worth talking about, which not. In such a dilemma, he is already well on the road to the world of dream.

The age itself provides plenty of examples of the collector's mania which we observe in Dickens, the delight in circumstance for its own sake, for the comfort of knowing that at least *there are things.* This worship of fact and event goes by many names—materialism, naturalism, representationalism, historicism, scientism—each emphasizing a slightly different bias of the same instinct. Finding the world more and more complicated than one thought, and simultaneously finding oneself less and less able to account for its multiplicity by means of a single set of values or a single intellectual system—faced, in other words, with loss of faith in the integrity of reality—one can either renounce the world entirely (madness or suicide) or accept it entirely, without distinction or hierarchy. The latter is the choice of compromise and eclecticism, not so much a choice at all as it is a paralysis of the will.* Ultimately one makes a virtue of necessity: thus the view that in data reside truth and wholeness, that things-as-they-are, being all there is, must be reality—for what else could we mean by "reality"! The inclination of the time seems, so far as such things can be pinned down at all, very much toward acquiescing and even delighting in the allegiance to fact. Material improvements in the conditions of life had a good deal to do with this acceptance—there is nothing so welcome as food and clothing for the poor, or plumbing for the middle classes. Such a welter of ameliorations and amenities might do much to keep one's attention from the condition of his heart and soul. Progress meant Things, as the Crystal Palace emphatically

*It is *not* choosing not-to-choose—the position, I take it, of much Eastern philosophy—but choosing-and-not-choosing, a shifty relativism.

declared. No doubt much of it was progress indeed, goods that were truly goods; but as fast as bellies and eyes filled, palates and tastes jaded without being sated, so that "goods" lost their use and value, and things were not always what they seemed. People went in for imitation things, flowers that turned out to be iron candelabra, bookcases that turned out to be painted doors (Dickens had such a door in his own house).* In the Victorian parlor, almost anything might turn out to be a papier-mâché imitation of something else. At the beginning of the century Londoners marveled at Daguerre's diorama, which made reality seem rather a poor show by comparison; they took similarly to panoramas, magic lanterns, stereopticons; by the end of the century the stereoscope had made the wonders of Niagara Falls and the Killarney Lakes available in every Victorian household. This is no simple materialism—enjoyment of things themselves—but a perverse delight in the thingness of things, in appearances, even, finally, in Pecksniffian hypocrisy.

The enormous vogue of photography, after its introduction to the public in 1839, is a particularly clear indication of the Victorian taste for imitation and representation, copies of things. In the popular mind, a daguerreotype, calotype, or ambrotype was superior to a drawing or painting simply because one could be sure that its subject had somewhere its own substantial reality, and that the camera's attention had been focused on that, whereas the painter, no matter how meticulous a representationalist, could never achieve the automatic response to his subject that guaranteed authenticity, the thingness of the thing. Paintings were things-in-themselves, whereas a daguerreotype, for all its own metallic beauty, was

*Done with flair this sort of imitation is not representationalism but Art Nouveau—a return to technique. In his private life—his dress, his letters—Dickens sometimes played the Dandy, but not in his fiction.

less an object than it was a magical window into a world somehow more real than one's own; looking at even the most literal of paintings, one was still conscious of the virtuosity of the artist. (How *does* he make it seem so real!)

So far as early photography catered in this way to popular taste the artists and critics who attacked the new medium as non- or even anti-artistic were surely right. Their point was that the medium afforded too little play for the artist's hand and mind, and of course this limitation, seen as a guarantee of fidelity to the object, was exactly what made Daguerre's invention such a success with the public. But many artists and critics welcomed photography (some of them, like David Octavius Hill, even had a part in its technical development). This is not surprising, in view of the predominance of representationalist painters, who in their own works strove chiefly for "photographic" accuracy and elaboration of detail, and who were quick to see the advantages of using photographs as models for their painstaking copies of real life—especially their panoramic scenes like Frith's *Derby Day*, on seeing which Oscar Wilde is supposed to have exclaimed, "And was it all done by hand!"[60] To twist another of Wilde's sharp phrases, art tried to imitate photography, especially that self-effacing quality which promotes the object at the expense of imagination and style. This tendency is seen not only in the passion for realistic detail, but also in the choice of subject matter—portraits, historical paintings, the "social realism" of Holman Hunt and the faithful-dog genre of Landseer. The importance to painters of the photographic ideal is strikingly illustrated in those anecdotal paintings where the action is arrested as in a snapshot (or "instantaneous photograph," as it was originally called); Hunt's *Awakening Conscience*, for example, shows the dissolute young man still singing, unaware of the change of heart in his paramour, who is "snapped" midway as she rises from his lap, in a position whose awkwardness curiously anticipates Muybridge's discoveries when—twenty years later—he used lens and shutter to capture a galloping horse with all four feet in the air—not, as painters had always thought, stretched out in front and behind like a hobbyhorse, but tightly drawn up under it. It is merely an accident of technology that painters were the first to record this sort of fleeting moment*; the coincidence of interest in this aspect of reality is not to be explained by any influence of photography on painting, or vice versa, but by the general hunger of artists, photographers, and the public alike for representations of real things, bits of truth which might be hung on the walls as a mirror of their own world, only more so.

Voyeurism and the quest for vicarious experience—always advertised as culturally broadening—are clearly at the heart of these preferences for realistic technique and subject matter, just as they are the source of the popularity of photography and representational painting in all their nineteenth-century drapings—the documentarianism and the exoticism, the sentimentalism and the lubricity, the hero-worshiping portraiture and the deathbed commemorations of the village daguerreotypist. The hunger for things, once sated, shifts and fades into an appetite for the mere thingness of things, a wish to have one's own immediacy soothed out of existence and replaced by a ready-made, vicarious world where the old struggles and passions can still be thinly tasted, but without commitment or risk. The Victorian attitude toward photography and

*Actually Fox Talbot's experiments with "flash" photography antedate *The Awakening Conscience* by a few years, but of course other painters had been in the field earlier, and instantaneous photography was extremely difficult until dry plates became practical in the seventies, when Muybridge did his work.

painting has its parallels in every area of nineteenth-century culture, but the example from the plastic arts illustrates the point best, since it emphasizes how a fanatically representational realism provides, as an every-ready alternative to the daily life of routine fact, a substitute world in which one can easily believe, for the sake of some drab, secondhand feeling.

Although Dickens does not fit into this class of representational artists (Trollope would be a better example), he does share certain traits with them. Thus his fondness for elaborate and minutely rendered detail seems to spring, like theirs, from an interest in things not so much for their own sake as for their "thingness," their membership in the class of tangibles or visibles—an interest seen at its most refined, perhaps, in what Orwell calls Dickens' "unnecessary detail." Similarly, the representationalist's concern to efface himself, to make his medium a totally transparent lens for the transmission of the look of things, as if they presented themselves directly to the viewer with no intermediate distorting consciousness, corresponds to Dickens' reluctance to take a hand in his novels, his withdrawn, camera-eye narrator, and his view of reality as offering (or not offering) itself to him, through no choice of his. And finally, the role-playing, which results from Dickens' taking himself as actor (of all the parts) rather than agent, matches the representationalist quest for vicarious experience, the anecdotal, "literary" approach to subject matter, indeed the whole crabbed view of the mimetic function of art. These similarities help to place Dickens as a Victorian artist, responding to the difficulties of the time in a characteristic way; but Dickens is not purely characteristic of his age, nor is its way entirely his. In spite of his lavish use of detail and his literalness of vision, his peculiarly disembodied narrative stance, and his unwillingness to place himself, Dickens does not create a representationalist world. On the contrary, his world is romantic, fantastic, even mad; in it objects take on human qualities, characters shrink to things; the perspective is askew, with the vantage point at once in and out of the scene; Dickens' vision combines literal report with magic and miracle, as in dreams. This can scarcely be described as acceptance of things-as-they-are, what we sometimes call "being realistic."

In *Hard Times* Dickens gives his own judgment of the popular deification of fact—which he sees as a debased utilitarianism—"Gradgrindism." The crucial passage, I suppose, is the opening scene in the schoolroom, where Sissy Jupe and Bitzer, the representatives of fancy and fact, are asked for their definitions of "horse." Because she has not been raised in the Gradgrind school of Hard Facts (her father "belongs to the horse-riding, if you please, Sir"), Sissy is unable to regurgitate the little pellets of information that constitute Bitzer's experience of "horse"—

Quadruped. Graminivorous. Forty teeth, namely twenty-four grinders, four eye-teeth, and twelve incisive. Sheds coat in the spring; in marshy countries, sheds hoofs, too. Hoofs hard, but requiring to be shod with iron. Age known by marks in mouth

—but Sissy clearly *knows* what a horse is, and knows it in a way that Bitzer cannot even comprehend, not as "factual" data abstracted from life, but as past and present experience of the real thing, met at first hand in daily life. When Dickens sets up his dichotomy between fact and fancy at the beginning of *Hard Times*, he has in mind some such distinction between what is known only vicariously and what has been humanly experienced. The same principle is applied to Coketown itself, where "what you couldn't state in figures, or show to be purchaseable in the cheapest market and saleable in the dearest, was not [Fact], and never should be, world without end, Amen" (1, v). The emphasis in this passage is not, as it may seem without its full context, merely on the money-grubbing of laissez-faire capitalists, but on the view of reality which underlies this greed—that only what can be labeled, classed, and tabulated has a meaningful existence. Dickens' charge is that his generation lives out of touch with reality, having put its trust in abstractions—data, rules and forms, money, empty superstructures of bureaucracy and tradition—rather than in concrete experience.

In other terms, the dichotomy between fact and fancy may be regarded as a split between belief (in what is) and desire (for what might or ought to be). Gradgrind and his school stand for the indicative mood of science and the system, while Sissy Jupe and Sleary's Horse-riding circus stand for the subjunctive/imperative of the imagination and morality. Stated in this way, it becomes clear just how desperate the case is: once the wedge is driven between fact and fancy, the whole of life is split down the middle. If one can believe only in facts, and desire only fancy, then one can no longer desire what is, or believe in what might be. Of course the split is never so absolute or life would be intolerable; but insofar as fact and fancy are regarded as antagonistic and mutually exclusive, the necessary result is the world of Coketown, where feeling no longer comes naturally but must be primed and pumped, where sentiment becomes sentimentality, where reform is humbug and there is no fervor in truth. It is appropriate that Dickens' only "industrial novel" should be his sharpest delineation of the split between fact and fancy, because these are the familiar problems of industrial society. The overlaying and obscuring of desire by the amelioration of physical want produce a deadening acceptance of and thus a lack of interest in things as they are. With the growth of specialization and economic bureaucracy, contact with the means of subsistence diminishes. Laissez-faire principles lead ironically to a sense of helplessness concerning one's own destiny, and finally—as a substitute for self-sufficiency—to a voyeuristic and narcissistic desire to play the passive audience to one's own dismal fate. This is a grim picture, but no more so than Dickens himself found it to be. For the representationalist there may be a face-saving consolation in accepting the facts, and by imitating them with meticulous care he may achieve a kind of identification with them. But Dickens can so little accept things as they are that even the look of his own face in the mirror revolts him; and yet no other way of life—as imagined, for example, in plays or poems—is believed possible; one *must* face the facts, for all else is merely imaginary, a pale fantasy which, if actually put to the test, would solidify into the same reality of cold brute circumstance (it is the horrific vision of Keats' "Lamia").

In *Hard Times* Dickens' grappling with the split between fact and fancy, between belief and desire, is a failure so far as plot and theme are concerned; he is unable to imagine a better world than the one he knows; Sleary's Horse-riding is hardly an alternative to Coketown factuality. In his use of the term "fancy" to stand for the realm of human feeling, of real experience—not "hard" facts, but "true," "brute" facts— Dickens apparently wants to say that if only one will pay attention to what fancy really is—a concern with what is truer than any fact—all our troubles will vanish. In a sense, he is suggesting that the way across the chasm between fact and fancy is to refuse to admit its existence. Yet at the same time he maintains the dichotomy; he too has fallen into the chasm, and advises us to climb out on the other side, the side of fancy, although he gives us no footing there. He knows well enough what knuckling under to fact means—the M'Choak-umchild school, Coketown, and all the rest—but fancy, our supposed deliverance, is thinly conceived, turns out at the end of the book to consist of nothing more than *not* looking the real facts in the face. In the epilogue to *Hard Times*, the characters are meted out their rewards and punishments: everyone gets what he deserves, namely the very life he has chosen to live—except for those anonymous creatures, the Hands in the factories of Coketown. who are consigned to the dirty red-brick buildings, and for whom Dickens can offer only the tender sympathy of Louisa Gradgrind, who is "to beautify their lives of machinery and reality with those imaginative graces and delights, without which the heart of infancy will wither up." This is what his Fancy finally comes to, a sugarwater glaze over the facts rather than a real facing of them. The notion of Louisa, her own life ruined by an unfortunate marriage, dedicating herself to making the lives of the Coketown Hands more palatable appeals to Dickens because it frees him from an impasse which appears again and again in his novels: the state of the poor and oppressed being as he has vividly and accurately described it, what possible relief can he envision for them? He does not trust the lower classes to make their own better world, nor does he imagine that legislative measures can really help; on the other hand, he continues to indulge a favorite daydream of the happy poor (Bob Cratchit, Joe Gargery, Caddy Jellyby Turveydrop), and when the impasse is inevitably reached at the end of a novel like *Hard Times*, this fantasy becomes the sole escape from the grim truth. For all his skill in describing the awful facts which give rise to the problem, Dickens is characteristically unable to imagine the practical details of his fantasy solution, and the lack of conviction is heard in the rhetoric, which combines the wheedling, promissory cadences of political oratory with the ritual harmonies of happily-ever-after. Just as he cannot desire what he believes are the facts, so he cannot believe in what his fancy desires.

The difficulty Dickens always encounters in imagining any reform of the abuses he writes about stems from this same dichotomy between belief and desire, for the imagination cannot invent solutions out of daydreams alone, any more than the intellect can propose desirable alternatives to conditions which it automatically judges not so much intolerable as inevitable.

The hallmark of nineteenth-century reform is its oscillation between sentimental hopefulness and hardheaded expediency. The Victorians, or at any rate some of them, still had notions about things-as-they-might-be or ought-to-be, so that while the nineteenth century is a great age of compromise, it is also a great age of utopias—though it is noteworthy that the utopian schemes of the period are more and more historically oriented, grounded in data and theories of data in such a way that they cannot result in anything more than "progressive" elaborations and projections of the status quo, or returns to some idealized status quo of the past. Even the notion, which persists into our own day, that utopias can only prove themselves by their durability (as if man could devise a way of life that would always suit him) is evidence of the century's desperate search for a system which would not only conform to the facts of life as they were then accepted, but also provide some moral imperatives of order and stability—with hierarchy, absolute touchstones of principle, and the like—in accord with those facts. But such a unification of the Is and the Ought, although still a possibility for some Victorians, was out of the question for Dickens, the energy of whose faith is used up in angry contemplation of things as they are, so that his vision of how things might be seems naive, out of touch with reality, and wavering in conviction.

*Hard Times* tests two different ways of coping with the

split between belief in facts and desire for fancies. One may stand for the way things are; this is the posture of Gradgrind and Bounderby, and it is equivalent to the representationalist position in Victorian art and culture, which eventuates stylistically in Bitzer's definition of "horse." Dickens rejects this solution to the dichotomy between belief and desire, and tries the alternative, the elevation of fancy over fact. This is the running stance of escapist literature, or the romantic vision of the greatest gothicists; there are as many ways of avoiding or dismissing facts as there are of embracing them. Actually, Dickens never really takes this direction, even though he does sometimes fall into it in the final chapters of his novels; indeed, no important English artist worked with fantasy in any of its extreme forms until late in the century, when attitudes like those of Beardsley and Wilde came into vogue.* Nevertheless the purveyors of fact and the apologists for the status quo had their opposite numbers in the flabby escapism of the lady novelists and the yellowback hacks, who wrote the Victorian equivalents of soap opera and the drugstore pulps.

Both of these varieties of escapist literature are akin to pornography, in their Victorian as well as their modern dress: their essence is the highly stylized presentation of fantasy situations, so totally denuded of texture and context that the characters are always verging on the archetypal, while the situations themselves, in spite of their wish-fulfilling (often taboo) content, seem peculiarly unequal to the emo-

---

*In America there were true fantasts, like Poe and Hawthorne, who must be taken seriously, but they had no English counterparts. In painting, Blake and Fuseli are surely great masters of fantastic art, but their example had only admirers, no successors (the dying out can be seen most poignantly in Blake's pupil, Samuel Palmer, whose genius unaccountably expired in midcareer).

tional response demanded of the reader, not so much because of the crudely abstract handling as because of a smell of insincerity and pretense that clings to the very language in which they are couched. Sentimental and sensational writers, having narrowed the world to a few paradigm cases abstracted from fantasy and daydreams, find themselves strangely unable to feel even these powerfully distilled situations (precisely because of their divorce from everyday life), and therefore, to compensate for the loss of affect, they lard their prose with the appropriate clichés of excitement and feeling—as some nineteenth-century sculptors painted blushes on their statues, with waxworklike results. The imposition of feeling not really felt is what distinguishes sentimentality from sentiment, sensationalism from sensation: when the writer begins not with concrete instances but with abstract formulas of fantasy and desire, the way to belief in the fantasy is blocked, there are no "objective correlatives" of the emotion, and the purported feelings are inevitably in excess of the facts since it is exactly the facts that have been bypassed. What verisimilitude there is in such works is an afterthought, superimposed upon an already conceived situation according to notions of how things might look in this or that case, just as the emotion is troweled on in simulation of how one might feel under those circumstances.

I do not mean to imply that Dickens belongs in the camp of sensationalism and sentimentality any more than he does in the opposite one of the literalists. But it can hardly be denied that his novels are sometimes sentimental or sensational, and in very nearly the way I have described. The end of *Hard Times* is one such sentimental frosting of a cake whose hard-fact ingredients are likely to prove indigestible. Dickens' sensationalism is perhaps an even more curious phenomenon than his sentimentalism, for it has a kind of power rarely found in even the best escape literature. Taken by themselves, the set pieces—Miss Wade's history, Doctor Manette's secret manuscript—are remarkably compelling and not sensationalist in the usual sense, that is to say, not especially forced or rhetorically puffed up. Dickens has no trouble imagining the details of the scene, and one does not feel that the language is loaded with demands for a response in excess of what the facts will bear. It is genuine horror. Nevertheless, when these scenes are examined in context, it becomes clear that they have some kinship with sensationalism, for they are astonishingly out of touch with their context—especially with the plot—and thus betray a disjunction quite similar to that found in typical blood-and-thunder literature. Dickens' unwillingness to bring his major characters into direct contact with sex and violence is no ordinary Victorian squeamishness; he is in some ways the least fastidious of writers, as his numerous scenes of squalor and degradation prove. But certain subjects are taboo for Dickens. That is, although he is continually writing about sex and violence, and even making them the core of motivation in his novels—as for example the outrages committed by the St. Evrémonde brothers—he is unable to integrate them in his plots: they fester behind the action, like a dreadful cancer, or they are encapsulated in the plot, like irritating bits of foreign matter which must be rendered harmless by layers of secretion. In this he is in a tradition which goes back, in English, at least to Spenser and the Bower of Bliss, and which has its great nineteenth-century practitioners in the American gothic manner—Hawthorne's *Scarlet Letter* being an extremely pure example of the type. The peculiarity of Dickens' use of such set pieces is that he is not primarily an allegorist. The consequence is a strangeness in the isolated scenes of violence and outrage: although their relation to the rest of the novel ought always to be explained in terms of plot instead of didactic purpose, the absence of a clear connection with the plot causes the reader instinctively to look for allegorical significance; thus, his expectations having been aroused and disappointed, he is left with an impression comparable to that produced by sensationalism—that the emotional effect of the scene is out of proportion to its circumstantial basis in the plot of the novel. A very clear example of this curious Dickensian trait is the scene in *Great Expectations* where Orlick captures and tries to kill Pip. This episode has puzzled critics because it seems so tangential to the story, although it occurs at a crucial juncture in what is otherwise a very carefully plotted narrative. Actually, the scene fits quite logically into the emotional progress of the novel: Magwitch, who up to this point had represented the violence and evil in Pip's life, just as Joe Gargery stands for serenity and goodness, has, with the revelation of Estella's parentage, suddenly become a "good" father-figure, to whom Pip is bound by love and duty; accepting the good in Magwitch means that Pip will somehow have to face the evil as well, and this is what Orlick provides.

But of course, all of this is completely behind the scenes. The appropriateness of the passage to the present stage of Pip's psychological development no doubt contributes to its power, but the peculiar quality of that power comes from the isolation of the incident from the major threads of plot. Dickens cannot make the violence arise directly out of Pip's character, any more than he can imagine Charles Darnay actually guilty of the sins of his uncle and his father; so the fantasies of evil are displaced, and float on the surface of the story, unattached to its circumstantial probabilities of character or action. Nevertheless, Dickens always grounds even his wildest fantasies in a strong pattern of emotional development, which underlies each novel, so that no matter how irrelevant the scene may be in the sequence of motivation and event, it still seems to have a right to be there. Fact and fancy collide—without being integrated, true enough, but also without either being completely blotted out by the other. The seemingly free-floating lump of violence and passion— like the sluice-house scene in *Great Expectations,* or the secret manuscript in *A Tale of Two Cities*—may be thought of as a kind of Dickensian iceberg, whose basis in repressed desire lies hidden under the calm, reflecting waters of plot and circumstance. Dickens does not manage to find any new synthesis of belief and desire; Orlick is never really integrated into Pip's life, and the placid Darnay is never touched by the brutal passions which break the surface all around him. The characteristic Dickensian handling of fact and fancy consists neither in choosing one in preference to the other, nor in managing any compromise or solution; rather, his success lies in allowing the problem to appear in his work, where it finds statement and embodiment, both a true reflection of the dilemma of his age and also an initial step in coping with it. Not a representationalist or an escapist, he finds a third alternative by separately accepting both belief and desire and binding them together in a single work of art, no matter how mutually repelling they continue to appear.

## The Collision of Belief and Desire

We have already seen in some detail the way in which Dickens brought fact and fancy together in his novels—a juxtaposition that is, after all, at the center of my analysis of his style, and may be regarded as the basis of the set of paradoxes (the photographic realism used to present a fantastic, magical world; the combined immediacy and detachment of the point of view; and so on) that are accounted for by the analogy to dream. His use of metonymy (interest in the details of things) and metaphor (interest in the alternatives to things) shows precisely the chasm he tried to bridge in his style, and his tendency to collapse the two figures of speech into one—the dream metaphor of the sea-mob or the Marquis' stone face—perfectly illustrates his usual means of connecting the worlds of fact and fancy.

It should now be clear why the dream quality of Dickens' vision is so crucial to understanding his contribution to Victorian culture. Caught between the extremes of total allegiance to fact or to fancy, Dickens found a way of satisfying both claims: he reports the world as he finds it, in all its multitudinous detail, but beneath the verisimilitude of the surface is an undercurrent of emotion which gives rise to strange displacements and distortions in the presented scene, and over all he superimposes a fairy-tale structure, thus making a weird sense out of the hodgepodge of hard, isolated bits of fact which sometimes coalesce in scenes of fiery passion or impossible fantasy. He does not provide an escapist daydream; rather he sees *this* world as though in a dream.

Dickens was not the only Victorian who, refusing to choose either fact or fancy, attempted to find some new adjustment of their claims. There are many parallels to his dreamer's stance in nineteenth-century art and culture, though none of them is so successful, either in managing a convincing blend of belief and desire, or in attuning that blend to the needs of a large popular audience. It will be useful to examine some of these parallels, if only in order to place Dickens more securely in the context of his age, and to see just what it was that ensured him a popularity unmatched in his time by any other great artist.

Although representationalism dominated the public taste, it is also true that sentimentalism and sensationalism—es-

capist tendencies basically opposed to the acceptance of fact—
were widely popular, and especially so in literature, while
the literalists held sway in the plastic arts and the sciences.
But what is notable about many of the men who attempted to
force belief and desire back together is their interest in
various combinations or juxtapositions of the arts and
sciences, as if the chasm could be closed merely by making a
new integration between, say, painting and poetry, or science
and literature. One thinks, for example, of Rossetti and
Morris, of Mill's *Autobiography*, of the remarkable illustrations made for Tennyson's poems by the Pre-Raphaelites
(woodcuts) and Julia Margaret Cameron (photographs), of
Lewis Carroll's fantasies of logic and mathematics, of Lear's
nonsense verse and drawings. The characteristic tone of these
different approaches to the unification of fact and fancy is
beautifully exemplified in the general culture by the fad of
pseudo-science, as varied a stew of science, moralizing, show-
manship, art, religion, and everything else as one could ask for.

Emerson, who had a keen sense of the spirit of his age,
makes some very interesting observations on the great popularity of such things as mesmerism, physiognomy, and phrenology, during the early and middle parts of the century:

It [pseudo-science] was human, it was genial, it affirmed unity
and connection between remote points, and as such was excellent
criticism on the narrow and dead classification of what passed
for science; and the joy with which it was greeted was an instinct
of the people which no true philosopher would fail to profit
by.... The popularity of Combe's Constitution of Man; the
humanity which was the aim of all the multitudinous works of
Dickens; the tendency even of Punch's caricature, was all on the
side of the people. There was a breath of new air, much vague
expectation, a consciousness of power not yet finding its deter-
minate aim.[61]

271

It is impossible to praise Emerson too highly for his insight here. Not only does he point out the connection between the Scottish phrenologist George Combe, Dickens' "humanity," and nineteenth-century caricature, but he also understands why those particular aspects of Victorian culture were so popular. The "remote points" connected by the pseudo-sciences are the poles of fact and fancy, as is indicated by Emerson's reference to an obvious instance of one side of the dichotomy, "the narrow and dead classification of what passed for science." What the pseudo-sciences attempted was a marriage of science and ethics, which was to give rise to a spiritualized kind of progress.

Phrenology and mesmerism today seem rather odd blends of hard- and soft-headedness, on the one hand comprising some of the best physiological and psychological thinking of the century, and on the other producing examples of gullibility, self-deception, and charlatanism matched only by our own Madison Avenue. Emerson and other reluctant admirers, while condemning the large measure of magic in the new disciplines, nevertheless found themselves attracted by the attempt to construct a science of man that would have room for both the moral imperatives and the mysteries which religion could no longer supply.* Emerson called Combe's *Constitution of Man* "the best Sermon I have read for some time," and in a letter to Combe William Ellery Channing reported a widespread intellectual reaction to it, "that the book is excellent, in spite of its phrenology."[62] Nor is there any doubt that the pseudo-scientific movement was, in fact, a new kind

---

*It is probably more than merely an irony that both Wallace and Darwin were converts, Wallace to both mesmerism and phrenology, Darwin to a genuinely scientific version of physiognomy, stemming from the physiological research of Sir Charles Bell and culminating in Darwin's classic *Expression of the Emotions in Man and Animals.*

of evangelicalism. The uplifting exhortations of Combe and his predecessor Spurzheim gave men like Horace Mann what seemed to be a scientific basis for an idealistic vision of the future; while as stubborn a mind as Harriet Martineau's might greedily accept Dr. John Elliotson's experiments in mesmerism as evidence of a supernatural world and as sufficient justification for a moral and spiritual crusade; and capping it all, the popular enthusiasm for the new sciences resembles nothing so much as religious revivalism—typically flavored in its later stages by a good dose of humbug.

The scientific credentials of such theorists as Gall, Spurzheim, Combe, Elliotson, and Braid gave a stamp of authority to the hopes and plans of all sorts of visionaries—educators, prison and asylum reformers, spiritualists, medical researchers—who used the pliable doctrines for their own pet projects. Especially appealing to its practitioners and its public alike was the divinatory power which seemed to belong to pseudo-science: by examining a young man's skull or putting him into a mesmeric trance, one might discover whether or not he would be a great scholar, or even whether it would rain on Sunday. The transition from what-is to what-might-be became one from what-is to what-will-be with the advantage over ordinary scientific prediction that one could very nearly write one's own ticket for the will-be. It was the answer to the reformer's prayer. Certain religious men felt in all this an encroachment on their own territory, and objected strongly to the determinism they recognized at the bottom of it; but only the shell of method was deterministic—the movement from evidence to promise generally had little to do with any systematic rules of cause and effect. What truths the pseudo-scientists had gotten on to—the principle of localization of some kinds of brain activity, the potentialities of hypnosis for anesthesia and "recall"—were the result of guesswork or unavoidable observation, and although these potentialities have proved themselves in the course of time (the claims made for them even in these areas continue to be pared down), very little else has remained, excepting only our continued fascination with visions of a reformed future based in some vague and rather magical way on science—namely, with science fiction.

Dickens himself is known to have been an expert mesmerist, though he does not seem to have taken much of the corollary spiritualism very seriously—but this is not the main point of Emerson's lumping of the pseudo-sciences with Dickens' "humanity." It begins to make sense, rather, when we compare Dickens' habits of style with those of modern science-fiction writers; so many similarities appear that it is not too far-fetched to say that his novels are in some ways the contemporary literary equivalent of pseudo-science, just as science fiction is its literary legacy. The emphasis on lavishly elaborated detail, the animism and its opposite "dehumanization" (these are carried to their extremes in science-fiction monsters), the pre-eminence of plot over character, the inclination to fantasize marvelous occurrences which are then defended as scientifically verifiable (for instance Krook's spontaneous combustion), the strong reforming instinct (compare the Circumlocution Office with, say, Orwell's Big Brother system, or any of numerous examples)—these analogies show both science fiction (as well as the early pseudo-science) and Dickens' dream fiction depending heavily on a bold juxtaposition of fact and fancy, the world of solid, statistical reality, and the world of mystery, passion, and ideality.

Emerson's use of the word "humanity" reminds us of Dickens' attack on Gradgrindism in *Hard Times*: Dickens had in common with the pseudo-scientists a hatred of the science that leaves human feelings and desires out of account, that lays down tables of statistics as models for the future, without ever asking whether the persons represented by those statistics might not want to change their lives. Furthermore, if insistence on the importance of the realm of feeling and desire was what Emerson understood by Dickens' "humanity," this does not close the door to still another, more literal application of the term, to Dickens' characters themselves, each of whom is individually an instance of his refusal to take human beings as mere facts, products of a million tiny stimuli in a totally conditioned world of statistical probability.

It would appear that Emerson must have the Dickensian grotesque in mind when he talks about his "humanity," since this is the link with the caricature in *Punch*. Nineteenth-century caricature is an interesting phenomenon precisely because it is so much at odds with the representationalist tendencies of the time. To our perception and understanding, Dickens' characters both as he describes them and as they appear in the illustrations for his books—especially those of George Cruikshank, perhaps the greatest of Victorian caricaturists—may seem exaggerated, not at all like humanity as we know it. But for the artists who invent such figures, caricature is character truly seen, not according to conventions of perspective and proportion, but according to active experience and knowledge of people. Thus, for example, Dickens is always recommending to his illustrators that they go and have a look at this or that real person, who is just like Mr. Fang or Mr. Dombey or Podsnap. If the final result seems exaggerated, it is no more so than the gruesome illustrations which fill the phrenological and physiognomical texts, purporting to represent the features of famous men (even the photographs that illustrate Darwin's *Expression of the Emotions* are hardly credible as images of real people). In all

these cases, the caricature is a product of conflicting intentions—at once to ground the interpretation in scientific ob-
jectivity and also to be true to the moral and emotional constitution of the character presented. The strange impression
one gets in looking at the work of Cruikshank or Tenniel, that
somehow realism and fantasy have been clamped together in
a single style, without being integrated, comes from their
elaborate use of detail, their strict definition of line, light,
and shadow, and their careful filling in of background—all in
order to convey an emotion, a settled disposition of feeling,
a "human" quality, which is conceived abstractly, indeed
fantasized, and thus is strangely at odds with the very medium.
Everything seems exaggerated and distorted because there
is a gap between the means (realistic, scientific, factual) and
the message (moralistic, emotional, fantastic). As in Alice's
Wonderland, a mushroom is really a mushroom but may
still have a caterpillar perched on it, smoking a hookah.

In any other age I suppose it would not be appropriate to
call all this an emphasis on "humanity," but with the Victorians' desperate need to reunite the worlds of belief and
desire, even so weird a vision of reality may seem humane and
humanitarian in its attempt to trace the mysteries of feeling
with rule and compass. The attempt is largely unsuccessful,
whether in the pseudo-sciences or in literary and graphic
caricature, because one cannot simply force the two worlds
back together; desire must grow out of belief, and belief must
draw its energy from desire, else neither is satisfying. The
reunion of the Is and the Ought or Might-be could not be
wished for, of course, unless a gap were felt between them; and
simply because the gap *was* felt, there could not be any
genuine synthesis, since that would have to consist precisely
in there being no gap felt. It is a genuine dilemma, and the
age was ill-equipped to cope with it. Traditional humanism

was scarcely possible, for it no longer seemed that man controlled his own destiny. The Victorian age was a remarkably eclectic one, a great age of fragmentation and tolerance, of allowing for variety and idiosyncrasy, of belief in many ways to the Celestial City; yet at the same time it was an age of unbelief, of self-distrust, compromise, unwillingness to take a chance. The breakdown of the old polarity of free will and predestination, which Buckle celebrates in the opening of his *History of Civilization in England,* is appropriately coupled with the birth of statistical probability, which is nothing more than an attempt to have the best of both worlds.* The resulting relativism was more debilitating to man's hope than the strictest absolutism, since it did away with both duty and reward, leaving habit and circumstance in the place of faith, fantasy and madness where there once had been desire. George Eliot, the great literary apologist for nineteenth-century relativism, admits the inevitability of failure, the hopelessness of all our visions, with a wise acceptance, and she even finds some cheer in the belief that our failures are such ordinary things as not to deserve the name of tragedy. Too many tiny influences operate in any man's life for him to do much about them, yet their very numerousness also makes anything possible—so one settles down like Fred Vincy to wait for old Featherstone's will to be opened. But those who strive win no greater victory: Tertius Lydgate might as well take satisfaction in having a pretty wife, since his youthful schemes must have come to naught anyway, had Rosamond Vincy been ever so ugly; and Dorothea Brooke is

*One of the reasons for the failure of the pseudo-sciences is this scientific relativism, a strange combination of the outdated determinism and free will; thus the phrenologists thought a man might enlarge any of his faculties—and hence the cranial manifestations of the appropriate organs—by "moral exercise."

apparently to be admired for finally recognizing her fate in Will Ladislaw, a paltry, charming version of Mr. Casaubon himself. Instead of an unopened will, the promise of the future turns out to be, like Dorothea's marriage, a contract with loopholes.

With the loss of the old absolutes went not merely a denial of the reality of evil, but also an inability to believe in any good. One believed in Progress instead. Dickens has not yet come to this pass, though he is on the verge of it sometimes. He tries to keep up his reader's (and his own) belief in the goodness and sweetness of life as his heroines always deserve it. Of course no one is fooled nowadays, and we suspect Dickens himself of remaining unconvinced when we hear how hollow the rhetoric rings at the crucial moment of married bliss. Still there is genuine feeling, beyond mere sentimentality, in Dickens' rage and tears at the death of poor Jo, or Little Nell, where at least some loss is felt, the end of promise and hope. (In George Eliot, such losses become a matter of course, and instead of mourning we are advised to retrench, by expecting less next time.)

The willing acceptance of loss is one of the most common symptoms of the Victorian failure to reconcile belief and desire. It is what one pays for the mystique of Progress. This transaction of the spirit is seen at its extreme in Tennyson, whose poetry veers extravagantly between the poles of wistful lyricism and a fat, complacent idyllicism. With his interest in mesmerism and photography, his memory for little authentic details, his romanticism, and his bourgeois tastes, Tennyson had much in common with Dickens and was in many ways equipped to satisfy the popular appetite for dream-reality. But in his poems belief and desire do not often come together as they must to produce the characteristic feeling of dream. In a few very exciting poems—"Maud" and "Lucretius," for instance—he manages to hold all the necessary elements in solution, but most of his work splits into either, on the one hand, yearning for a lost mythic paradise—desired but no longer believed in, so that there is a compulsive concern with technique, to enforce resignation—or, on the other hand, apologetics for the status quo—believed in but not much desired, as the drugged, flatfooted quality of the verse itself suggests. *In Memoriam* brings the two together in a revealing configuration: Hallam's loss is finally made good when Tennyson gives himself up to a thinly realized mythic world (here Christian rather than pagan), and after that comes the typical Victorian happy ending, marriage, and an uninspired affirmation of Progress—he confidently (but without apparent joy) awaits "the crowning race/ Of those that, eye to eye, shall look/ On knowledge.../ No longer half-akin to brute...,/ Whereof the man [Hallam], that with me trod/ This planet, was a noble type/ Appearing ere the times were ripe...."

Tennyson's most interesting poems are those that combine the sensuous and fantastic qualities of his lyric style with the narrative and dramatic structure of his domestic idyls. The result never has the wholeness of form that he achieved in his lesser verse, but the fragmented and hallucinatory "Maud," to name the best example, has a power beyond anything else he ever wrote. It stands in the same relation to most of his other verse as "Childe Roland" does to Browning's; in both, the poet has dropped his usual manner to produce a masterpiece of the realistic-fantastic. In contrast, Dickens might be said to dwell habitually in the realm of dream, with occasional lapses into sentimentalism or unearned optimism (though he rarely succumbs to the historicism that so enthralled Browning).

Tennyson's illustrators furnish an interesting range of parallels to his various poetic postures. Some of the Pre-Raphaelite painters had hit upon a formula that combined representationalist precision and authenticity of detail with romantic, dreamlike conceptions—although the degree to which they took Ruskin's advice that they should ground their fancies and moralities in botany varied from artist to artist. Thus Millais' illustrations perfectly suit such poems as "Dora" and "Locksley Hall"; Hunt's are just right for "The Lady of Shalott"; and Rossetti is brilliantly successful with "The Palace of Art" and might have done a great "Maud," as indeed he did produce a drawing of Tennyson reading the poem which gets its tone marvelously. Rossetti is by far the most in tune with Tennyson's fantastic mood, no doubt because his own bent was toward the same combination of realism and romanticism. His imagination turned not merely to gothic subjects, but especially to situations fundamentally magical—that is, situations in which some spiritual meaning is in the process of being materialized, as for example in his greatest painting, *The Annunciation*, or his weird drawing of "How They Met Themselves," the *Doppelgänger* legend pictorialized. Rossetti is fascinated with moments of sudden possession, of epiphany, of translation from physical to spiritual or from spiritual to physical; and almost all his work has an open-mouthed ecstasy about it.

A distinction ought to be made here between Rossetti's major and minor works, as between those of Tennyson. There is a failure in taste that runs through almost every major effort Rossetti made in painting or poetry, which I suppose must be put down to the inadequacy of his technique to the conception he attempted. Wishing as he does to portray the very moment of transfiguration, he is torn between the real and the ideal, and cannot choose, so that his figures are strangely both ethereal and earthy, not—as in, say, Botticelli—to the enhancement of each, but rather with the effect of cheapening the spiritual and devitalizing the animal nature. Rossetti painted moments of ecstasy, one guesses, in order to live them vicariously (his endless portraits of Elizabeth Siddal, Jane Morris, and Fanny Cornforth impress me as extremely voyeuristic); but this suggests that he did not himself experience the union of the physical and spiritual which he tried to portray. His technique betrays exactly such a failure of integration; the spiritual quality never grows out of the concrete instance, out of the painstaking attention to detail (although that attention surely was given), but rather seems to be painted in as an afterthought, contrived by means of cluttered and cloudy backgrounds, auras of light, allegorical props, a whole bag of tricks all curiously inappropriate to the realistic underpainting.* The same tasteless juxtaposition vitiates much of Rossetti's poetry; the Blessed Damozel, with her realistic bosom warming the coldly allegorical bar of heaven, is an especially clear case, since the same composite of verisimilitude and fantasy may be seen both in the poetry and in the painting which matches it. Even in his own life Rossetti was guilty of the same bad taste, as in his attempt to unite this world and the next by burying the manuscripts of his poems with his wife's body—only to have them dug up later for publication.

But if Rossetti failed rather consistently in his major efforts to achieve the dreamlike combination of the real and the ideal, many of his minor attempts are relatively success-

---

*I say "underpainting" instead of "veneer" because Rossetti seems to differ most strikingly from Hunt and others in just this—that he tries to spiritualize the physical, while their attempt is to clothe some poor, naked spiritual meaning in a nice warm overcoat. Thus one always feels the model lurking in the depths of Rossetti's work, though it is less realistic than Hunt's.

ful. He is at his best as an illustrator, probably because there he did not use models and thus could escape into a world more allegorical and magical than was possible for him when he had his eye on flesh and blood. There is still plenty of careful detailing in the illustrations—the backgrounds are if anything even more cluttered—but the verisimilitude is replaced by something closer to the intellectual concreteness of allegory. His designs for "Goblin Market," for instance, are nicely adjusted to the tone of his sister's poem, which is not quite allegorical but rather like fairy tale, magic, and dream. It was a style perfectly suited to a wildly gothic fancy, and Rossetti's illustrations for the *Idylls of the King* show what Tennyson might have done with his medievalism if only he had been a little more willing to let himself go.

From this brief analysis of Rossetti's work, and from our earlier glance at caricature, an interesting conception of Victorian art begins to emerge. At least so far as the attempt to reunite fact and fancy is concerned, the more instructive examples are to be found not in painting, which was predominantly representationalist, but in illustration, the area where the literary medium regularly encounters the plastic. It may also be said that the writing most typical of the dream style is highly susceptible to illustration, and it was in fact illustrated profusely. Partly this is an instance of the general feeling in the century—especially among those who experienced the gap between belief and desire most acutely in their own lives—that every effort was to be bent toward the redintegration of all aspects of life. But it is also possible to view the particular juxtapositions of writing and drawing as still another evidence of the need to make art more like dream: writing, by itself, lacked the visual quality that lends conviction to the most fantastic version of reality, whereas drawing, by itself, was unable to render the experience of insubstantiality, the possibility that things may not be what they seem, which is fundamental to the dream world. Of course, there were many ventures toward reuniting belief and desire, or fact and fancy, which did not aim at creating a dreamlike vision of reality. A fuller treatment of the subject would deal with Hopkins, Carlyle, Newman, and Arnold, to mention some of the obvious figures. But my concern has been to notice those aspects of Victorian art and culture with which Dickens has the closest affinity. Remembering that the Pickwick Club had its birth as a mere vehicle for a proposed series of comic drawings, and that throughout his career Dickens worked closely with, and took great pains in choosing, his illustrators, we can see how naturally he falls into place with the artists we have been examining here, not only in his struggle with the poles of fact and fancy, but also in his concern with the representation of his dream-reality in the line and shadow of Cruikshank, "Phiz," and others. Dickens' novels do not need illustration, any more than Tennyson's poems require to be read in the Moxon edition, but that they are perfectly suited to illustration can hardly be disputed; and this suitability may be traced finally to the dreamer's stance which Dickens takes, and especially to his habit of "seeing" all the visible aspects of a scene, his hypostatizing of such scenes, so that they offer themselves to the imagination almost cinematically, in tableaux and "all-at-once."

The whole question of medium, and of the mixing of media, is important to Dickens' peculiar position in Victorian culture, including his tremendous popularity. Not every art form can lend itself to the requirements of dream-making, or to the needs of a public that craves such dreams—increasingly lethargic and complacent in its situation as audience to its own story, instead of actor in it. In Dickens' hands, fiction provided more than a reflection or a comment upon the life led by the ordinary man; it offered an alternative to that life, a world in which he could regularly lose himself, and where his beliefs and desires were embodied and wedded as they rarely could be elsewhere. Fiction offers itself to the creation of such public dreams through its great flexibility and its ability to command total attention while ranging over whole territories of experience and imagination. The author is free to decide whether to present a world of fancy or of fact, or some combination of the two; whether to exercise a high degree of selectivity in the details of the setting, or to include everything that comes to hand and eye, as if without discrimination; whether to create characters that remind us of the way people ordinarily look, or make them grotesques such as we see only in certain moods and states of consciousness; whether to invent actions that seem to grow out of the confrontation of characters and their societies, or to impose abstractly conceived, fairy-tale plots on changeless stock types; whether to tell the reader everything in his own person, or in that of some persona in the story, or leave the tale to "tell itself"; whether, in sum, his novels are to be like dreams, or like some other kind of reality. Dickens, out of the hunger and the genius of his nature, chose to write the sort of fiction which satisfied the public appetite for some relief from life as it is. His art is not so much that of the novelist, although he is a very great novelist, as it is that of a master magician, a latterday sorcerer who performs for his audiences an act of ritual healing, by bringing the halves of their lives back together—not merely in a mimetic mirror, by a conjuring trick, but actually, in the core of the reader's own experience, by giving him a dream to dream, an experience to live through and savor, a purging and a refreshment of the spirit. If this has its drawbacks—tending as it does to perpetuate the complacency and inertia of an audience out of touch with its own reality, its own beliefs and desires—still Dickens' gift was also to remind us of our plight by making us live through it again and again, according to his own painful and delightful vision of the dismal facts and impossible fancies, never himself reconciled to the difference between them.

Finally to understand Dickens, we must take him into our own century, which has resigned itself to habits of compromise which the Victorians never even approached. We value more the virtues of tact and flexibility (that we can call them "virtues" is symptomatic) than the manners and morals by which men judge and live. It never shocks us to be told that we must choose the lesser of two evils, or what is even more likely, that we must swallow both at once, ground so fine and homogeneous that we shan't taste them at all. Here at least the Victorians had the advantage of us: less accustomed to living without principle, they were often of two minds about a question—rather than of no mind at all—and could be astonishingly inconsistent and pig-headed, whereas we deplore inconsistency as much as we do intolerance. Who can read Carlyle or Ruskin—or Dickens—without a patience *they* never commanded?

Yet in spite of differences, it is clear enough that we are the heirs of the Victorian age, and that the gap between what is dispiritedly believed and what is hopelessly desired appears wider than ever. Our main palliative—the great art form (such as it is) of the twentieth century—has been the movies, and it is therefore not surprising that Dickens' novels should have so much in common with them, and should have proved so notably translatable into the film medium. The dream analogy, of course, has often been applied to motion pictures. The audience settles into a comfortable trance while a sequence of images takes up the whole attention, playing out one's favorite fantasy situations in the most realistic of settings, so that for the moment belief and desire appear to be reunited—one's dreams have come true. It is no accident that early film-makers such as Griffith and Eisenstein should have gone to school to Dickens' novels. Even the accompanying circumstances are the same: the star system corresponds to the public adulation of characters like Little Nell or Sam Weller, who call up so powerful a response in their audiences that they are taken as real people; the Saturday-night movie, like the appearance of the latest serial installment, renews the fantasy world as regularly as the night offers its dreams; even the cult of Hollywood has its parallel in the topographers and travelers who keep the Dickens Fellowship going, unwilling to give up the notion that their dream world somewhere has a magical equivalent in reality.

The primary reason why Dickens' novels and modern motion pictures have both succeeded so completely in answering a public craving for some bridge between belief and desire lies in the ingenious use of their media. Dreams, like hallucinations, have their power in the combination of the fantastic and the usual, the hoped-for and the actualized— or as Freud put it, in wish-fulfillment; and this is possible because under certain conditions (extreme limitation of sensory input from the outside world) the inner desires as it were project themselves upon the screen of the senses, so that it seems as if one's fantasies were actually taking place, realized in the objective world.[63] To show how this occurs in Dickens has been one of the aims of the present study. With motion pictures, the conditions of the medium itself so lend themselves to hallucination and dream that the use of the screen for dreamlike effects would seem unavoidable, even though very few movie-makers have come near to realizing the potentialities of their medium.* But Dickens' imagination is so powerful, even compared with the silver screen, that movie-makers would do well to take another leaf from his book. In order to create a public dream that is more than mere respite and escape, one must give oneself up to the vision. The role-playing of which I have accused Dickens, in his life and in his identification with all the characters of his novels, may not be so deplorable after all; for in a world which provides so thin a sense that the facts around one are desirable, or that the desires one has are also possibilities, it is hard to feel oneself, to place oneself; in such circumstances, to be able to take any role at all—let alone so many and so strongly as Dickens did—is surely not a bad thing. He can give us these many roles, his great characters, because he plays them himself; they are part of his dream. That finally is Dickens' humanity. Each attempt to find himself was undertaken with all his energies and talents, as if he were starting out anew, with every hope of success. That *he* was never satisfied has finally nothing to do with whether *we* are satisfied; we ask of him much less than he gives us—that is why, in reading Dickens, we are so continually astonished, because he goes beyond what anyone might have expected.

*It should be pointed out that surrealist films—attempts to imitate dreams quite literally—have never achieved any popular success, perhaps because the makers did not recognize that the dream illusion depends in great part on the audience's not knowing that a dream experience is what is being offered. In dreams one is utterly convinced of the reality of the vision, simply because the attention is completely usurped by it. To match this totality of illusion, the movies must avoid whatever might lead the viewer to question the "everyday reality" of his cinematic experience. (Of course, if more studios were to try surrealist techniques, conventions might soon grow up among audiences that would allow for total suspension of disbelief, no matter how weird the fantasies portrayed.)

# Notes

[1]George Orwell, "Charles Dickens," *A Collection of Essays* (New York, 1954), pp. 99–102.

[2]*The Letters of Charles Dickens,* ed. Walter Dexter ("The Nonesuch Dickens" [3 vols.; Bloomsbury, 1938]), III, 462.

[3]John Forster, *The Life of Charles Dickens,* ed. J. W. T. Ley (London, 1928), p. 76.

[4]See facsimile of the number plan, in Forster, facing p. 625.

[5]Robert Morse, "*Our Mutual Friend,*" *Partisan Review,* XVI (1949), 281. On Dickens' *Märchenrealismus,* cf. Wilhelm Dibelius, *Charles Dickens* (Leipzig, 1916), pp. 382–387 and *passim.*

[6]H. A. Taine, "The Novel—Dickens," *History of English Literature,* trans. H. Van Laun (New York, 1873), p. 587.

[7]See L. A. Riggs *et al.,* "The Disappearance of Steadily Fixated Visual Test Objects," *Journal of the Optical Society of America,* XLIII (1953), 495–501.

[8]"Two Aspects of Language and Two Types of Aphasic Disturbances," in Roman Jakobson and Morris Halle, *Fundamentals of Language (Janua Linguarum,* Nr. 1 ['s Gravenhage, 1956]), pp. 76–77.

[9]Kenneth Burke, *The Philosophy of Literary Form* (rev. ed.; New York, 1957), p. 24.

[10]H. A. Taine, p. 596.

[11]J. Hillis Miller, "Dickens' Symbolic Imagery" (unpublished Ph.D dissertation; Harvard University, 1952), p. 306.

## NOTES

[12]Joseph Frank, "Spatial Form in Modern Literature," *Sewanee Review*, LIII (1945), 231.

[13]J. Hillis Miller, "Dickens' Symbolic Imagery," p. 306.

[14]Paul Goodman, "Literary Method and Author-Attitude," in *Art and Social Nature* (New York, 1946), p. 88.

[15]Northrop Frye, *Anatomy of Criticism* (Princeton, 1957), pp. 303–314.

[16]E. M. Forster, *Aspects of the Novel* (New York, 1954), pp. 67–68.

[17]Henry James, "*Our Mutual Friend*," a review reprinted in *Henry James: The Future of the Novel*, ed. Leon Edel (New York, 1956), p. 77; George Orwell, p. 75; Mario Praz, "Charles Dickens," *The Hero in Eclipse in Victorian Fiction*, trans. Angus Davidson (London, 1956), p. 172.

[18]George Gissing, *Charles Dickens: A Critical Study* (New York, 1904), p. 15; Robert Liddell, *A Treatise on the Novel* (London, 1947), p. 17.

[19]George Santayana, "Charles Dickens," *Soliloquies in England and Later Soliloquies* (London, 1922), pp. 65–66.

[20]G. H. Lewes, "Dickens in Relation to Criticism," *The Fortnightly Review*, XI n.s. (1872), 144–145.

[21]John Forster, p. 720.

[22]The "Memoranda" book is in the Henry W. and Albert A. Berg Collection of the New York Public Library. It has been printed, with a great many inaccuracies, transpositions, and omissions, both in Forster's *Life* and in the final volume of the Nonesuch edition of the *Letters*. Mr. K. J. Fielding is preparing a new edition for the *New York Public Library Bulletin*. The passages quoted in my text follow the manuscript, which is not paginated.

[23]Morton Zabel, Introduction to the Riverside edition of *Bleak House* (Boston, 1956), p. xxii.

[24]Knud Sørensen, "Subjective Narration in *Bleak House*," *English Studies*, XL (1959), 431–439.

[25]J. Hillis Miller, *Charles Dickens: The World of His Novels* (Cambridge, Mass., 1958), pp. 165–166.

[26]Wolfgang Wickardt, *Die Formen der Perspektive in Charles Dickens' Romanen* (Neue Forschung: Arbeiten zur Geistesgeschichte der germanischen und romanischen Völker, 22 [Berlin, 1933]), pp. 49–50.

[27]Roman Jakobson, "Randbemerkungen zur Prosa des Dichters Pasternak," *Slavische Rundschau*, VII (1935), 363–364.

[28]Ernst Cassirer, *Language and Myth*, trans. Susanne K. Langer (New York, 1946), p. 94.

[29]H. A. Taine, p. 585.

[30]Sigmund Freud, *The Interpretation of Dreams*, in *The Basic Writ-*

*ings of Sigmund Freud*, trans. and ed. Dr. A. A. Brill (New York, 1938), pp. 88–89.

[31]Norman Malcolm, *Dreaming* (London, 1959), p. 86.

[32]Freud, p. 183.

[33]Freud, p. 189.

[34]Sylvère Monod, *Dickens Romancier* (Paris, 1953), pp. 370–372.

[35]John Forster, p. 26.

[36]Edmund Wilson, "Dickens: The Two Scrooges," *Eight Essays* (Garden City, N.Y., 1954), pp. 15–16.

[37]*Letters*, III, 462.

[38]The outline is printed in John Butt and Kathleen Tillotson, *Dickens at Work* (London, 1957), p. 30.

[39]Humphry House, *The Dickens World* (London, 1941), p. 156.

[40]Humphry House, pp. 219–220.

[41]*Letters*, II, 695.

[42]Percy Lubbock, *The Craft of Fiction* (New York, 1957), p. 214.

[43]John Forster, p. 565.

[44]*Letters*, II, 776.

[45]Lionel Trilling, Introduction to *Little Dorrit* (New Oxford Illustrated Dickens [London, 1953]), p. xi.

[46]The number plan is published, with reasonable accuracy, in Ernest Boll, "The Plotting of *Our Mutual Friend*," *Modern Philology*, XLII (1944), 96–122.

[47]Henry James, p. 75.

[48]Eugene Goodheart, "Dickens's Method of Characterisation," *Dickensian*, LIV (1958), 35.

[49]F. R. Leavis, "*Hard Times*: An Analytic Note," *The Great Tradition* (Garden City, N.Y., 1954), p. 280.

[50]George Orwell, p. 91.

[51]Sergei Eisenstein, *Film Form and The Film Sense*, ed. and trans. Jay Leyda (New York, 1957), pp. 234–235.

[52]George Orwell, p. 93.

[53]Humphry House, p. 55.

[54]*Letters*, II, 621; John Forster, p. 639.

[55]*Letters*, II, 765; John Forster, p. 639.

[56]John Forster, p. 513.

[57]John Forster, p. 511.

[58]Letter in the Pierpont Morgan Library, quoted by Edgar Johnson in his biography, *Charles Dickens: His Tragedy and Triumph* (2 vols.; New York, 1953), II, 878.

[59]*Letters*, II, 6.

[60]See Helmut Gernsheim, *Masterpieces of Victorian Photography* (London, 1951), p. 12. Frith, as Gernsheim notes, was no great friend to photography, although he used it in his work. I do not know the source for Wilde's remark.

[61]"Historic Notes on Life and Letters in New England," in *The Complete Works of Ralph Waldo Emerson* (12 vols.; Boston, 1903–1904), X, 337–339.

[62]*The Letters of Ralph Waldo Emerson,* ed. Ralph L. Rusk (6 vols.; New York, 1939), I, 291. Channing's remark is recorded in Charles Gibbon, *The Life of George Combe* (2 vols.; London, 1878), I, 221. John D. Davies quotes both Emerson and Channing in his *Phrenology: Fad and Science* (New Haven, Conn., 1955), pp. 15, 165.

[63]This theory of hallucination and dream is Coleridge's—from Essay III of the section called "The First Landing–Place" in *The Friend.* See Louis Jolyon West, "A General Theory of Hallucination and Dreams," in *Hallucinations,* ed. Louis Jolyon West (New York, 1962), pp. 275–290, for a modern physiological hypothesis based on this metaphor.

# Index

293